Fodor's 2001

Excerpted from Fodor's Hawaii 2001

Maui and Lanai

Fodor's Travel Publications • New York, Toronto, London, Sydney, Auckland
www.fodors.com

CONTENTS

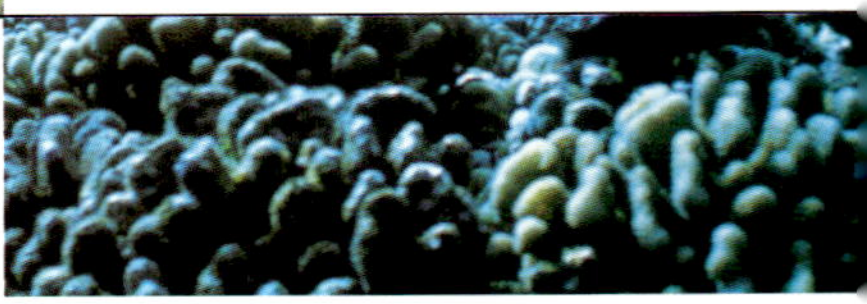

Destination Maui & Lāna`i 5

Fodor's Choice 14

1 EXPLORING MAUI 17

West Maui 19

Central Maui 26

Close-Up *Hawaiian Myths and Legends* 27

The South Shore 31

Haleakalā and Upcountry 33

Close-Up *Hawai`i's Flora and Fauna* 35

The Road to Hāna 37

2 DINING 42

West Maui 43

Central Maui 48

The South Shore 49

East Maui 50

3 LODGING 52

West Maui 53

The South Shore 58

East Maui 60

Guest Houses and Bed-and-Breakfasts 61

4 NIGHTLIFE AND THE ARTS 65

Bars and Clubs 66

Dinner and Sunset Cruises 67

Film 68

Lū`au and Revues 68

Close-Up *Hula, the Dance of Hawai`i* 69

Music 70

Theater 70

5 OUTDOOR ACTIVITIES, BEACHES, AND SPORTS 71

Beaches 72

Participant Sports 73

Spectator Sports 80

CLOSE-UP *Whale-Watching* 81

6 SHOPPING 84

Specialty Stores 86

7 SIDE TRIP TO LĀNA'I 90

Exploring Lāna'i 92

CLOSE-UP *Hawaiian Music* 96

Beaches 98

Dining 99

Lodging 100

Nightlife and the Arts 101

Outdoor Activities and Sports 101

Shopping 103

Lāna'i A to Z 104

8 BACKGROUND AND ESSENTIALS 107

Portraits of Maui 108

Books and Videos 124

Chronology 127

Smart Travel Tips A to Z 136

Hawaiian Vocabulary 164

Menu Guide 168

INDEX 169

ABOUT OUR WRITERS 176

MAPS

MAUI 20–21, 134–135

Lahaina 23

Kahului-Wailuku 28

Maui Dining 44–45

Maui Lodging 54–55

LĀNA'I 94

HAWAIIAN ISLANDS 131

WORLD TIME ZONES 132–133

Circled letters in text correspond to letters on the photographs. For more information on the sights pictured, turn to the indicated page number Ⓐ on each photograph.

DESTINATION MAUI & LĀNAʻI

Survey just one of Maui's flawless beaches, and you'll wonder how this island ever could have been a travel backwater. Yet that's what it was until savvy locals built championship golf courses and invited the world to tee off. Now two million visitors a year flock to Maui, for everything from water sports to whale-watching to not watching their waistlines. You can hike a volcano here, along the way admiring exotic, spiky silversword plants found nowhere else in the world. At night, you can enjoy cuisine of a sophistication found only in New York and London. Later, you can party in Lahaina, in a former brothel district once frequented by whalers. Or pack for a retreat to Lānaʻi, the backwater of present-day Hawaiʻi.

MAUI

Ⓐ 32

The Valley Isle never runs out of ways to enchant. Its lush, verdant beauty would be reason enough to visit. So would its world-class golf, water sports, and whale-watching, and its surprisingly hip dining scene. But of all things Mauian and enchanting, the finest is the warmth of the people. You encounter it everywhere. It infuses both posh resorts and the just-as-friendly rustic stands along the ⒷⒺ**Hāna Highway,** one of the world's most beautiful drives. Easier on suspensions

Ⓑ 37

©▷25

after considerable roadwork, the highway's 55 miles offer breathtaking overlooks, drowsy little towns, magical waterfalls, and flower-scented breezes (roll down your windows). Step into the past on the passenger run between Lahaina and Kā'anapali aboard the 1890s-vintage ©**Sugarcane Train,** or in the community of Lahaina, where whalers once came for lusty R&R and where missionaries, fellow New Englanders, made landfall to clean up the whalers' act (with less than impressive results). Today it is a National Historic Landmark, and the good times are safe and sanitized, at shows like the ⓓ**Old Lahaina Lū'au.** Even when Lahaina gets crowded and commercial—and it can—the mood is mellow. Neptune rules at the Ⓐ**Maui Ocean Center,** where without even changing your clothes you're virtually plunged to the ocean floor, surrounded by the finny creatures of a great Pacific reef.

ⓓ▷68

Ⓔ▷37

7

SPORTS AND OUTDOORS

Gym class was never like this. Whatever your outdoor pleasure, Maui provides not only superb conditions for indulging in it, but spectacular backdrops, too. The local name for stretches of the island's western shore—the Golf Coast—broadly hints at what you'll find here: championship courses designed by some of the biggest names in the sport, Arnold Palmer among them. But beware of a peculiar local hazard: the scenery may make it hard to keep your head down. (Ditto when you try to keep your eye on the tennis ball.) Higher up, hikers who venture along ancient Polynesian footpaths are rewarded in the still bamboo forest of Ⓑ**Haleakalā National Park** and by the sublime vistas at its ⒶⒹ**Haleakalā Crater.** The Ⓒ**Kula Botanical Gardens** showcase such native flora as the protea as well as orchids and koa and kukui trees. By the shore, spectators are wowed by the most agile of big-wave experts at places like Hoʻokipa Beach Park. Top windsurfers seek out perfect breezes here and at Kanahā Beach in Ⓔ**Kahului.** During calving season, in winter, whales breach offshore, many favoring Lahaina waters. No one has seen a whale give birth, but passengers on the whale-watching excursions that depart from several points along the coast observe many other behaviors in a show as diverting as any episode of *Hawaii Five-0*.

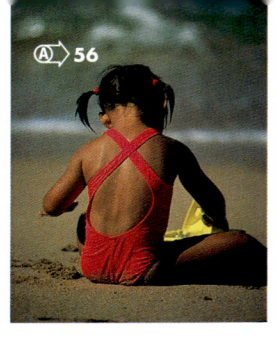

Thanks to creative local chefs, Maui's food scene is cosmopolitan, and you'll find everything from classic coq au vin to contemporary Pacific Rim fare, as at ⓒ**A Pacific Cafe,** and one-of-a-kind delicacies at the ⓔ**Komoda Store & Bakery**. The cream puffs here are what you'd expect in heaven—or, in this world, on Maui. At bedtime, you will be reminded that Maui was not made for roughing it. Although you may head to Haleakalā National Park's camp-

DINING AND LODGING

grounds and cabins, the island's hotels and resorts may beckon more seductively. There are vintage charmers like the Hotel Hāna-Maui as well as stylish town-house complexes that are good for families, such as ⒶKapalua Bay Villas. Children's programs like the one available in summer at the ⒷSheraton Maui have enabled many a mom and dad to explore Maui on their own. Meanwhile, budget travelers find their comfort zone at the ⒻPioneer Inn, in Lahaina's historic district, or in any number of other bed-and-breakfasts. Side-trippers to Lāna'i retreat to the gracious ⒹLodge at Kō'ele, on 21 mountainous acres, or sit on the expansive porch of the quaint Hotel Lāna'i, which has enjoyed this scenery since 1923.

LĀNA'I

For all its charm, Maui sometimes feels crowded. Fortunately, Lāna'i is just a hop away, full of serenity. Once known as the "Pineapple Island," it was rechristened "Hawai'i's Most Secluded Island" after giant Dole Foods opened two luxurious hotels here. Whether you stay in one of them or opt for simpler quarters, rare pleasures await, like snorkeling off Hulopo'e Beach or scuba diving among the angelfish at the submerged rock pinnacles known as the ⒶCathedrals, both off Lāna'i's south shore. Never quite a cathedral, even during the sugarcane boom, the 19th-century church in ⒷKeōmuku is still lovely in its desolation. So is the rest of this eerie ghost town of ruined homes and crumbling stone walls poignantly cradled by paradise. Long before missionaries built here, the first Hawaiians were moved to awe and fear by the lunar ⒸGarden of the Gods. Come late in the day, when the shadows grow long, and a spooky beauty descends—or connect with the past at the ⒹLu'ahiwa Petroglyphs, boulders inscribed with figures by Hawaiians just 200 years ago. To reach the island's high point and a spectacular view of nearly all Hawai'i's islands, ascend the Ⓔ **Munro Trail.** Back at home base, settle in on the front porch after dinner and appreciate the textures of the Pacific night. Commotion lies across the water. This is why you came to Lāna'i.

FODOR'S CHOICE

FODOR'S CHOICE

Even with so many special places on Maui and Lāna'i, Fodor's writers and editors have their favorites. Here are a few that stand out.

QUINTESSENTIAL MAUI AND LĀNA'I

Garden of the Gods, Lāna'i. For photography it's hard to top this surreal landscape scattered with red and black lava formations and rocks, with the blue Pacific in the background. ☞ p. 97

Ⓐ **Maui flightseeing.** Gaze down on the moonscape craters of Haleakalā volcano or zoom over rain forests, waterfalls, beaches, and emerald-green-carpeted canyons. ☞ p. 157

Munro Trail, Lāna'i. In your ramblings through the forest here, pass over Lāna'ihale, the "House of Lāna'i," and view the Hawaiian islands from its peak. ☞ p. 98

Old Lahaina Lū'au. Some consider this traditional, low-key lū'au to be Maui's best. Digest your fresh fish and *kālua* (roasted) pig to the tune of old Hawaiian chants and songs. ☞ p. 68

Whale-watching off Maui. Humpback whales breach and blow right offshore between November and April. ☞ p. 81

BEACHES

Hulopo'e Beach, Lāna'i. The island's only swimming beach, also a Marine Life Conservation District, is great for snorkeling. The underwater coral and lava formations, not to mention the jewel-tone fish, are dazzling. ☞ p. 98

Ⓓ **Mākena Beach State Park, Maui.** Protected by their state-park status, "Big Beach" and "Little Beach" are free from the clutter of development. ☞ p. 73

Nāpili Beach, Maui. This sparkling white beach forms a secluded cove that's tailor-made for romantics. ☞ p. 72

Shipwreck Beach, Lāna'i. Though the waters aren't friendly, the broad beach and view of Moloka'i across the Kalohi Channel make this 8-mi-long stretch of sand a beautiful place to stroll and take pictures. ☞ p. 99

DRIVES

Coming down Mt. Haleakalā, Maui. Drive to Haleakalā's summit without stopping, to arrive as early as possible, and take your time coming down. The views are stunning. ☞ p. 33

From Lahaina to Ma'alaea, Maui. The road along the northwest shore offers plenty of good stopping places from which to watch for whales wintering off the coast. ☞ p. 19

Ⓕ **Road to Hāna, Maui.** This trip is all about the drive, not the destination. The route, across bridges and past waterfalls, is unforgettable. ☞ p. 37

FLAVORS

Formal Dining Room, Lāna'i. Fresh local ingredients create an inventive island cuisine in this elegant country restaurant. $$$$ ☞ p. 99

Ⓖ **David Paul's Lahaina Grill, Maui.** Also known as the best restaurant on Maui, this classic spot in a creaky old building has wine in the cellar and a piano in the lounge. $$–$$$$ ☞ p. 46

Ⓙ **Hāli'imaile General Store, Maui.** A former camp store, this lofty old structure is a legendary fine-dining spot for creative Pacific Rim fare. $$–$$$ ☞ p. 50

Mama's Fish House, Maui. Mama's 1940s-era trucks mark the entrance to this clifftop thatch-roof restaurant, where you can enjoy the view of the ocean with your sautéed fish and macadamia nuts. $$–$$$ ☞ p. 51

A Pacific Cafe, Maui. Hawaiian Regional cuisine is at its best here. Rather than simply add a tropical flourish to traditional fare, these chefs create new flavors with innovative combinations that reflect Hawai'i's cultural diversity. $$–$$$ ☞ p. 50

Trattoria Ha'ikū, Maui. This dinner house, once a mess hall for pineapple cannery workers, brings white linens to the jungle and serves country-style Italian fare made from local ingredients. $$–$$$ ☞ p. 51

COMFORTS

Ⓔ **Four Seasons, Maui.** Set on one of the South Shore's finest beaches, with fountains, gardens, and waterfalls on the property, the resort caters to those who prefer luxury. $$$$ ☞ p. 58

Lodge at Kō'ele, Lāna'i. Fireplaces warm this sprawling mountain retreat in the cool highlands. Local artwork and rare Pacific artifacts embellish the interiors. $$$$ ☞ p. 100

Ritz-Carlton, Maui. A magnificent setting, terraced swimming pools, exemplary service, and beautifully appointed rooms (most with ocean views) make for an island idyll. $$$$ ☞ p. 56

Hāmoa Bay House & Bungalow, Maui. At this secluded jungle sanctuary in Hāna, choose between a room in the house, with an ocean view and outdoor lava-rock shower, and a treetop bungalow with a hot tub on the veranda. $$$ ☞ p. 61

Ⓒ **Lahaina Inn, Maui.** In the heart of town, seemingly in another time, this 12-room period inn has quilts in the rooms and your breakfast in the parlor. $$–$$$ ☞ p. 58

SIGHTS

Ⓐ **Haleakalā, Maui.** You couldn't miss seeing it if you tried, but take the drive to see it up close. ☞ p. 33

Ⓗ **Ho'okipa Beach, Maui.** This is the place to watch world-class windsurfing but not the place to learn the sport yourself. The north-shore windsurfers will earn your respect. ☞ p. 73

Ⓑ **'Īao Needle, 'Īao Valley State Park, Maui.** You don't have to be a nature lover to find this 2,000-ft-high rock formation, and the surrounding park, awe-inspiring. ☞ p. 29

Ⓘ **Sunsets.** Of course.

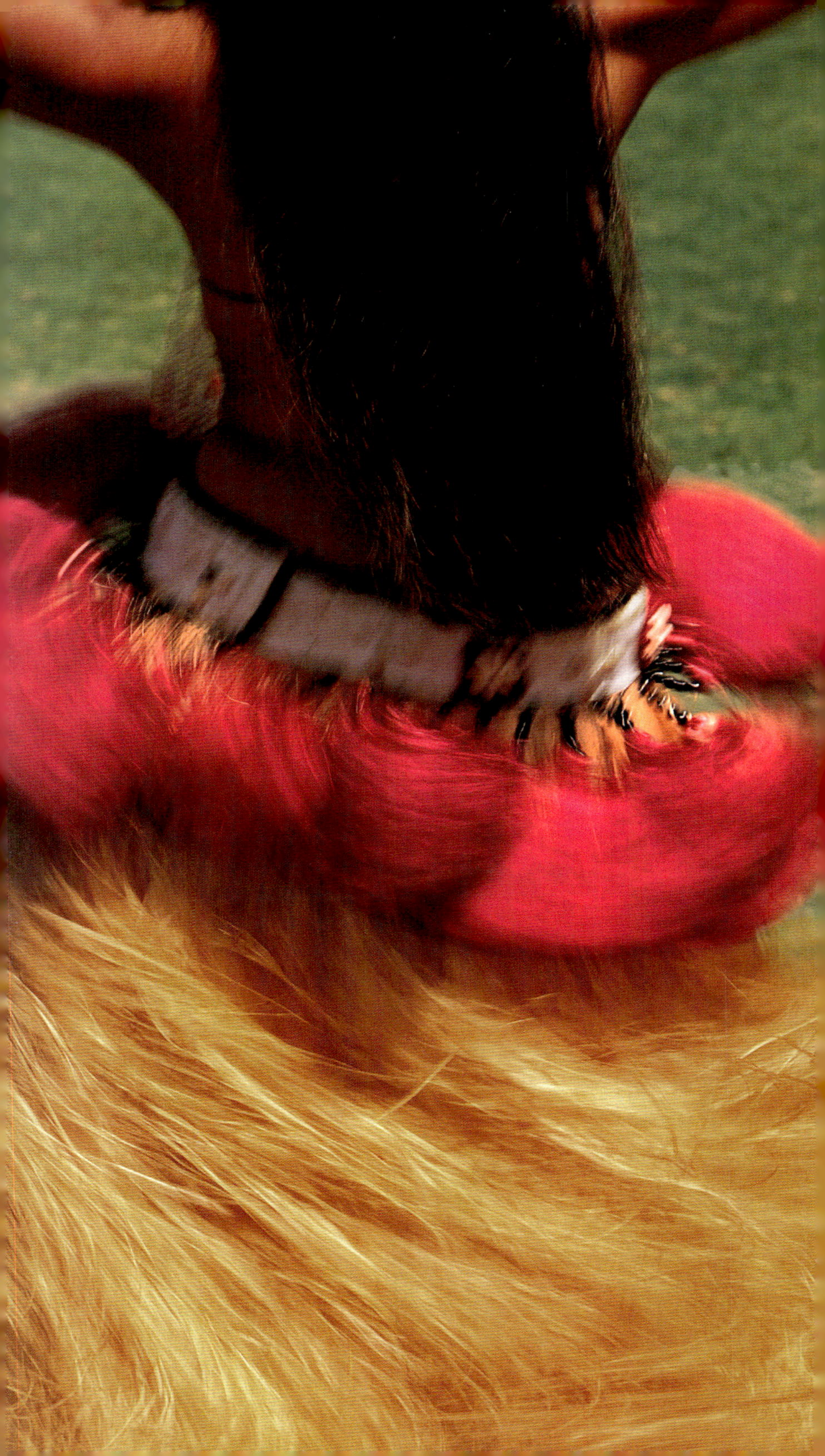

1 EXPLORING MAUI

Lush Maui's tropical sun, surf, and sports activities have gained it an international reputation. In laid-back Hāna, on the eastern shore, you can get a taste of what Hawai'i was like before T-shirt tourism. West Maui's gorgeous "Golf Coast" resorts draw eager putters, while shoppers head for the old whaling town of Lahaina.

Exploring Maui

Updated by Pablo Madera

THERE IS PLENTY TO SEE AND DO on the Valley Isle besides spending time on the beach. The island can be split up into five exploring areas—West Maui, Central Maui, the South Shore, Upcountry (including Haleakalā), and the Road to Hāna (East Maui). You can spend half a day to a full day or more in each area, depending on how long you have to visit. The best way to see the whole island is by car, but there are opportunities for good walking tours.

To get yourself oriented, first look at a map of the island. You will notice two distinct circular landmasses. These are volcanic in origin. The smaller landmass, on the western part of the island, consists of 5,788-ft Pu'u Kukui and the West Maui Mountains. The interior of these mountains is one of the earth's wettest spots. Annual rainfall of 400 inches has sliced the land into impassable gorges and razor-sharp ridges. Oddly enough, the area's leeward shore—what most people mean when they say "West Maui"—is sunny and warm year-round.

The large landmass on the eastern portion of Maui was created by Haleakalā, the cloud-wreathed volcanic peak at its center. One of the best-known mountains in the world, Haleakalā is popular with hikers and sightseers. This larger region of the island is called East Maui. Its dry, leeward South Shore is flanked with resorts, condominiums, beaches, and the busy town of Kīhei. Its windward shore, largely one great rain forest, is traversed by the Road to Hāna.

Between the two mountain areas is Central Maui, the location of the county seat of Wailuku, from which the islands of Maui, Lāna'i, Moloka'i, and Kaho'olawe are governed. It's also the base for much of the island's commerce and industry.

In the Islands, the directions *mauka* (toward the mountains) and *makai* (toward the ocean) are often used.

Great Itineraries

Many visitors never get over the spell of the sea, and never go inland to explore the island and its people. Those who do, though, launch out early from their beachside hotel or condo, loop through a district, then wind up back "home" for sunsets and *mai tais* (potent rum drinks with orange and lime juice). When you live on an island, you get used to going in circles. Don't be too goal-oriented as you travel around. If you rush to "get there," you might find you've missed the point of going, which is to encounter one of the most beautiful islands in the world, still largely unpopulated.

Numbers in the text correspond to numbers in the margin and on the Maui, Lahaina, and Kahului-Wailuku maps.

IF YOU HAVE 1 DAY

This is a tough choice. But how can you miss the opportunity to see **Haleakalā National Park** ㊳ and the volcano's enormous, otherworldly crater? Sunrise at the summit has become the thing to do. It's quite dramatic (and chilly), but there are drawbacks. Namely, you miss seeing the landscape and views on the way up in the dark. You also have to get up early. How early? You'll need an hour and a half from the bottom of **Haleakalā Highway** (Highway 37) ㊲ to the summit. Add to that the time of travel to the highway—at least 45 minutes from Lahaina or Kīhei. *The Maui News* posts the hour of sunrise every day. The best experience of the crater takes all day and good legs. Start at the summit, hike down Sliding Sands trail, cross the crater floor, and come back up the Halemau'u switchbacks. (This works out best if you leave your car at the Halemau'u trailhead parking lot and get a lift for

West Maui

the last 20-minute drive to the mountaintop.) All you need is a packed lunch, water, and decent walking shoes. If you don't hike, leave the mountain early enough to go explore **'Īao Valley State Park** ㉙ above Wailuku. This will show you the island's jungle landscape and will compensate for the fact that you're missing the drive to Hāna.

IF YOU HAVE 3 DAYS

Give yourself the Haleakalā volcano experience one day, and then rest up a little with a beach-snorkel-exploring jaunt on either East or West Maui. The East Maui trip will have to include the **Maui Ocean Center** ㉜ at Ma'alaea. Then drive the South Shore, sampling the little beaches in **Wailea** ㉞ and getting a good dose of big, golden **Mākena Beach State Park** ㉟. Be sure to drive on past Mākena into the rough lava fields, the site of Maui's last lava flows, which formed rugged **La Pérouse Bay** ㊱. The 'Āhihi-Kīna'u Marine Preserve has no beach, but it's a rich spot for snorkeling.

Or take the West Maui trip over the pali through Olowalu, **Lahaina** ④–⑰, and **Kā'anapali** ③, and dodge off the highway to find small beaches in Nāpili, Kahana, **Kapalua** ①, and beyond. The road gets narrow and sensational around **Kahakuloa** ②. If you're enjoying it, keep circling West Maui and return through the Central Valley.

On your third day, explore **Hāna** ㊸. Stop in **Pā'ia** ㊹ for a meal, pause at **Ho'okipa Beach** ㊺ for the surf action, and savor the sight of the taro fields of **Ke'anae Arboretum** ㊺ and **Wailua Overlook** ㊾. Nearly everyone keeps going past Hāna town to **'Ohe'o Gulch** ㊿, the "seven pools."

IF YOU HAVE 5 DAYS

Explore Upcountry. Get to **Makawao** ㊷ and use that as your pivot point. Head north at the town's crossroads and drive around Ha'ikū ㊻ by turning left at the first street (Kokomo Road), right at Ha'ikū Road, then coming back uphill on any of those leafy, twisting gulch-country roads. After you've explored Makawao town, drive out to Kula on the Kula Highway. This is farmland, with fields of flowers and vegetables and small ranches with well-nourished cattle. Stop in little Kēōkea for coffee, and keep driving on Highway 37 to the 'Ulupalakua Ranch History Room at the **Tedeschi Vineyards and Winery** ㊵. Add some time in Central Maui to really get to the heart of things, especially **Wailuku** ㉓–㉖, with its old buildings and curious shops. From here you can loop out to **Pā'ia** ㊹ and spend some time enjoying beaches in the Spreckelsville area and poking around the shops of this old plantation town.

When to Tour Maui

Although Maui has the usual temperate-zone shift of seasons—a bit rainier in the winter, hotter and drier in the summer—these seasonal changes are negligible on the leeward coasts, where most visitors stay. The only season worth mentioning is tourist season, when the roads around Lahaina and Kīhei get crowded. Peak visitor activity occurs from Christmas to March and picks up again in summer. If traffic is bothering you, get out of town and explore the countryside. During high season, the Road to Hāna tends to clog—well, not clog exactly, but develop little choo-choo trains of cars, with everyone in a line of six or a dozen driving as slowly as the first car. The solution: leave early (dawn) and return late (dusk). And if you find yourself playing the role of locomotive, pull over and let the other drivers pass.

West Maui

West Maui, anchored by the amusing old whaling town of Lahaina, was the focus of development when Maui set out to become a premier tourist destination. The condo-filled beach towns of Nāpili, Kahana,

Maui

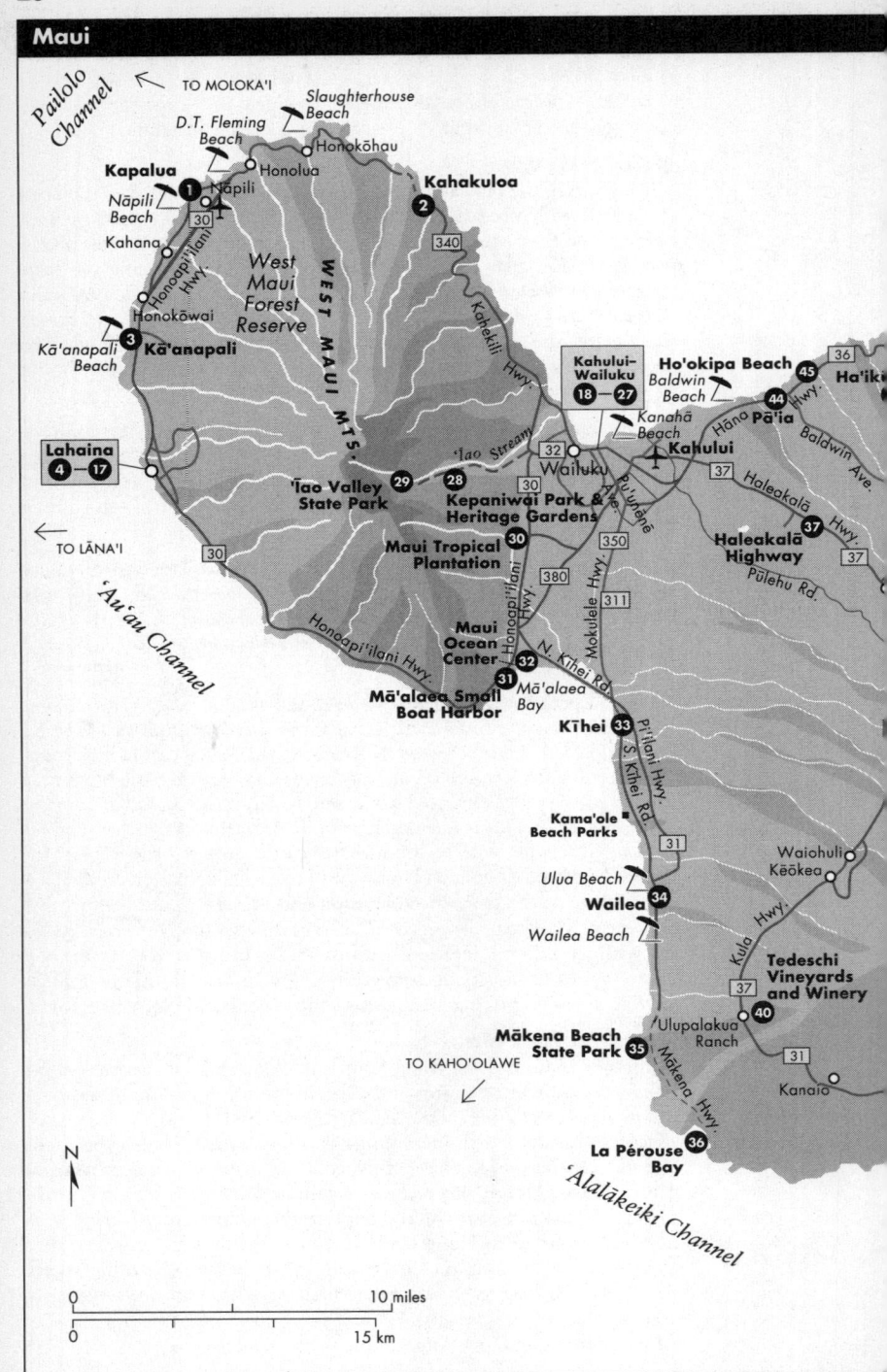

21

PACIFIC OCEAN

'Alenuihāhā Channel

TO THE BIG ISLAND OF HAWAI'I

and Honokōwai are arrayed between the stunning resorts of Kapalua and Kā'anapali, north of Lahaina.

A Good Drive

Begin this tour in **Kapalua** ①. Even if you're not staying there, you'll want to have a look around the renowned Kapalua Bay Hotel and enjoy a meal or snack before you begin exploring. From Kapalua drive north on the Honoapi'ilani Highway (Hwy. 30). This road is paved, but storms now and then make it partly impassable, especially on the winding 8-mi stretch that is only one lane wide, with no shoulder and a sheer drop off into the ocean. However, you'll discover some gorgeous photo opportunities along the road, and if you go far enough, you'll come to **Kahakuloa** ②, a sleepy fishing village tucked into a cleft in the mountain. The road pushes on to Wailuku, but you may be tired of the narrow and precipitously winding course you have to take.

From Kahakuloa turn around and go back in the direction from which you came—south toward Kā'anapali and Lahaina, past the beach towns of Nāpili, Kahana, and Honokōwai. If you wish to explore these towns, get off the Upper Honoapi'ilani Highway and drive closer to the water. If you're not staying there, you may want to visit the planned resort community of **Kā'anapali** ③, especially the Hyatt Regency Maui and the Westin Maui. To reach them, turn right at Kā'anapali Parkway. Next, head for Lahaina. Before you start your Lahaina trek, take a short detour by turning left from Honoapi'ilani Highway onto Lahainaluna Road, and stop at the **Hale Pa'i** ④, the printing shop built by Protestant missionaries in 1837. Return down Lahainaluna Road until you reach Front Street and turn left.

Since Lahaina is best explored on foot, use the drive along Front Street to get oriented and then park at or near **505 Front Street** ⑤, at the south end of the town's historic and colorful commercial area. Heading back into town, turn onto Prison Street and you'll come to the **Hale Pa'ahao** ⑥, which was built from coral blocks. Then return to Front Street, where it's a short stroll to the **Banyan Tree** ⑦, one of the town's best-known landmarks, and behind it, the old **Court House** ⑧. Next door, also in Banyan Park, stand the reconstructed remains of the waterfront **Fort** ⑨. About a half block northwest, you'll find the site of Kamehameha's **Brick Palace** ⑩. The **Brig Carthaginian II** ⑪ is anchored at the dock nearby and is open to visitors. If you walk from the brig to the corner of Front and Dickenson streets, you'll find the **Baldwin Home** ⑫, restored to reflect the decor of the early 19th century and now home to the Lahaina Restoration Foundation. Next door is the **Master's Reading Room** ⑬, Maui's oldest building.

Wander about Front Street to explore Lahaina's commercial side. At the Wharf Cinema Center, see the **Spring House** ⑭, built over a freshwater spring. Continue north on Front Street and you'll come to the **Wo Hing Museum** ⑮; another two blocks north is the **Seamen's Hospital** ⑯. If it's before dusk and you still have a hankering for just one more stop, try the **Waiola Church and Cemetery** ⑰. Walk south on Front Street, make a left onto Dickenson Street, and then make a right onto Waine'e Street and walk another few blocks.

TIMING

You can walk the length of Lahaina's Front Street in less than 30 minutes if you don't stop along the way. Just *try* not to be intrigued by the town's colorful shops and historic sites. Realistically, you'll need at least half a day—and can easily spend a full day—to check out the area's coastal beaches, towns, and resorts. The Banyan Tree in Lahaina is a terrific spot to be when the sun sets—mynah birds settle in here for a

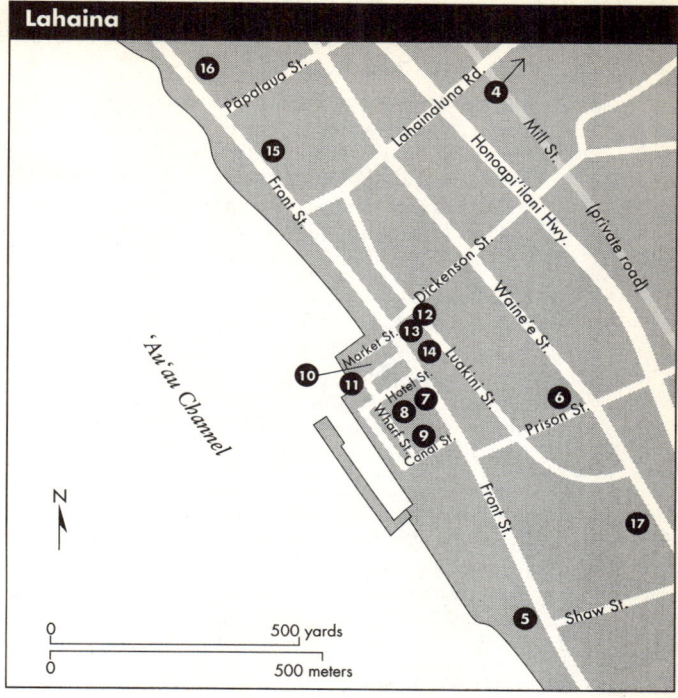

Baldwin
Home 12
Banyan Tree . . 7
Brick
Palace 10
Brig
Carthaginian
II 11
Court House . . 8
505 Front
Street 5
Fort 9
Hale
Pa'ahao (Old
Prison) 6
Hale Pa'i 4
Master's
Reading
Room 13
Seamen's
Hospital 16
Spring
House 14
Waiola
Church and
Cemetery . . . 17
Wo Hing
Museum 15

Lahaina

screeching symphony, which can be an event in itself. If you arrange to spend a Friday afternoon exploring Front Street, you can dine in town and hang around for Art Night, when the galleries stay open into the evening and entertainment fills the streets.

Sights to See

🖘 *following the text of a review is your signal that the property has a Web site where you will find details and, usually, images; for a link, visit www.fodors.com/urls.*

★ ⓬ **Baldwin Home.** In 1835 an early missionary to Lahaina, Ephraim Spaulding, built this attractive thick-walled house of coral and stone. In 1836 Dr. Dwight Baldwin—also a missionary—moved in with his family. The home has been restored and furnished to reflect the period. You can view the living room with the family's grand piano, the dining room, and Dr. Baldwin's dispensary. The Lahaina Restoration Foundation occupies the building, and its knowledgeable staff is here to answer almost any question about historic sites in town. Ask for its walking-tour brochure. ⊠ *696 Front St., Lahaina,* ☎ *808/661–3262.* 🖾 *$3.* ⊙ *Daily 10–4.*

❼ **Banyan Tree.** This massive tree, a popular and hard-to-miss meeting place if your party splits up for independent exploring, was planted in 1873. It is the largest of its kind in the state and provides a welcome retreat for the weary who come to sit under its awesome branches. ⊠ *Front St., between Hotel and Canal Sts., Lahaina.*

❿ **Brick Palace.** All that's left of the palace built by King Kamehameha I around 1802 to welcome the captains of visiting ships are the excavated cornerstones and foundation in front of the Pioneer Inn. Hawai'i's first king lived only one year in the palace because his favorite wife,

Ka'ahumanu, refused to stay there. It was then used as a warehouse, storeroom, and meeting house for 70 years, until it collapsed. ✉ *Makai end of Market St., Lahaina.*

★ ⑪ **Brig Carthaginian II.** This vessel's sailing days are over, but it makes an interesting museum. It was built in Germany in the 1920s and is a replica of the type of ship that brought the New England missionaries around Cape Horn to Hawai'i in the early 1800s. A small museum belowdecks features the "World of the Whale," a colorful multimedia exhibit about whaling and local sea life. ✉ *At dock opposite north end of Wharf St., Lahaina,* ☎ *808/661-3262.* 🎫 *$3.* ⊙ *Daily 10–4.*

⑧ **Court House.** This old civic building was erected in 1859, rebuilt in 1925, and restored to its 1925 condition in 1999. At one time or another it served as a customs house, post office, vault and collector's office, governor's office, police court, and courtroom. Now it houses museum displays, the Lahaina Arts Society, a visitor center—where volunteers will answer your questions—and, perhaps best of all, a water cooler. ✉ *649 Wharf St., Lahaina,* ☎ *808/661-0111.* 🎫 *Free.* ⊙ *Daily 9–5.*

⑤ **505 Front Street.** Quaint New England–style architecture characterizes this mall, which houses small shops and casual restaurants connected by a wooden sidewalk. It isn't as crowded as some other areas in Lahaina, probably because between here and the nearby Banyan Tree the town turns into a sleepy residential neighborhood and some people, walking from the more bustling center of Front Street, give up before they reach the mall. ✉ *South end of Front St. near Shaw St., Lahaina.*

⑨ **Fort.** Used mostly as a prison, this fortress was positioned so that it could police the whaling ships that crowded the harbor. It was built after sailors, angered by a law forbidding local women from swimming out to ships, lobbed cannonballs at the town. Cannons raised from the wreck of a warship in Honolulu Harbor were brought to Lahaina and placed in front of the fort, where they still sit today. The building itself is an eloquent ruin. ✉ *Canal and Wharf Sts., Lahaina.*

⑥ **Hale Pa'ahao (Old Prison).** This jailhouse dates back to rowdy whaling days. Its name means "stuck-in-irons house," referring to the wall shackles and ball-and-chain restraints. The compound was built in the 1850s by convict laborers out of blocks of coral that had been salvaged from the demolished waterfront ☞ Fort. Most prisoners were there for desertion, drunkenness, or reckless horse riding. Today, a wax figure representing an imprisoned old sailor tells visitors his recorded tale of woe. ✉ *Waine'e and Prison Sts., Lahaina.* 🎫 *Free.* ⊙ *Daily 8–5.*

④ **Hale Pa'i.** Six years after the Protestant missionaries established Lahainaluna Seminary as a center of learning and enlightenment in 1831, they built this printing shop. Here at the press they and their young native scholars created a written Hawaiian language and used it to produce a Bible, history texts, and a newspaper. An exhibit features a replica of the original Rampage press and facsimiles of early printing. The oldest U.S. educational institution west of the Rockies, the seminary now serves as Lahaina's public high school. ✉ *980 Lahainaluna Rd., Lahaina.* 🎫 *Donation.* ⊙ *Weekdays 10–3.*

③ **Kā'anapali.** The theatrical look of Hawai'i tourism—planned resort communities where luxury homes mix with high-rise hotels, fantasy swimming pools, and a theme-park landscape—all began right here in the 1960s. Three miles of uninterrupted white beach and placid water form the front yard for this artificial utopia, with its 40 tennis courts and two championship golf courses. The six major hotels here are all worth visiting just for a look around, especially the Hyatt Regency Maui,

West Maui

which has a multimillion-dollar art collection. At the Whalers Village shopping complex, a small **Whaling Museum** tells the story of the 19th-century *Moby-Dick* era. ✉ 2435 Kā'anapali Pkwy., Suite H16, ☎ 808/661–5992. 💰 Donation. 🕒 Daily 9:30 AM–10 PM.

❷ **Kahakuloa.** This tiny fishing village seems lost in time. Untouched by progress, it's a relic of pre–jet travel Maui. Many remote villages similar to Kahakuloa used to be tucked away in the valleys of this area. This is the wild side of West Maui. True adventurers will find terrific snorkeling and swimming along this coast, as well as some good hiking trails. ✉ North end of Honoapi'ilani Hwy.

❶ **Kapalua.** This resort, set in a beautifully secluded spot surrounded by pineapple fields, got its first big boost in 1978, when the Maui Land & Pineapple Company built the luxurious Kapalua Bay Hotel. It was joined in 1992 by a dazzling Ritz-Carlton. The hotels host dedicated golfers, celebrities who want to be left alone, and some of the world's richest folks. Kapalua's shops and restaurants are among Maui's finest, but expect to pay big bucks. By contrast, the old **Honolua Store** serves informal plate lunches, popular with locals. ✉ Bay Dr., Kapalua.

Lahaina. This little whaling town has a notorious past. There are stories of lusty whalers who met head-on with missionaries bent on saving souls. Both groups journeyed to Lahaina from New England in the early 1800s. At first, Lahaina might look touristy, but there's a lot that's genuine here as well. The town has renovated most of its old buildings, which date from the time when it was Hawai'i's capital. Much of the town has been designated a National Historic Landmark, and any new buildings must conform in style to those built before 1920. ✉ Honoapi'ilani Hwy., 3 mi south of Kā'anapali.

🖐 **Lahaina–Kā'anapali & Pacific Railroad.** Affectionately called the Sugarcane Train, this is Maui's only passenger train. It's an 1890s-vintage railway that once shuttled sugar but now moves sightseers between Kā'anapali and Lahaina. This quaint little attraction with its singing conductor is a big deal for Hawai'i but probably not much of a thrill for those more accustomed to trains. The kids will like it. ✉ 1½ blocks north of the Lahainaluna Rd. stoplight on Honoapi'ilani Hwy., Lahaina, ☎ 808/661–0089. 💰 $14.50. 🕒 Daily 9–5:30.

⑬ **Master's Reading Room.** This could be Maui's oldest residential building, constructed in 1834. In those days the ground floor was a mission's storeroom, and the reading room upstairs was for sailors. ✉ Front and Dickenson Sts., Lahaina, ☎ 808/661–3262.

⑯ **Seamen's Hospital.** Built in the 1830s to house King Kamehameha III's royal court, this property was later turned over to the U.S. government, which used it as a hospital for whalers. Next door is a typical **sugar plantation camp residence**, circa 1900. ✉ 1024 Front St., Lahaina, ☎ 808/661–3262.

⑭ **Spring House.** Built by missionaries to shelter a freshwater spring, this historic structure is now home to a huge Fresnel lens, once used in a local lighthouse that guided ships to Lahaina. ✉ Wharf Cinema Center, 658 Front St., Lahaina.

NEED A BREAK?	The sandwiches have real Gruyère and Emmentaler cheese at **Maui Swiss Cafe** (✉ 640 Front St., Lahaina, ☎ 808/661–6776)—expensive ingredients with affordable results. The friendly owner scoops the best and cheapest locally made ice cream in Lahaina. Daily lunch specials are less than $6. Courtyard tables are set back from Front Street. Open from 9 to 7 daily, this is an informal local favorite.

⑰ **Waiola Church and Cemetery.** The Waiola Cemetery is actually older than the neighboring church, dating from the time when Kamehameha's sacred wife, Queen Keōpūolani, died and was buried there in 1823. The first church here was erected in 1832 by Hawaiian chiefs and was originally named Ebenezer by the queen's second husband and widower, Governor Hoapili. Aptly immortalized in James Michener's *Hawai'i* as the church that wouldn't stand, it was burned down twice and demolished in two windstorms. The present structure was put up in 1953 and named Waiola (water of life). ✉ *535 Waine'e St., Lahaina,* ☎ *808/661–4349.*

⑯ **Wo Hing Museum.** Built by the Wo Hing Society in 1912 as a fraternal society for Chinese residents, this eye-catching building now contains Chinese artifacts and a historic theater that features Thomas Edison's films of Hawai'i, circa 1898. Upstairs is the only public Taoist altar on Maui. ✉ *858 Front St., Lahaina,* ☎ *808/661–3262.* 🎟 *Donation.* ⊙ *Daily 10–4.*

Central Maui

Kahului, an industrial and commercial town in the center of the island, is home to many of Maui's permanent residents, who find their jobs close by. The area was developed in the early '50s to meet the housing needs of workers for the large sugarcane interests here, specifically those of Alexander & Baldwin. The large company was tired of playing landlord to its many plantation workers and sold land to a developer who promised to create affordable housing. The scheme worked, and Kahului became the first planned city in Hawai'i. Ka'ahumanu Avenue (Hwy. 32), Kahului's main street, runs from the harbor to the hills. It's the logical place to begin your exploration of Central Maui.

A Good Tour

Begin at the **Alexander & Baldwin Sugar Museum** ⑱ in Pu'unēnē, directly across from the HC&S sugar mill. The mill has been processing cane and belching steam and smoke since it opened in 1902. For a while it was the biggest sugar mill in the world. By 1930 Pu'unēnē had a population of 10,000 workers and families living in "camps" around the mill, and it had a school, churches, and a bowling alley. All of that is gone today, but the museum tells the story of these people and of the industry they helped create.

From here, explore **Kahului,** which looks nothing like the lush tropical paradise most people envision as Hawai'i. Head back on Pu'unēnē Avenue all the way to its end at Ka'ahumanu Avenue and turn left. Three blocks ahead you'll see the sputniklike canvas domes of Ka'ahumanu Center, Maui's largest shopping center. If you turn right at the signal just before that, you'll follow the curve of Kahului Beach Road and see many ships in port at **Kahului Harbor** ⑲. On your left are the cream-and-brown buildings of **Maui Arts & Cultural Center** ⑳. Continue past the harbor, turn right at Waiehu Beach Road, and about a mile later as you cross the 'Īao Stream you'll see **Haleki'i-Pihana Heiau State Monument** ㉑ on the hilltop to your left. Return along the harbor road and make a right turn at Kanaloa Avenue. Return to Ka'ahumanu Avenue on this road, passing the new **Keōpūolani Park** ㉒ and the War Memorial Stadium, site of the annual Hula Bowl game. Turn right to reach Wailuku (Ka'ahumanu eventually becomes Wailuku's Main Street). To get a closer look at **Wailuku's Historic District** ㉓, turn right from Main Street onto Market Street, where you can park for free within view of the landmark **'Īao Theater** ㉔. The theater is a good place to begin your walking tour. Many amusing shops line **Market Street** ㉕ between Vineyard and Main streets. From here, it's a short walk along Main Street to **Ka'ahumanu Church** ㉖ on High Street, just around the

Close-Up
HAWAIIAN MYTHS AND LEGENDS

The best-known deity in Hawaiian lore is Pele, the volcano goddess. Although visitors are warned not to remove lava rocks from Pele's domain without her permission, some do and find themselves dogged by bad luck until they return the stolen items. The Hawai`i Volcanoes National Park Service often receives packages containing chunks of lava along with letters describing years of misfortune.

Tales of Pele's fiery temper are legion. She battled Poli`ahu, ruler of snow-capped Mauna Ke`a on the Big Island, in a fit of jealousy over the snow goddess's extraordinary beauty. She picked fights with her peace-loving sister, Hi`iaka, turning the younger goddess's friends into pillars of stone. And her recurring lava-flinging spats with suitor Kamapua`a, a demigod who could change his appearance at will, finally drove him into the sea, where he turned into a fish to escape from her wrath.

But Pele can be kind if the mood suits her. It is said that before every major eruption, she appears in human form as a wrinkled old woman walking along isolated back roads. Those who pass her by find their homes devastated by molten lava. Those who offer her a ride home return home to find a river of boiling magma abruptly halted inches from their property or diverted around their houses. Many hula *hālau* (schools) still make pilgrimages to the rim of Kīlauea—Pele's home—where they honor the fickle goddess with prayers, chants, and offerings of gin and flower leis.

A less volatile but equally intriguing figure in Hawaiian lore is Māui, a demigod who is credited with pulling the Hawaiian Islands up from the bottom of the sea with a magic fishhook, pushing the sky away from the treetops because it had flattened all the leaves, and, his most prestigious feat—lassoing the sun as it came up over the top of Haleakalā and demanding that it move more slowly across the sky in summer so that Māui's mother would have longer daylight hours to dry her *kapa* (cloth made from bark).

In addition to battling the elements and each other, gods were thought to have intervened in the daily lives of early Hawaiians. Storms that destroyed homes and crops, a fisherman's poor catch, or a loss in battle were blamed on the wrath of angry gods. And according to legend, an industrious race of diminutive people called *menehune* built aqueducts, fishponds, and other constructs requiring advanced engineering knowledge unavailable to early Hawaiians. Living in remote hills and valleys, these secretive workers toiled only in darkness and completed complex projects in a single night. Their handiwork can still be seen on all the islands.

Also at night, during certain lunar periods, a traveler might inadvertently come across the Night Marchers—armies of dead warriors, chiefs, and ancestral spirits whose feet never touch the ground as they tread the ancient highways, chanting and beating their drums, and pausing only to claim the spirits of their brethren who died that night. It was believed that such an encounter would mean certain death unless a relative among the marchers pleaded for the victim's life.

The moral? Leave the lava rocks as they are and pick up any elderly hitchhikers you might come across. Straightforward enough. But I'd still hightail it in the other direction if I heard mysterious chanting or drum beating.

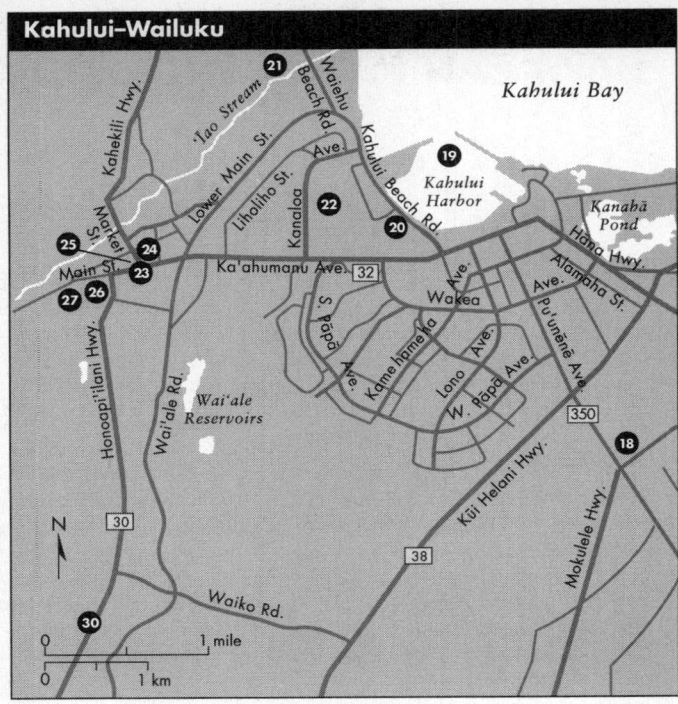

Alexander & Baldwin Sugar Museum	18
Bailey House	27
Haleki'i–Pihana Heiau State Monument	21
'Iao Theater	24
Ka'ahumanu Church	26
Kahului Harbor	19
Keōpūolani Park	22
Market Street	25
Maui Arts & Cultural Center	20
Maui Tropical Plantation and Country Store	30
Wailuku's Historic District	23

Kahului–Wailuku

corner from Main and across the way from the County Court House. Retrieve your car and return to Main Street, where you'll turn right. After a few blocks, on your left, you'll see **Bailey House** ㉗.

Continue driving uphill, into the mountains. Main Street turns into 'Iao Valley Road, the air cools, and the hilly terrain gets more lush. Soon you'll come to **Kepaniwai Park & Heritage Gardens** ㉘. 'Iao Valley Road ends at **'Iao Valley State Park** ㉙, home of the erosion-formed gray and moss-green rock called 'Iao Needle. This is a great place to picnic, wade in the stream, and explore the paths. Then return to Wailuku and, at the traffic light, turn right onto Highway 30. Drive south a couple of miles to the **Maui Tropical Plantation & Country Store** ㉚.

TIMING

The complete itinerary will take a full day. But you can explore Central Maui comfortably in little more than half a day if you whiz through the Maui Tropical Plantation, or save it for another day. If you want to combine sightseeing with shopping, this is a good itinerary for it, but you'll need more time. Hikers may want to expand their outing to a full day to explore 'Iao Valley State Park.

Sights to See

★ ⑱ **Alexander & Baldwin Sugar Museum.** "A&B," Maui's largest landowner, was one of five companies known collectively as the Big Five that spearheaded the planting, harvesting, and processing of the valuable agricultural product sugarcane. Although Hawaiian cane sugar is now being supplanted by cheaper foreign versions—as well as by sugar derived from inexpensive sugar beets—the crop was for many years the mainstay of the Hawaiian economy. You'll find the museum in a small, restored plantation manager's house next to the post office and the still-operating

Central Maui

sugar refinery (black smoke billows up when cane is burning). Historic photos, artifacts, and documents explain the introduction of sugarcane to Hawai'i and how plantation managers brought in laborers from other countries, thereby changing the Islands' ethnic mix. Exhibits also describe the sugar-making process. ✉ *3957 Hansen Rd., Pu'unēnē,* ☎ *808/ 871–8058.* 🎟 *$4.* ⊙ *Mon.–Sat. 9:30–4:30.*

★ ㉗ **Bailey House.** This was the home of Edward and Caroline Bailey, two prominent missionaries who came to Wailuku to run the first Hawaiian girls' school on the island, the Wailuku Female Seminary. The school's main function was to train the girls in the "feminine arts." It once stood next door to the Baileys' home, which they called Halehō'ike'ike (House of Display), but locals always called it the Bailey House, and the sign painters eventually gave in. Construction of the house, between 1833 and 1850, was supervised by Edward Bailey himself. The Maui Historical Society runs a museum in the plastered stone house, with a small collection of artifacts from before and after the missionaries' arrival and with Mr. Bailey's paintings of Wailuku. Some rooms have missionary-period furniture. The Hawaiian Room has exhibits on the making of tapa cloth, as well as samples of pre–Captain Cook weaponry. ✉ *2375A Main St., Wailuku,* ☎ *808/244–3326.* 🎟 *$4.* ⊙ *Mon.–Sat. 10–4.* ✎

㉑ **Haleki'i-Pihana Heiau State Monument.** Stand here at either of the two *heiau* (ancient temple platforms) and imagine the king of Maui surveying his domain. That's what Kahekili, Maui's last fierce king, did, and so did Kamehameha the Great after he defeated Kahekili's soldiers. Today the view is most instructive. Below, the once-powerful 'Iao Stream has been sucked dry and boxed in by concrete. Before you is the urban heart of the island. The suburban community behind you is all Hawaiian Homelands. ✉ *End of Hea Place, off Kuhio Place from Waiehu Beach Road (Hwy. 340), Kahului,* 🎟 *Free.* ⊙ *Daily 7–7.*

㉔ **'Iao Theater.** One of Wailuku's most photographed landmarks, this charming movie house went up in 1927 and served as a community gathering spot. When restoration work was completed on the Art Deco building in 1996, the Maui Community Theatre resumed its longtime residence here in its historic Wailuku headquarters. ✉ *68 N. Market St., Wailuku,* ☎ *808/242–6969.*

NEED A BREAK? **Maui Bake Shop & Deli Ltd.** (✉ 2092 Vineyard St., Wailuku, ☎ 808/ 242–0064) serves salads, sandwiches, and a variety of light entrées, but what you're really going to crave are the pastries—a feast for the eyes as well as the palate. The pastel-frosted frogs, chicks, rabbits, and mice, made of orange butter-cream cookie dough, are irresistible.

★ ㉙ **'Iao Valley State Park.** When Mark Twain saw this park, he dubbed it the Yosemite of the Pacific. Yosemite it's not, but it is a lovely deep valley with the curious 'Iao Needle, a spire that rises more than 2,000 ft from the valley floor. You can take one of several easy hikes from the parking lot across 'Iao Stream and explore the junglelike area. This park offers a beautiful network of well-maintained walks, where you can stop and meditate by the edge of a stream or marvel at the native plants and flowers. Mist occasionally rises if there has been a rain, which makes being here even more magical. ✉ *Western end of Hwy. 32.* 🎟 *Free.* ⊙ *Daily 7–7.*

㉖ **Ka'ahumanu Church.** It's said that Queen Ka'ahumanu attended services on this site in 1832 and requested that a permanent structure be erected. Builders first tried adobe, which dissolved in the rain, then stone. The present wooden structure, built in 1876, is classic New England style, with white exterior walls and striking green trim. You won't be able to see the interior, however, unless you attend Sunday services. There's a service entirely in the Hawaiian language each Sunday morning at 9:30. ✉ *Main and High Sts., Wailuku,* ☎ *808/244-5189.*

Kahului. The town of Kahului is the industrial and commercial center for Maui's year-round residents, as close to a bustling urban center as Maui gets. Most visitors arrive at the airport here and see all they will see of the town as they drive on to their hotels. But this is the home of Maui's largest mall, Ka'ahumanu Center, which is virtually the social center of island life. It's also the site of the newly revived Maui Mall (with a 12-theater "megaplex") and the island's big mainland-style box stores, which are all visible on the main road from the airport.

⑲ **Kahului Harbor.** This is Maui's chief port, since it's the island's only deep-draft harbor. American-Hawaii's 800-passenger S.S. *Independence* and S.S. *Constitution* each stop here once a week, as do cargo ships and smaller vessels, including the occasional yacht. Surfers sometimes use this spot to catch some good waves, but it's not a good swimming beach. ✉ *Kahului Beach Rd., Kahului.*

㉒ **Keōpūolani Park.** Maui's new "Central Park" covers 101 acres, and—reflecting Maui residents' traditional love of sports—it has seven playing fields. Named for the great Maui queen who was born near here and is buried in Lahaina's Waiola Church cemetery, the park is planted with native species that will take a few years to reach their potential. The park also includes a native-plant botanical garden and a 3-mi walking path. ✉ *Kanaloa Ave. next to the YMCA.*

㉘ **Kepaniwai Park & Heritage Gardens.** This county park is a memorial to Maui's cultural roots, with picnic facilities and ethnic displays dotting the landscape. There's an early Hawaiian shack, a New England–style saltbox, a Portuguese-style villa with gardens, and dwellings from such other cultures as China and the Philippines. Next door the **Hawai'i Nature Center** has an interactive exhibit and hikes good for children.

The peacefulness here belies the history of the area. During his quest for domination, King Kamehameha I brought his troops from the Big Island of Hawai'i to the Valley Isle in 1790 and engaged in a particularly bloody battle against the son of Maui's chief, Kahekili, near Kepaniwai Park. An earlier battle at the site had pitted Kahekili himself against an older Big Island chief, Kalani'ōpu'u. Kahekili prevailed, but the carnage was so great that the nearby stream became known as Wailuku (water of destruction) and the place where fallen warriors choked the stream's flow was called Kepaniwai (the water dam). ✉ *Valley Rd., Wailuku.* 🎟 *Free.* ⓧ *Daily 7–7.*

NEED A BREAK?	If you're in Central Maui at lunchtime, try local favorite **Cafe O'Lei** (✉ 2051 Main St., Wailuku, ☎ 808/244–6816), right in downtown Wailuku. The food is healthy, fresh, and tasty. The prices are great, and the people are friendly.

㉕ **Market Street.** An idiosyncratic assortment of shops—with proprietors to match—makes Wailuku's Market Street a delightful place for a stroll. Shops like the Good Fortune Trading Company and Brown-Kobayashi have affordable antiques and home furnishings. Merchants are happy to recommend a restaurant and offer advice or directions.

★ ⑳ **Maui Arts & Cultural Center.** This $32-million facility opened in 1994 after an epic fund drive led by the citizens of Maui. The top-of-the-line Castle Theater seats 1,200 people on orchestra, mezzanine, and balcony levels. Rock stars play the A&B Amphitheater. The Center (as it's called) also includes a small black box theater, an art gallery with interesting exhibits,

The South Shore

and classrooms. The building itself is worth the visit. It incorporates work by Maui artists, and its signature lava-rock wall pays tribute to the skills of the Hawaiians. ✉ *Above the harbor on Kahului Beach Rd., Kahului,* ☎ *808/242–2787; 808/242–7469 box office.* ⊘ *Weekdays 9–5.*

③⓪ **Maui Tropical Plantation & Country Store.** When Maui's once-paramount crop declined in importance, a group of visionaries decided to open an agricultural theme park on the site of this former sugarcane field. The 60-acre preserve, on Highway 30 just outside Wailuku, offers a 30-minute tram ride through its fields with an informative narration covering growing processes and plant types. Children will probably enjoy the historical-characters exhibit, as well as fruit-testing, coconut-husking, and lei-making demonstrations, not to mention some entertaining spider monkeys. There's a restaurant on the property and a "country store" specializing in "Made In Maui" products. ✉ *Honoapi'ilani Hwy. (Hwy. 30), Waikapu,* ☎ *808/244–7643.* 🎟 *Free; tram ride with narrated tour $9.50.* ⊘ *Daily 9–5.*

②③ **Wailuku's Historic District.** The National Register of Historic Places lists many of this area's buildings. At the Wailuku Main Street Association (2062 Main St., ☎ 808/244–3888), you can pick up a free brochure that describes a good walking tour. The little town is sleepy, and you wouldn't guess that it's Maui's county seat. The mayor sits on the top floor of the tallest building in town, on the corner of Main and High streets. ✉ *High, Vineyard, and Market Sts., Wailuku.*

The South Shore

Twenty years ago almost no one lived in Kīhei. Now about one-third of the Maui population lives here in what was, for a while, one of the fastest-growing towns in America. Traffic lights and mini-malls may not fit your notion of tropical paradise, but Kīhei does offer sun, heat, and excellent beaches. Besides that, the town's relatively inexpensive condos and small hotels make this a home base for many Maui visitors. At one end of this populous strip, you have Mā'alaea Small Boat Harbor and the Maui Ocean Center, a world-class seawater aquarium. At the other end, lovely Wailea—a resort community to rival those on West Maui—gives way to truly unspoiled coastline.

A Good Drive

Start with a look at **Mā'alaea Small Boat Harbor** ③①, the setting-out place for many whale-watch trips, snorkel excursions (often out to the tiny crescent island Molokini), and sunset dinner cruises. Then tour the **Maui Ocean Center** ③②, an aquarium dedicated to the sea life of the North Pacific. When you leave the aquarium, turn right onto Highway 30 and then turn right again at the first traffic signal—Highway 31 or North Kīhei Road. You're headed toward the town of **Kīhei** ③③ on a straight road following the long sandy coastline of Mā'alaea Bay. On your left is marshy Keālia Pond, a state-managed wildlife sanctuary. On your right, ecologically fragile dunes run between the road and the sea. A turnout provides some parking stalls, information about the dunes, and a boardwalk so you can cross the dunes and use the beach. When you get to the long, thin town of Kīhei, you have a choice. You can turn right at the fork in the road and experience the colorful stop-and-go beach route of South Kīhei Road. Or you can turn left and bypass the town on the Pi'ilani Highway, hastening to the resort community of **Wailea** ③④. If you're looking for the best beach, you might as well flip a coin. There are great beaches all along this coast. At Wailea, you'll drive past grand resorts interspersed with stretches of golf courses and access roads leading down to small but excellent beaches. Then the manicured look of Wailea gives way to wildness and, after a couple of miles, to **Mākena Beach State Park** ㉟. Mākena is such a big beach that it has two paved parking areas. Beyond this point the landscape gets wilder and the road gradually fades away in black fields of cracked lava. This is **La Pérouse Bay** ㊱.

TIMING

Because it includes so many fine beach choices, this is definitely an all-day excursion—especially if you include a visit to the aquarium. A good way to do this trip is to get active in the morning with exploring and snorkeling, then shower in a beach park, dress up a little, and enjoy the cool luxury of the Wailea resorts. At sunset, settle in for dinner at one of the area's many fine restaurants.

Sights to See

㉝ **Kīhei.** This is a community that's still discovering itself. Much of it is less than 10 years old, inhabited by recent Maui immigrants. An abundance of condos, moderately priced hotels, and sprawl-malls makes the town convenient for visitors. The beaches and the reliably sunny weather make it a draw. The county beach parks such as Kama'ole One, Two, and Three provide lawns, showers, and picnic tables. Remember: beach park or no beach park, the public has a right to the entire coastal strand, and this one in Kīhei has many off-road delights.

㊱ **La Pérouse Bay.** Beyond Mākena Beach, the road fades away into a vast territory of black lava flows, the result of Haleakalā's last eruption some 200 years ago. This is where Maui received its first official visit by a European explorer—the French admiral Jean-François de Galaup, Comte de La Pérouse, in 1786. Before it ends, the road passes through 'Āhihi-Kīna'u Marine Preserve, an excellent place for morning snorkel adventures.

㉛ **Mā'alaea Small Boat Harbor.** With only 89 slips and so many good reasons to take people out on the water, this active little harbor needs to be expanded. The Army Corps of Engineers has a plan to do so, but harbor-users are fighting it—particularly the surfers, who say the plan would destroy their surf breaks. In fact, the surf here is world renowned, especially the break to the left of the harbor called "freight train," said to be the fastest anywhere.

★ ㉟ **Mākena Beach State Park.** "Big Beach" they call it—a huge stretch of coarse golden sand without a house or hotel for miles. A decade ago, Maui citizens campaigned successfully to preserve this beloved beach from development. At the right-hand end of the beach rises the beautiful hill called Pu'u Ōla'i, a perfect cinder cone. A climb over the rocks at this end leads to "Little Beach," where the (technically illegal) clothing-optional attitude prevails.

★ ㉜ **Maui Ocean Center.** This aquarium, which focuses on Hawaii and the Pacific, will make you feel as though you're walking from the seashore down to the bottom of the reef, and then through an acrylic tunnel in the middle of the sea. Special tanks get you close up with turtles, rays, and the bizarre creatures of the tide pools. ✉ *Enter from Honoapi'ilani Hwy. (Hwy. 30) as it curves past Mā'alaea Harbor, Mā'alaea,* ☎ *808/ 270-7000.* 🎟 *$17.50.* ☉ *Daily 9–5.*

★ ㉞ **Wailea.** Wailea is to Kīhei as Kā'anapali—Maui's original fantasy resort development—is to the town of Lahaina. In both cases, the town is real and the resort community is ideal. The luxury of the Grand Wailea, the Moorish near-silliness of the Kea Lani, the simple grandeur of the Four Seasons, the public displays of fine art and architecture make Wailea a unique Maui attraction. A handful of perfect little beaches all have

Haleakalā and Upcountry

public access, and a paved beachwalk allows you to stroll between all the properties, restaurants, and sandy coves.

Haleakalā and Upcountry

The west-facing upper slopes of Haleakalā are locally called "Upcountry." This region is responsible for much of Hawai'i's produce—lettuce, tomatoes, and sweet Maui onions—but the area is also a big flower producer. As you drive along you'll notice cactus thickets mingled with jacaranda, wild hibiscus, and towering eucalyptus trees. Upcountry is also fertile ranch land, with the historic 20,000-acre 'Ulupalakua Ranch and 32,000-acre Haleakalā Ranch. In Makawao each July 4, the Maui Roping Club throws its annual rodeo and parade.

A Good Drive

Take the **Haleakalā Highway** ㊲ (Hwy. 37) to **Haleakalā National Park** ㊳ and the mountain's breathtaking summit. Make sure you have a full gas tank. There are no service stations above Kula.

Watch the signs: Haleakalā Highway divides. If you go straight it becomes Kula Highway, which is still Highway 37. If you veer to the left it becomes Highway 377, the road you want. After about 6 mi, make a left onto Highway 378. The switchbacks begin here. Near the top of the mountain is the Park Headquarters/Visitor Center, a good spot to stretch your legs and learn a little bit about the park.

Continuing up the mountain, you'll come to several overlooks, including Leleiwi Overlook and Kalahaku Overlook, both with views into the crater. Not far from Kalahaku Overlook you'll find the Haleakalā Visitor Center. Eventually you'll reach the highest point on Maui, the Pu'u 'Ula'ula Overlook.

On the return trip, turn left when you reach Highway 377. Go about 2 mi, and you'll come to **Kula Botanical Gardens** ㊴ on your left. It's worth a stop here to admire the abundant tropical flora. Continue on Highway 377, away from Kahului, and you'll soon join Highway 37 again. Turn left and, about 8 mi farther on, you'll reach 'Ulupalakua Ranch headquarters and **Tedeschi Vineyards and Winery** ㊵, where you can sample Hawai'i's only homemade wines.

Return toward Kahului on Highway 37, the Kula Highway. **Enchanting Floral Gardens** ㊶ is clearly visible on the right side of the road near Mile Marker 10, about 2 mi before the Highway 37/377 junction. If you're pressed for time you can take Highway 37 from here back to Kahului. Otherwise, head north on Highway 365 toward **Makawao** ㊷, a classic old Hawaiian town. The **Hui No'eau Visual Arts Center** ㊸ is about a mile from the Makawao crossroads as you head down Baldwin Avenue. From here it's a 7-mi drive down toward the ocean to the Hāna Highway at the town of Pā'ia. Make a left on the Hāna Highway to return to Kahului.

TIMING

This can be an all-day outing even without the detours to Tedeschi Vineyards and Makawao. If you start early enough to catch the sunrise from Haleakalā's summit, you'll have plenty of time to explore the mountain, have lunch in Kula or at 'Ulupalakua Ranch, and end your day with dinner in Makawao or Ha'ikū.

Sights to See

㊶ **Enchanting Floral Gardens.** This 8-acre flower garden shines with blooms from every part of the globe. There are excellent collections of bromeliads and proteas, but this garden doesn't specialize. You'll find some of everything, and the signage is very good. A paved path winds through the display, under blooming arbors, and past three colorful gazebos. ✉ *Hwy. 37 near Omaopio Rd., Kula,* ☎ *808/878–2531,* FAX *808/878–1805.* 🎫 *$5.* ⊙ *Daily 9–5.*

③⑦ **Haleakalā Highway.** On this road, you'll travel from sea level to an elevation of 10,023 ft in only 38 mi—a feat you won't be able to repeat on any other car route in the world. It's not a quick drive, however. It'll take you about two hours—longer if you can't resist the temptation to stop and enjoy the spectacular views. ✉ *Hwy. 37.*

★ ③⑧ **Haleakalā National Park.** Haleakalā Crater is the centerpiece of this 27,284-acre national park, first established in 1916. The crater is actually an "erosional valley," flushed out by water pouring from the summit through two enormous "gaps." The small hills within the crater are volcanic cinder cones (called *puʻu* in Hawaiian), each with a small crater at its top, and each the site of a former eruption. The mountain has terrific camping and hiking opportunities, including a trail that loops through the crater.

Before you head up Haleakalā, call for the latest park weather conditions (☎ 808/871–5054). Extreme gusty winds, heavy rain, and even snow in winter are not uncommon—even if it's paradise as usual down at beach level. Because of the high altitude, the mountaintop temperature is often as much as 30 degrees cooler than that at sea level. Be sure to pack an extra jacket.

You can learn something of the volcano's origins and eruption history at the Park Headquarters/Visitor Center, at 7,000-ft elevation on Haleakalā Highway. Maps, posters, and other memorabilia are available at the gift shop here.

Leleiwi Overlook, at about an 8,800-ft elevation on Haleakalā, is one of several lookout areas in the park. If you're here in the late afternoon, it's possible you'll experience a phenomenon called the Brocken Specter. Named after a similar occurrence in East Germany's Harz Mountains, the "specter" allows you to see yourself reflected on the clouds and encircled by a rainbow. Don't wait all day for this, because it's not a daily occurrence.

The famous silversword plant grows amid the desertlike surroundings at **Kalahaku Overlook**, at the 9,000-ft level on Haleakalā. This endangered flowering plant grows only here in the crater at the summit of this mountain. The silversword looks like a member of the yucca family and produces a 3- to 8-ft-tall stalk. At this lookout the silversword is kept in an enclosure to protect it from souvenir hunters and nibbling wildlife.

The **Haleakalā Visitor Center**, at 9,740-ft elevation on Haleakalā, has exhibits inside, and a trail from here leads to White Hill—a short, easy walk that will give you an even better view of the valley. Hosmer Grove, just off the highway before you get to the visitor center, has campsites and interpretive trails. Park rangers maintain a changing schedule of talks and hikes both here and at the top of the mountain. Call the park for current schedules.

Just before the summit, the **Crater Observatory** offers warmth and shelter, informative displays, and an eye-popping view of the cinder-cone-studded, 7-mi by 3-mi crater. The highest point on Maui is the **Puʻu ʻUlaʻula Overlook**, at the 10,023-ft summit. Here you'll find a glass-enclosed lookout with a 360-degree view. The building is open 24 hours a day, and this is where visitors gather for the best sunrise view. Dawn begins between 5:45 and 7, depending on the time of year. On a clear day you can

Close-Up
HAWAI'I'S FLORA AND FAUNA

Hawai'i has the dubious distinction of claiming more extinct and endangered animal species than all of the North American continent. The Hawaiian crow, or 'alalā, for example, has been reduced to a population of only 15 birds, and most of these have been raised in captivity on the Big Island. The 'alalā is now facing a serious threat from another endangered bird—the 'io, or Hawaiian hawk. Still "protected" although making a comeback from its former endangered status, the nēnē goose, Hawai'i's state bird, roams freely in parts of Maui, Kaua'i, and the Big Island, where mating pairs are often spotted ambling across roads in Hawai'i Volcanoes National Park.

The mongoose is not endangered, although some residents wish it were. Alert drivers can catch a glimpse of the ferretlike mongoose darting across country roads. The mongoose was brought to Hawai'i in 1883 in an attempt to control the rat population, but the plan had only limited success, since the hunter and hunted rarely met: mongooses are active during the day, rats at night. Another creature, the rock wallaby, arrived in Honolulu in 1916 after being purchased from the Sydney Zoological Garden. Two escaped, and today about 50 of the small, reclusive marsupials live in remote areas of Kalihi Valley.

At the Kīlauea Point National Wildlife Refuge on Kauai'i, hundreds of Laysan albatross, wedge-tail shearwaters, red-footed boobies, and other marine birds glide and soar within photo-op distance of visitors to Kīlauea Lighthouse. Boobie chicks hatch in the fall and emerge from nests burrowed into cliffside dirt banks and even under stairs—any launching pad from which the fledgling flyer can catch the nearest air current.

Hawai'i has only two native mammals. Threatened with extinction, the rare Hawaiian bat hangs out primarily at Kealakekua Bay on the Big Island. Also on the endangered species list, doe-eyed Hawaiian monk seals breed in northwestern Islands. With only 1,500 left in the wild, you won't catch many lounging on the beaches of Hawai'i's populated islands, but you can see rescued pups and adults along with Hawaiian green sea turtles at Sea Life Park and the Waikīkī Aquarium on O'ahu.

Tropical flowers such as plumeria, orchids, hibiscus, red ginger, heliconia, and anthuriums grow wild on all the islands. Pīkake blossoms make the most fragrant leis, and fragile orange 'ilima (once reserved only for royalty) the most elegant leis. The lovely wood rose is actually the dried seed pod of a species of morning glory. Mountain apple, Hawaiian raspberry, thimbleberry, and strawberry guava provide refreshing snacks for hikers; and giant banyan trees, hundreds of years old, spread their canopies over families picnicking in parks, inviting youngsters to swing from their hanging vines.

Sprouting ruby pom-pomlike lehua blossoms—thought to be the favorite flower of Pele, the volcano goddess—'ōhi'a trees bury their roots in fields of once-molten lava. Also growing on the Big Island as well as the outer slopes of Maui's Haleakalā, exotic protea flourish only at an elevation of 4,000 ft; within Haleakalā's moonscape crater, the rare and otherworldly silversword—a 7-ft stalk with a single white spike and pale yellow flower found nowhere else on earth—blooms once and then dies.

The moral? Leave the lava rocks as they are and pick up any elderly hitchhikers you might come across. Straightforward enough. But I'd still hightail it in the other direction if I heard mysterious chanting or drum beating.

36 **Exploring Maui** Chapter 1

see the islands of Moloka'i, Lāna'i, Kaho'olawe, and Hawai'i. On a *really* clear day you can even spot O'ahu glimmering in the distance.

On a small hill nearby, you'll see **Science City**, a research and communications center straight out of an espionage thriller. The University of Hawai'i and the Department of Defense don't allow visitors to enter the facility. The university maintains an observatory here, and the Department of Defense tracks satellites. ⊠ *Haleakalā Crater Rd. (Hwy. 378), Makawao,* ☎ *808/572–4400.* ⊡ *$10 per car.* ⊙ *Park Headquarters/Visitor Center daily 7:30–4; Haleakalā visitor center daily sunrise–3.*

NEED A BREAK? **Kula Lodge** (⊠ Haleakalā Hwy., Kula, ☎ 808/878–2517) serves hearty breakfasts from 6:30 to 11:15, a favorite with visitors coming down from a sunrise visit to Haleakalā's summit, as well as those on their way up for a later-morning tramp in the crater. Spectacular ocean views fill the windows of this mountainside lodge (☞ East Maui *in* Chapter 3).

㊸ Hui No'eau Visual Arts Center. This nonprofit cultural center is on the old Baldwin estate, just outside the town of Makawao. The main house, an elegant two-story Mediterranean-style villa designed in the 1920s by C. W. Dickey, shines from the efforts of renovations. "The Hui," more than 60 years old, is the grande dame of Maui's well-known arts scene. The acreage seems like a botanical garden, and the nonstop exhibits are always satisfying. The Hui also offers classes and maintains working artists' studios. ⊠ *2841 Baldwin Ave., Makawao,* ☎ *808/572–6560.* ⊡ *Free.* ⊙ *Tues.–Sun. 10–4.*

㊴ Kula Botanical Gardens. This well-kept 35-year-old garden has assimilated itself naturally into its craggy 6-acre habitat. There are beautiful trees here, including native koa (prized by woodworkers) and kukui (the state tree, a symbol of enlightenment). There's also a good selection of proteas, the flowering shrubs that have become a signature flower crop of Upcountry Maui. A natural stream feeds into a koi pond, which is also home to a pair of African cranes. ⊠ *R.R. 2, Upper Kula Rd., Kula,* ☎ *808/878–1715.* ⊡ *$4.* ⊙ *Daily 9–4.*

㊷ Makawao. This once-tiny town has managed to hang on to its country charm (and eccentricity) as it has grown in popularity. The district was settled originally by Portuguese and Japanese immigrants, who came to Maui to work the sugar plantations and then moved "upcountry" to establish small farms, ranches, and stores. Descendants now work the neighboring Haleakalā and 'Ulupalakua ranches. Every July 4 the *paniolo* (Hawaiian cowboy) set comes out in force for the Makawao Rodeo. The crossroads of town, lined with places to shop, see art, and get food, reflects a growing population of people who came here just because they liked it. ⊠ *Hwy. 365, East Maui.*

NEED A BREAK? One of Makawao's most famous landmarks is **Komoda Store & Bakery** (⊠ 3674 Baldwin Ave., ☎ 808/572–7261)—a classic mom-and-pop store that has changed little in more than 70 years—where you can get a delicious cream puff if you arrive early enough in the day. They make hundreds, but sell out each day.

★ **㊵ Tedeschi Vineyards and Winery.** You can take a tour of the winery and its historic grounds, the former Rose Ranch, and sample the island's only wines: a pleasant Maui Blush, the Maui Brut-Blanc de Noirs Hawaiian Champagne, and Tedeschi's annual Maui Nouveau. The top-selling products, however, are pineapple wines. The tasting room is a cottage built in the 1800s for the frequent visits of King Kalākaua. The cottage also contains the **'Ulupalakua Ranch History Room,** which tells colorful stories of the ranch's owners, the paniolo tradition that developed here, and Maui's polo teams. The old General Store may look like a museum, but in fact it's an excellent pit stop. The ranch and winery are not too far out of the way when you're returning from a visit to Haleakalā. ✉ *Kula Hwy., 'Ulupalakua Ranch,* ☎ *808/878-6058.* 🆓 *Free.* ⊙ *Daily 9–5, tours daily 9–2:30.*

The Road to Hāna

Don't let anyone tell you the Hāna Highway is impassable, frightening, or otherwise unadvisable. Because of all the hype, you're bound to be a little nervous approaching it for the first time. But once you try it, you'll wonder if somebody out there is making it sound tough just to keep out the hordes. The 55-mi road begins in Kahului, where it's a well-paved highway. The eastern half of the road is riddled with turns and bridges, and you'll want to stop often so the driver can enjoy the view, too. But it's not a grueling all-day drive. The challenging part of the road takes only an hour and a half.

A Good Drive

The Hāna Highway is the main street in the little town of **Pā'ia** ㊹. You'll want to begin with a full tank of gas. There are no gas stations along the Hāna Highway, and the stations in Hāna close by 6 PM. You can also pick up a picnic lunch here. Lunch and snack choices along the way are limited to local fare from rustic fruit stands. Once the road gets twisty, remember that many residents make this trip frequently. You'll recognize them because they're the ones who'll be zipping around every curve. They've seen this so many times before that they don't care to linger. Pull over to let them pass.

Two miles east of Pā'ia you'll see **Ho'okipa Beach** ㊺, arguably the windsurfing capital of the world. Two miles later the bottom of Ha'ikū Road offers a right-turn side trip to **Ha'ikū** ㊻, Maui's verdant gulch country. About 6 mi later, at the bottom of Kaupakalua Road, the roadside mileposts begin measuring the 36 mi to Hāna town. The road's trademark noodling starts about 3 mi after that. All along this stretch of road, waterfalls are abundant. Open the windows to enjoy the sounds and smells. There are plenty of places to pull off and park. You'll want to plan on doing this a few times, since the road's curves make driving without a break difficult. When it's raining (which is often), the drive is particularly beautiful.

As you drive on, you'll pass the sleepy country villages of **Huelo** ㊼ and Kailua. At about Mile Marker 11 you can stop at the bridge over **Puahokamoa Stream** ㊽, where there are more pools and waterfalls. If you'd rather stretch your legs and use a flush toilet, continue another mile to the **Kaumahina State Wayside Park** ㊾. Near Mile Marker 13 you'll find yourself driving along a cliffside plunging down into deep, lush **Honomanū Bay** ㊿. Another 4 mi brings you to the **Ke'anae Arboretum** ㈎, where you can add to your botanical education or enjoy a challenging hike into a forest. Nearby you'll find the **Ke'anae Overlook** ㈏. Coming up is the halfway mark to Hāna. If you've had enough scenery, this is as good a time as any to turn around and head back to civilization.

Don't expect a booming city when you get to Hāna. It's the road that's the draw. Continue from Mile Marker 20 for about ¾ mi to **Wailua Overlook** ㈐. After another ½ mi you'll hit the best falls on the entire drive, **Waikāne Falls** ㈑. At about Mile Marker 25 you'll see a road that heads down toward the ocean and the village of **Nāhiku** ㈒, once a populous settlement. Just after Mile Marker 31, the left turn at 'Ula'ino Road doubles back for a mile, loses its pavement, and even crosses a streambed just before Kahanu Garden and **Pi'ilanihale Heiau** ⑯, the largest in the state. Back on the road and less than ½ mi farther is the turnoff for Hāna Airport. Just beyond Mile Marker 32 you'll pass **Wai'ānapanapa State Park** ⑰. Stop at the black-sand beach for a swim. **Hāna** ⑱ is just minutes from here. **Hotel Hāna-Maui** ⑲, with its surrounding ranch, is the mainstay of Hāna's economy.

Once you've seen Hāna, you might want to drive 10 mi past the town to the pools at **'Ohe'o Gulch** ⑳. Many people travel the mile past 'Ohe'o Gulch to see the **Grave of Charles Lindbergh** ㉑. You'll see a ruined sugar mill with a big chimney on the right side of the road and then, on the left, a rutted track leading to Palapala Ho'omau Congregational Church. The simple one-room church sits on a bluff over the sea, with the small graveyard on the ocean side. From here, you'll want to return the way you came. The road ahead is quite rough and not recommended for rental cars.

TIMING

With stops, the drive from Pā'ia to Hāna should take you between two and three hours. Lunching in Hāna, hiking, and swimming can easily turn the round-trip into a full-day outing. Since there's so much lush scenery to take in, try to plan your Road to Hāna drive for a day that promises fair, sunny weather. And be prepared for car trains that form spontaneously during the busier tourist seasons. (If you find one forming behind you, pull over and let the other drivers pass.)

Sights to See

㉑ **Grave of Charles Lindbergh.** The world-renowned aviator chose to be buried here because he and his wife, writer Anne Morrow Lindbergh, spent a lot of time living in the area in a home they'd built. He was buried here in 1974, next to Palapala Ho'omau Congregational Church. Since this is a churchyard, be considerate and leave everything exactly as you found it. Next to the churchyard on the ocean side is a small county park, a good place for a peaceful picnic. ✉ *Palapala Ho'omau Congregational Church, Kīpahulu.*

OFF THE BEATEN PATH

KAUPŌ ROAD – The road to Hāna continues all the way around Haleakalā's "back side" through 'Ulupalakua Ranch and into Kula. It's a bad road, sometimes impassable in winter. The car-rental agencies are smart to call it off-limits to their passenger cars. Most of the residents along the road in these wild reaches also prefer that you stick to the windward side of the mountain. The danger and dust from increasing numbers of speeding jeep drivers are making life tough for the natives, especially in Kaupō, with its 4 mi of unpaved road. The small communities around East Maui cling tenuously to the old ways. Please keep them in mind if you do pass this way.

㊻ **Ha'ikū.** At one time this town vibrated around a couple of enormous pineapple canneries. Now the place is reawakening and becoming a self-reliant community. At the town center, the old cannery has been turned into a rustic mall. Nearby warehouses are following suit. Continue 2 mi up Kokomo Road to see a large pu'u capped with a grove of columnar pines, and the 4th Marine Division Memorial Park. During World War II, American GIs trained here for battles on Iwo Jima and Saipan. Locals have nicknamed the cinder cone "Giggle Hill," because it was a popular place for Maui girls to entertain their favorite servicemen. You might want to return to Hāna Highway by following Ha'ikū Road east. This is one of Maui's prettiest drives, and it passes West Kuiaha Road, where a left turn will bring you to a second renovated cannery. ✉ *Intersection of Ha'ikū and Kokomo Rds.*

The Road to Hāna

★ ⑤⑧ **Hāna.** For many years, the ☞ **Hotel Hāna-Maui** was the only attraction for diners and shoppers determined to spend some time and money in Hāna after their long drive. The **Hāna Cultural Center Museum** (☎ 808/248–8622), on Ukea Street, helps to meet that need. Besides operating a well-stocked gift shop, it displays artifacts, quilts, a replica of an authentic *kauhale* (an ancient Hawaiian living complex, with thatched huts and food gardens), and other Hawaiiana. The knowledgeable staff can explain it all to you.

This is a company town. Although sugar was once the mainstay of Hāna's economy, the last plantation shut down in the '40s. In 1946 rancher Paul Fagan built the Hotel Hāna-Maui and stocked the surrounding pastureland with cattle. Suddenly, it was the ranch and its hotel that were putting food on most tables. The cross you'll see on the hill above the hotel was put there in memory of Fagan.

The town centers on its lovely circular bay, dominated on the right-hand shore by a pu'u called Ka'uiki. A short trail here leads to a cave, the birthplace of Queen Kā'ahumanu. Two miles beyond town another pu'u presides over a loop road that passes Hāna's two best beaches—Koki and Hāmoa. The hill is called Ka Iwi O Pele (Pele's Bone). This area is rich in Hawaiian history and legend. Offshore here, at tiny 'Ālau Island, the demigod Maui supposedly fished up the Hawaiian islands. ✉ *Hāna Hwy., Mile Marker 35.*

Hāna Airport. Think of Amelia Earhart. Think of Waldo Pepper. If these picket-fence runways don't turn your thoughts to the derring-do of barnstorming pilots, you haven't seen enough old movies. Only the smallest planes can land and take off here, and when none of them happen to be around, the lonely wind sock is the only evidence that this is a working airfield. ✉ *Hāna Hwy. past Mile Marker 30,* ☎ *808/248–8208.*

⑤⓪ **Honomanū Bay.** At Mile Marker 14 the Hāna Highway drops into and out of this enormous valley, with its rocky black-sand beach. The Honomanū Valley was carved by erosion during Haleakalā's first dormant period. At the canyon's head there are 3,000-ft cliffs and a 1,000-ft waterfall, but don't try to reach them. There's not much of a trail, and what does exist is practically impassable. ✉ *Hāna Hwy. before Ke'anae.*

★ ④⑤ **Ho'okipa Beach.** There is no better place on this or any other island to watch the world's best windsurfers in action. The surfers know five different surf breaks here by name. Unless it's a rare day without wind or waves, you're sure to get a show. It's not safe to park on the shoulder. Use the ample parking lot at the county park entrance. ✉ *2 mi past Pā'ia on Hwy. 36.*

⑤⑨ **Hotel Hāna-Maui.** It's pleasant to stroll around the lobby of this low-key but beautiful property, perhaps on the way to dinner at the restaurant, drinks at the bar, or shopping in the gift stores. The newer Sea Ranch cottages across the road are also part of the Hāna-Maui. The cottages were built to look like authentic plantation housing, but only from the outside. ✉ *Hāna Hwy., Hāna,* ☎ *808/248–8211.*

④⑦ **Huelo.** This sleepy little farm town has two quaint and lovely churches but little else of interest. Yet it's a good place to meet local residents and learn about a rural lifestyle you might not have expected to find in the Islands. The same could be said, minus the churches, for nearby Kailua (Mile Marker 6), home to Alexander & Baldwin's irrigation employees. ✉ *Hāna Hwy. near Mile Marker 5.*

④⑨ **Kaumahina State Wayside Park.** The park has a picnic area, rest rooms, and a lovely overlook to the Ke'anae Peninsula. Hardier souls can camp here, with a permit. ✉ *Hāna Hwy., Mile Marker 12, Kailua,* ☎ *808/984–8109 weekdays 8–4.* 🎫 *Free.*

(51) **Ke'anae Arboretum.** Here you can learn the names of the many plants and trees now considered native to Hawai'i. The meandering Pi'ina'au Stream adds a graceful touch and provides a swimming pond besides. You can take a fairly rigorous hike from the arboretum, if you can find the trail at one side of the large taro patch. Be careful not to lose the trail once you're on it. A lovely forest waits at the end of the hike. ✉ *Hāna Hwy., Mile Marker 17, Ke'anae.* 🎫 *Free.*

(52) **Ke'anae Overlook.** From this observation point, you'll notice the patchwork-quilt effect the taro farms create below. The people of Ke'anae are working hard to revive this Hawaiian agricultural art and the traditional cultural values that the crop represents. The ocean provides a dramatic backdrop for the farms. In the other direction there are awesome views of Haleakalā through the foliage. This is a great spot for photos. ✉ *Hāna Hwy. near Mile Marker 17, Ke'anae.*

(55) **Nāhiku.** This was a busy settlement in ancient times, with hundreds of residents. Now only about 80 people live in Nāhiku, mostly native Hawaiians and some back-to-the-land types. A rubber grower planted trees here in the early 1900s. The experiment didn't work out, so Nāhiku was essentially abandoned. The road ends at the sea in a pretty landing. This is the rainiest, densest part of the East Maui rain forest. ✉ *Makai side of Hāna Hwy., Mile Marker 25.*

★ (60) **'Ohe'o Gulch.** One branch of Haleakalā National Park runs down the mountain from the crater and reaches the sea here, where a basalt-lined stream cascades from one pool to the next. Tour guides used to call this area by the silly name "Seven Sacred Pools." You can park here and walk to the lowest pools for a cool swim. The place gets crowded, though, since most people who drive the Hāna Road make this their last stop. If you can hike at all, go up the stream on the 2-mi hike to **Waimoku Falls.** The trail crosses a spectacular gorge, then turns into a boardwalk that takes you through an amazing bamboo forest. You can pitch a tent in the grassy campground down by the sea. *Pi'ilani Hwy., 10 mi south of Hāna.*

★ ㊹ **Pā'ia.** This little town on Maui's north shore was once a sugarcane enclave, with a mill and plantation camps. Shrewd immigrants quickly opened shops to serve the workers, who probably found it easier to buy supplies near home. The town boomed during World War II when the marines set up camp in nearby Ha'ikū. The HC&S sugar mill, on Baldwin Avenue about a mile above the traffic light at Hāna Highway, is still in full production. After the war, however, workers moved to other parts of Maui, and the town's population began to dwindle. In the '70s Pā'ia became a hippie town as dropouts headed for Maui to open boutiques, galleries, and unusual eateries. In the '80s windsurfers discovered nearby Ho'okipa Beach and brought an international flavor to Pā'ia. You can see this in the youth of the town and in the budget inns that have cropped up to offer accommodations to those who windsurf for a living. Pā'ia is certainly a fun place.

If you want to do some shopping, you can find clothing and handcrafted keepsakes or snacks and sweets in abundance in the friendly town of Pā'ia. Pā'ia is also home to Lama Tenzin, a Tibetan monk who lives and teaches at a small open temple called **Karma Rimay O Sal Ling,** on Baldwin Avenue half a mile from the traffic light. ✉ *Hwys. 390 and 36, north shore.*

NEED A BREAK? Pā'ia has become a great place to find food. It used to be that **Picnics** (☎ 808/579–8021) was the one place to eat on Baldwin Avenue, and

The Road to Hāna

Charley's Saloon (☎ 808/579–8085), an easygoing local hangout with pool tables, was the place on Hāna Road. Now, right near the intersection of Baldwin Avenue and Hāna Road, you have a number of choices. **Pā'ia Fishmarket** (☎ 808/579–8030) specializes in fresh island fish both by the pound and served as tasty lunches and dinners. **Anthony's Coffee Company** (☎ 808/579–8340) serves ice cream, smoothies, and picnic lunches. The little town also has an excellent wine store, **The Wine Corner** (☎ 808/579–8940), and an admirable natural-foods store called **Mana Foods** (☎ 808/579–8078).

★ ⑤⑥ **Pi'ilanihale Heiau.** The largest prehistoric monument in Hawai'i, this temple platform was built for a great 16th-century Maui king named Pi'ilani and his heirs. This king also supervised the construction of a 10-ft-wide road that completely encircled the island. (That's why his name is part of most of Maui's difficult-to-pronounce highway titles.) Hawaiian families continue to maintain and protect this sacred site as they have for centuries, and they have not been eager to turn it into a tourist attraction. However, they now offer a brochure so you can tour the property yourself. Parties of four or more can reserve a guided tour by calling 48 hours in advance. Tours include 122-acre **Kahanu Garden**, a federally funded research center focusing on the ethnobotany of the Pacific. ✉ *Left on 'Ula'ino Rd. at Mile Marker 31; the road turns to gravel; continue 1½ mi,* ☎ *808/248-8912.* 🎟 *$5 self-guided, $10 guided.* ⊙ *Weekdays 9–3.*

④⑧ **Puahokamoa Stream.** The bridge over Puahokamoa Stream is one of many you'll cross en route from Pā'ia to Hāna. It spans pools and waterfalls. Picnic tables are available, so many people favor this as a stopping point, but there are no rest rooms. ✉ *Hāna Hwy. near Mile Marker 11.*

★ ⑤⑦ **Wai'ānapanapa State Park.** The park is right on the ocean, and it's a lovely spot to picnic, hike, or swim. An ancient burial site is nearby, as well as a heiau. Wai'ānapanapa also has one of Maui's only black-sand beaches and some freshwater caves for adventurous swimmers to explore. With a permit you can stay in state-run (and rather shabby) cabins here for less than $30 a night—the price varies depending on the number of people—but reserve early. They often book up a year in advance. ✉ *Hāna Hwy. near Mile Marker 32, Hāna,* ☎ *808/984-8109.* 🎟 *Free.*

⑤④ **Waikāne Falls.** Though not necessarily bigger or taller than the other falls, these are the most dramatic—some say the best—falls you'll find on the road to Hāna. That's partly because the water is not diverted for sugar irrigation. The taro farmers in Wailua need all the runoff. This is a particularly good spot for photos. ✉ *Hāna Hwy. past Mile Marker 21, Wailua.*

⑤③ **Wailua Overlook.** From the parking lot you can see Wailua Canyon, but you'll have to walk up steps to get a view of Wailua Village. The landmark in Wailua Village is a church made of coral, built in 1860. Once called St. Gabriel's Catholic Church, the current Our Lady of Fatima Shrine has an interesting legend surrounding it. As the story goes, a storm washed just enough coral up onto the shore to build the church but then took any extra coral back to sea. ✉ *Hāna Hwy. near Mile Marker 21, Wailua.*

2 DINING

In many of Maui's eateries, Continental classics such as chateaubriand and veal scallopine have given way to dishes such as coconut-chili beef and yellowfin tuna–breadfruit cakes. Although most of the island's food was once shipped in frozen, it is now passé to order goods from the mainland. The island's abundance of ingredients, from some 20 types of wild bananas to fresh fish caught off the island's shores, together with Asian and Western techniques has spawned a new style of cooking—contemporary Hawaiian cuisine. The result: exciting and glorious fare.

IN THE RESORTS YOU'LL FIND some of Maui's finest Continental restaurants and some good cafés and bistros as well. In addition, because many of the upscale hotels sit right on the beach, you'll often have the benefit of an oceanfront ambience. Outside the resorts, you'll find great places to dine formally or grab a bite informally (to use the pidgin term, "grind").

Except as noted, reservations are not required, but it's never a bad idea to phone ahead to book a table. Restaurants are open daily unless otherwise noted. Few restaurants on Maui require jackets. An aloha shirt and pants for men and a simple dress or pants for women are acceptable in all but the fanciest establishments. For price category explanations, *see* Smart Travel Tips A to Z.

West Maui

American

$$–$$$
★ ✕ **Longhi's.** This Lahaina establishment has been around since 1976, serving great Italian pasta as well as sandwiches, seafood, beef, and chicken dishes. All the pasta is homemade, and the in-house bakery turns out breakfast pastries, desserts, and fresh bread. Even on a warm day, you won't need air-conditioning here with two spacious, breezy, open-air levels to choose from. The black-and-white tile floors are a nice touch. ✉ 888 Front St., Lahaina, ☎ 808/667–2288. AE, D, DC, MC, V.

$–$$
★ ✕ **Lahaina Coolers.** This breezy little café with a surfboard hanging from its ceiling serves such tantalizing fare as Evil Jungle Pasta (grilled chicken in spicy Thai peanut sauce) and linguine with prawns, basil, garlic, and cream. It also has pizzas, steaks, burgers, and such desserts as a chocolate taco filled with tropical fruit and berry salsa. Pastas are made fresh in-house. Don't be surprised to see a local fisherman walk through the dining area with a freshly caught snapper, or a harbor captain reeling in a hearty breakfast. ✉ 180 Dickenson St., Lahaina, ☎ 808/661–7082. AE, MC, V.

Chinese

$–$$ ✕ **Red Lantern.** This true Maui novelty is a good place to eat that stays open until 2 AM. This oceanfront restaurant wins a lot of local awards, and for good reason. The owners are native Chinese, and they are serious about food. The menu lists 138 items, including specials like shark fin or sea cucumber in oyster sauce, but less-adventurous dishes are numerous as well. Dim sum is one of the specialties. Takeout is available, too. ✉ 1312 Front St., Lahaina, ☎ 808/667–1884. AE, D, DC, MC, V.

Continental

$$$–$$$$
★ ✕ **Swan Court.** You enter this elegant eatery via a grand staircase and what seems like a tropical, cathedral-ceiling ballroom, where black and white swans glide across a waterfall-fed lagoon. The menu applies European and Pacific Rim flavors to fresh, locally grown vegetables, seafood, and meats. Try the crispy scallop dim sum (a type of wonton) in plum sauce; creamy lobster-coconut bisque brimming with chunks of fish, lobster, shrimp, and button mushrooms; or charbroiled lamb chops in macadamia satay sauce. Arrive early and ask for a table on the left side, where the swans linger in the evening. The restaurant serves a breakfast buffet. ✉ Hyatt Regency Maui, Kā'anapali Beach Resort, 200 Nohea Kai Dr., Lahaina, ☎ 808/661–1234. AE, D, DC, MC, V.

$$–$$$$
★ ✕ **Bay Club.** A candlelit dinner at this spot on a rocky promontory overlooking the ocean is a romantic way to cap off a day in the sun, especially if you've been swimming at Kapalua Beach just a few yards from

Maui Dining

- 'Ānuenue Room 2
- A Pacific Cafe 22
- A Saigon Café 31
- Bay Club 3
- Bella Luna Ristorante 26
- BJ's Chicago Pizza 15
- Casanova Italian Restaurant & Deli 33
- Chez Paul 19
- David Paul's Lahaina Grill 14
- Erik's Seafood Grotto 6
- Gerard's 13
- Hāli'imaile General Store 32
- Hapa's Brewhouse 21
- Hula Grill 7
- Hula Moons 25
- I'o 18
- Joe's Bar & Grill 23
- Kimo's 12
- Lahaina Coolers 16
- Longhi's 11
- Mā'alaea Waterfront Restaurant 20
- Makawao Steak House 35
- Mama's Fish House 37
- Marco's Grill & Deli 27
- Orient Express 4
- Pacific'O 17
- Picnic's 38
- Plantation House Restaurant 1
- Polli's 34
- Red Lantern 9
- Restaurant Matsu 28
- Roy's Kahana Bar & Grill 5
- Ruth's Chris Steak House 10
- Saeng's Thai Cuisine 29
- Seasons 24
- Siam Thai 30
- Swan Court 8
- Trattoria Ha'ikū 36

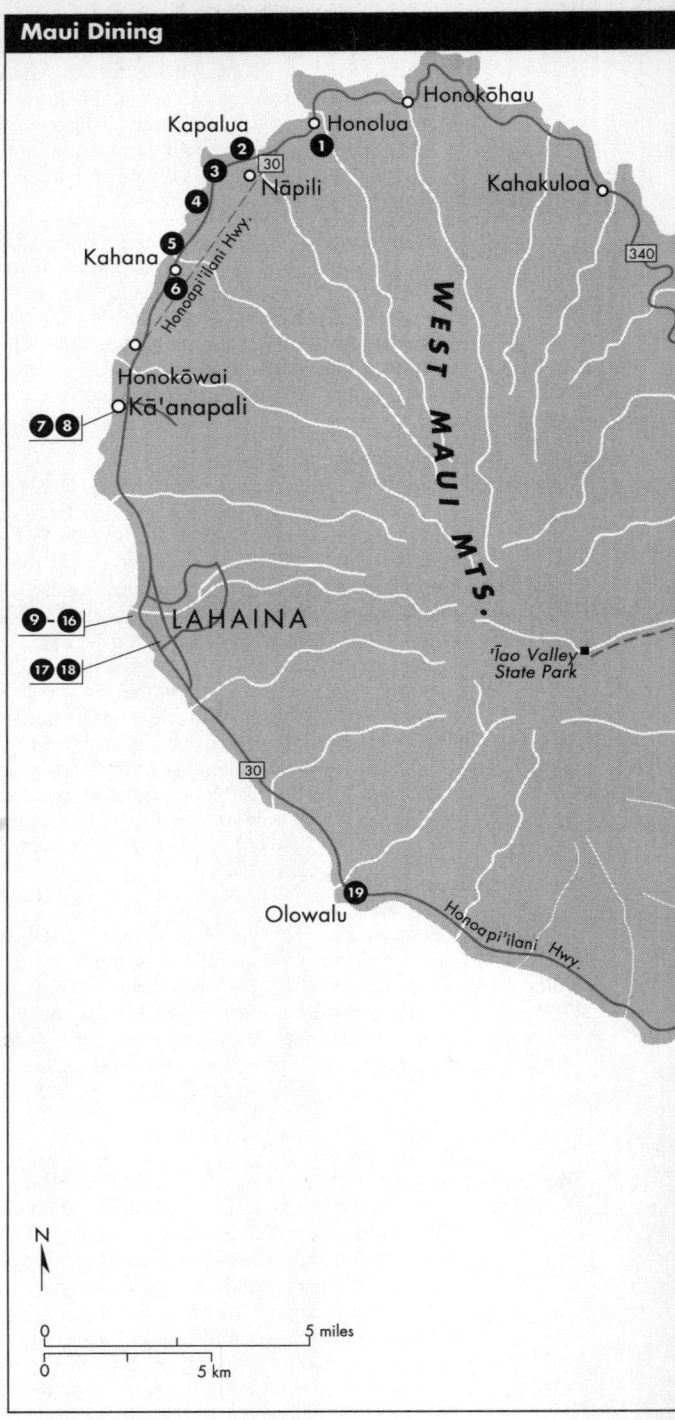

45

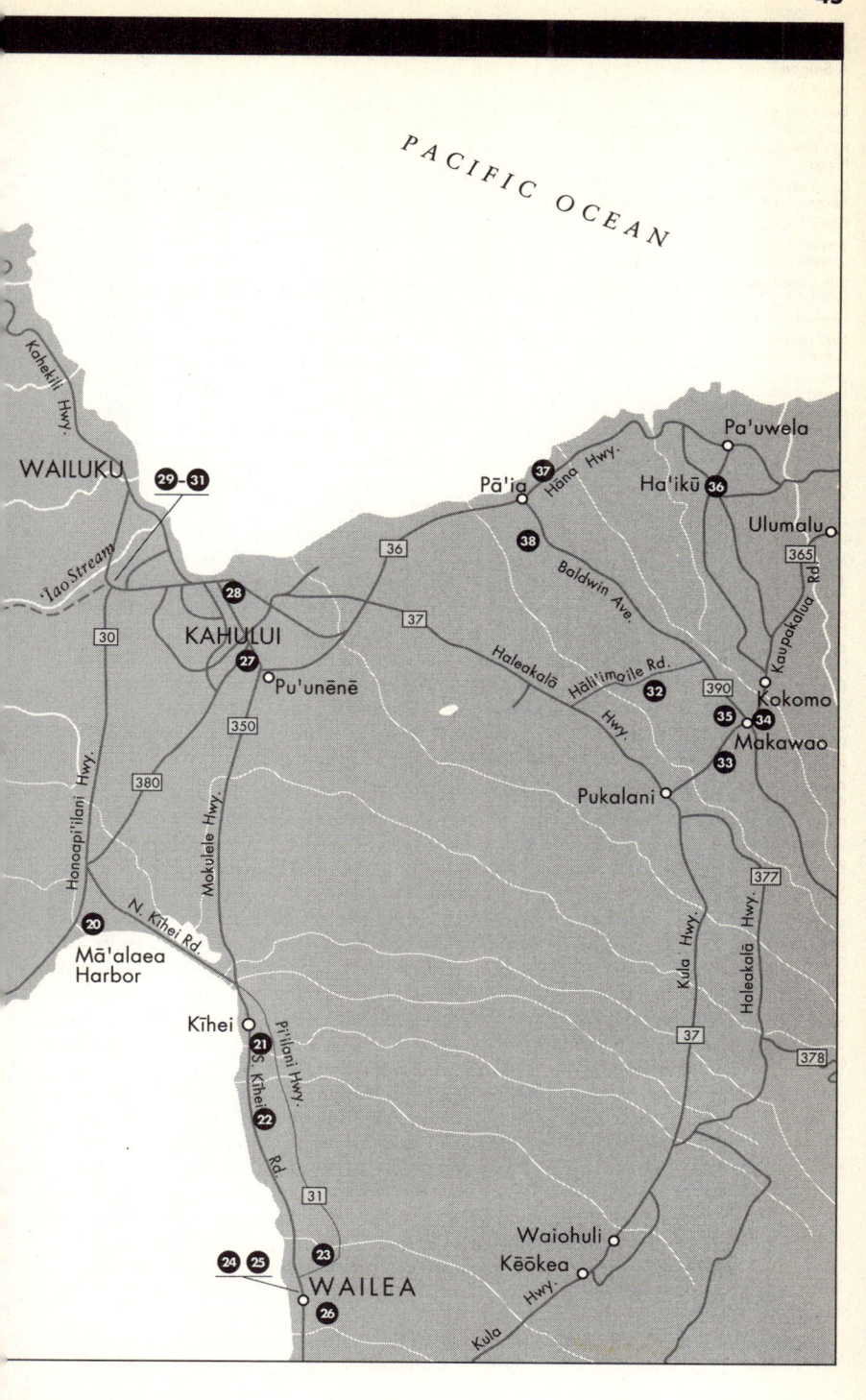

PACIFIC OCEAN

- Kahekili Hwy.
- WAILUKU
- 29 - 31
- 'Iao Stream
- 28
- KAHULUI
- 30
- 27
- Pu'unēnē
- 36
- 37
- Pā'ia
- 38
- Hāna Hwy.
- Pa'uwela
- Ha'ikū 36
- Ulumalu
- 365
- Baldwin Ave.
- Hāli'imaile Rd.
- Haleakalā Hwy.
- 32
- 390
- 35
- 34 Kokomo
- Makawao
- 33
- Pukalani
- Kaupakalua Rd.
- 350
- 380
- Honoapi'ilani Hwy.
- 20
- Mā'alaea Harbor
- N. Kīhei Rd.
- Mokulele Hwy.
- Kīhei
- 21
- S. Kīhei Rd.
- 22
- Pi'ilani Hwy.
- 31
- 24 25 23
- WAILEA
- 26
- Kula Hwy.
- 377
- Haleakalā Hwy.
- 378
- 37
- Waiohuli
- Kēōkea
- Kula Hwy.

the door. You won't want to walk through the richly paneled, elegant interior with sandy feet, however. For a truly relaxing evening, shower and dress first and then lean back, sip a glass of cabernet or Riesling from the excellent wine list, and watch the sun slip gloriously past the Maui horizon. Island seafood is the emphasis here, starting with appetizers like the seared 'ahi tartare and foie gras and building to main courses such as the Hawaiian seafood pan roast of prawns, lobster, and scallops cooked in sweet basil broth. ✉ *Kapalua Bay Hotel, 1 Bay Dr., Kapalua,* ☏ *808/669–5656. AE, D, DC, MC, V.*

French

$$$–$$$$ ★ ✕ **Gerard's.** Owner and celebrated chef Gerard Reversade started cooking at the age of 10, and at 12 he was baking croissants. Since 1982 he has been honoring the French tradition at this charming restaurant with such exquisitely prepared dishes as rack of lamb in mint crust with thyme jus; venison cutlets in a port sauce with confit of chestnuts, walnuts, fennel, and pearl onions; and impeccably fresh fish. The menu changes once a year, but many favorites—such as the sinfully good crème brûlée—remain. A first-class wine list, a lovely room, and celebrity-spotting round out the experience. ✉ *Plantation Inn, 174 Lahainaluna Rd., Lahaina,* ☏ *808/661–8939. AE, D, DC, MC, V. No lunch.*

$$–$$$$ ★ ✕ **Chez Paul.** Since 1975 this tiny roadside restaurant between Lahaina and Māʻalaea in Olowalu has served excellent French cuisine to a packed house of repeat customers. Such dishes as fresh local fish poached in white wine with shallots, cream, and capers typify the classical menu with island touches. The restaurant's nondescript exterior belies the fine art, 14 linen-draped tables, 22-seat private dining room, wine cellar, and charming atmosphere inside. Don't blink or you'll miss this small group of buildings huddled in the middle of nowhere. ✉ *Hwy. 30, 4 mi south of Lahaina,* ☏ *808/661–3843. Reservations essential. AE, D, MC, V. No lunch.*

Hawaiʻi Regional/Pacific Rim

$$$–$$$$ ✕ **ʻĀnuenue Room.** In Hawaiian, *ʻānuenue* means rainbow. The name, however, doesn't really characterize the Ritz-Carlton's elegant signature restaurant, with its dark-wood walls and massive chandeliers. The cuisine is pure Hawaiian, inventively elevated. Appetizers include *opihi* (sea snail) with island goat cheese in pastry, and crispy corn-and-sea-urchin fritters served with shrimp, seaweed, and Hawaiian chili-lobster sauce. For the main course, how about kālua suckling pig served with Hawaiian sticky rice, cabbage, port wine, and *ʻohelo* berries (the island equivalent of cranberries)? Service is excellent, as you might expect at the Ritz. ✉ *Ritz-Carlton, Kapalua, 1 Ritz-Carlton Dr., Kapalua,* ☏ *808/669–1665. AE, D, DC, MC, V.*

$$–$$$$ ★ ✕ **David Paul's Lahaina Grill.** This beautifully designed restaurant sits arm-in-arm with the elegant Lahaina Inn in a historic, creaky building on Lahainaluna Road. It's won numerous awards since it opened in 1990, including *Honolulu* magazine's selection as "Best Restaurant on Maui" seven years in a row. It offers an extensive wine cellar, an in-house bakery, and a baby grand in the lounge. The chef's celebrated menu is revised seasonally, but you can count on finding the signature tequila shrimp and firecracker rice along with such scrumptious desserts as triple-berry pie. ✉ *127 Lahainaluna Rd., Lahaina,* ☏ *808/667–5117. AE, DC, MC, V.*

$$–$$$ ✕ **Hula Grill.** This bustling, family-oriented restaurant is the informal counterpart to genial chef-restaurateur Peter Merriman's first popular eatery, Merriman's, on the Big Island, and the food is every bit as good. South Pacific snapper is baked with tomato, chili, and cumin aioli and served with black bean, Maui onion, and avocado relish. Spare ribs are steamed in banana leaves, then grilled with mango barbecue

sauce over mesquite-like *kiawe*. The restaurant is set in a re-created 1930s Hawaiian beach house, and every table has an ocean-beach view. Or you can actually dine on the beach, toes in the sand, at the Barefoot Bar, where Hawaiian entertainment is presented every evening. ✉ *Whalers Village, 2435 Kā'anapali Pkwy., Kā'anapali,* ☎ *808/667-6636. AE, DC, MC, V.*

$$–$$$ ✗ **I'o.** Opened in 1999, this restaurant immediately established itself as the hippest place in Lahaina—both for its theatrical, sculpted interior designed by the artist Dado and for its eclectic menu of contemporary Pacific cuisine. The most popular appetizer is the "silken purse"—steamed wontons stuffed with roasted peppers, mushrooms, macadamia nuts, and tofu and served with jalapeño-scented tomato sauce and yogurt purée. Favorite dinners include the crispy 'ahi, sashimi-grade tuna wrapped in nori and served with a salad of green papaya and sweet peppers; and lemongrass-coconut fish served with fresh hearts-of-palm salad and chilled spicy soba noodles. ✉ *505 Front St., Lahaina,* ☎ *808/661-8422,* FAX *808/661-8399. AE, D, DC, MC, V. No lunch.*

$$–$$$ ✗ **Plantation House Restaurant.** It's hard to decide which is best here, the food or the view. Rolling hills, grassy volcanic ridges lined with pine trees, and fairways that appear to drop off into the ocean provide an idyllic setting. The specialty is fresh island fish prepared according to different "tastes"—Upcountry Maui, Asian-Pacific, Provence, and others. The "Taste of the Rich Forest" includes roasted wild mushrooms served on tender tot soi greens and garlic mashed potatoes with a Maui onion meunière. The breeze through the large shuttered windows can be cool, so you may want to bring a sweater or sit by the fireplace. ✉ *Plantation Course Clubhouse, 2000 Plantation Club Dr., past Kapalua,* ☎ *808/669-6299. AE, MC, V.*

$$–$$$ ✗ **Roy's Kahana Bar & Grill.** Anyone who's ever eaten at one of Roy Yamaguchi's restaurants knows how good the food is, and this Roy's is no exception. Such Asian-Pacific specialties as shrimp with sweet-and-spicy chili sauce keep regulars returning for more. Locals find this is a great place to get together with friends for fun and good food. Next door is the somewhat quieter Roy Yamaguchi's Nicolina, which caters to a spice-loving crowd with grilled Southwestern-style chicken with chili hash and smoked tomato sauce, and smoked-and-peppered duck with gingered sweet potatoes and Szechuan-Mandarin sauce. ✉ *Kahana Gateway Shopping Center, 4405 Honoapi'ilani Hwy., Kahana,* ☎ *808/669-6999 (Roy's); 808/669-5000 (Nicolina). AE, D, DC, MC, V.*

Italian

$–$$ ✗ **BJ's Chicago Pizza.** If you're in the mood for pizza, this is the place to go on Maui. Residents have consistently voted it the island's best, and *Bon Appétit* magazine even went so far as to call it one of the country's best. The restaurant sits right on the seawall in Lahaina. The sound of live music by contemporary island stars tempts you inside because it all looks like so much fun. It is. ✉ *730 Front St., Lahaina,* ☎ *808/661-0700. AE, DC, MC, V.*

Seafood

$$–$$$ ✗ **Erik's Seafood Grotto.** This seafood diner is so proud of its large selection of fresh fish that it displays the whole offering nightly as a photo opportunity. Additional house specialties include bouillabaisse brimming with clams, scallops, lobster, shrimp, and fish and served with toasted garlic bread; and *cioppino,* a seafood stew served over homemade fettuccine. A stop at the oyster bar is a worthwhile detour. Try half shells topped with horseradish mayonnaise and baked with Gruyère cheese. Come to this nautical spot between 5 and 6 and catch the $12.95–$13.95 early bird specials. ✉ *Kahana Villas, 4242 Lower Honoapi'ilani Hwy., Kahana,* ☎ *808/669-4806. AE, D, DC, MC, V.*

$$-$$$ ✗ **Pacific'O.** You can sit outdoors at umbrella-shaded tables near the water's edge, or find a spot in the breezy, marble-floored interior. The menu is exciting, with the likes of a fresh 'ahi-and-*ono* tempura (ono is a makerel-like fish), in which the two kinds of fish are wrapped around *tobiko* (flying-fish roe), then in nori, and wok-fried. There's a great lamb dish, too—a whole rack of sweet New Zealand lamb, sesame-crusted and served with roasted macadamia sauce and Hawaiian chutney. Live jazz is offered Thursday through Saturday nights from 9 to midnight. George Benson likes to sit in. ✉ *505 Front St., Lahaina,* ☎ *808/667–4341. AE, D, DC, MC, V.*

$-$$ ✗ **Kimo's.** Outstanding seafood is just one of the options here. Also good are Hawaiian-style chicken and pork dishes, burgers, sandwiches, vegetarian pasta, and sashimi. The smoked marlin appetizer is especially tasty. On a warm Lahaina summer day, it's a treat to relax at an umbrella-shaded table on the open-air lānai, sip a pineapple-passion-fruit-guava drink, and watch sailboats and parasailers glide in and out of the harbor. Try the signature dessert, hula pie: vanilla–macadamia-nut ice cream topped with chocolate fudge and whipped cream in an Oreo-cookie crust. ✉ *845 Front St., Lahaina,* ☎ *808/661–4811. AE, DC, MC, V.*

Steak

$$-$$$$ ✗ **Ruth's Chris Steak House.** This chain claims to be the "home of serious steaks"—corn-fed midwestern beef, and only the top 2% of the cuts. When you hear your own immense, broiled-to-order portion sizzling as it approaches from across the room, you may believe the claim. The meat cuts like butter, and butter is a main feature of the '40s-style, classic steak-house menu (creamed spinach, scalloped potatoes). The ambience is appropriately old-fashioned and elegant: candlelight, lots of wood, and etched glass. The windows look right out over the Lahaina seawall. ✉ *Lahaina Shopping Center, 900 Front St., Lahaina,* ☎ *808/661–8815. AE, DC, MC, V.*

Thai

$-$$ ✗ **Orient Express.** Have your Thai food hot, medium, or mild at this decidedly Asian locale with red lacquer and yellow flowers evident everywhere. Eating Thai is always an adventure with such menu choices as beef satay marinated in coconut milk and spices, skewered on bamboo sticks and grilled; or shrimp cooked with bamboo shoots, water chestnuts, and dried chilies. ✉ *Nāpili Shores Resort, 5316 Lower Honoapi'ilani Hwy., Nāpili,* ☎ *808/669–8077. AE, MC, V. No lunch.*

Central Maui

Italian

$$ ✗ **Marco's Grill & Deli.** This convenient eatery outside the Kahului airport (look for the green awning) is home to some of the best-priced and best-tasting Italian fare on Maui. Fettuccine Alfredo, linguine with sausage, and vodka rigatoni are all on the extensive menu, along with an unforgettably good Reuben sandwich and the best Greek salad you'll ever find. The local business crowd fills the place for breakfast, lunch, and dinner. ✉ *444 Hāna Hwy., Kahului,* ☎ *808/877–4446. AE, D, DC, MC, V.*

Japanese

$ ✗ **Restaurant Matsu.** The Maui Mall just got a face-lift and a movie megaplex, but it's fortunately held on to a few real gems from the old days—including this tiny, nondescript kitchen and lunch room. Sit at a common table and eat authentic Japanese fare along with the locals—*katsus* (cutlets) and curries served with white rice, or bowls of saimin or udon noodles with tempura. ✉ *Maui Mall, Ka'ahumanu Ave., Kahului,* ☎ *808/871–0822. No credit cards.*

Thai

$–$$ ✕ **Saeng's Thai Cuisine.** Making a choice from the six-page menu here requires determination, but the food is worth the effort, and most dishes can be tailored to your taste buds: hot, medium, or mild. Begin with spring rolls and a dipping sauce, move on to such entrées as Evil Prince Chicken (cooked in coconut sauce with Thai herbs) or red curry shrimp, and finish up with tea and tapioca pudding. The dining room is decorated with Asian artifacts, flowers, and a waterfall, and tables on a veranda will satisfy outdoor lovers. ✉ *2119 Vineyard, Wailuku,* ☏ *808/244–1567. AE, MC, V.*

$–$$ ✕ **Siam Thai.** Behind a slightly weathered storefront you'll find some of the best Thai food on Maui. This local favorite serves traditional chicken-coconut soup, beef and chicken sautéed with ginger and bamboo shoots, curries, and vegetarian dishes—about 60 selections in all. The food tends to be spicy, the portions small, and huge crowds arrive at lunchtime. Some patrons opt for takeout because there's not much in the way of decor. ✉ *123 Market St., Wailuku,* ☏ *808/244–3817. AE, D, DC, MC, V.*

Vietnamese

$–$$ ✕ **A Saigon Café.** The only storefront sign announcing this small, delightful hideaway is one reading OPEN. Once you find it, treat yourself to *banh hoi chao tom,* more commonly called "shrimp pops burritos" (ground marinated shrimp, steamed and grilled on a stick of sugarcane). It's fun and messy. Vegetarian fare is also well represented here. The white interior serves as a backdrop for Vietnamese carvings and other interesting artwork. ✉ *1792 Main St., Wailuku,* ☏ *808/243–9560. D, MC, V.*

The South Shore

American

$$–$$$ ✕ **Joe's Bar & Grill.** With friendly service, a great view of Lāna'i, and such dishes as New York strip steak with caramelized onions, wild mushrooms, and Gorgonzola cheese crumble, there are lots of reasons to stop in at this spacious, breezy spot. Owners Joe and Bev Gannon, who run the immensely popular Hāli'imaile General Store (☞ East Maui, *below*), have brought their flair for food home to roost in this comfortable treetop-level restaurant at the Wailea Tennis Club, where you can dine while watching court action from a balcony seat. ✉ *131 Wailea Ike Pl., Wailea,* ☏ *808/875–7767. AE, MC, V.*

$–$$ ✕ **Hapa's Brewhaus & Restaurant.** This friendly place has an assortment of great eats that includes pizza, calzones, pastas, chicken-teriyaki burgers, vegetarian stir-fry, sashimi, and lobster bisque. There are seven kinds of beer on tap, including Kona Longboard Lager. The adjoining room, Hapa's Rockin' Sushi, is open till one in the morning. ✉ *Lipoa Center, 41 E. Lipoa St., Kīhei,* ☏ *808/879–9001. D, DC, MC, V.*

Continental/Eclectic

$$$$ ✕ **Seasons.** Acclaimed executive chef George Mavrothalassitis prepares standout dishes that marry fresh island ingredients with flavors from his native Provence as well as from China, Japan, Thailand, and the Pacific islands. Consider, for example, *onaga* (pink or red snapper) and summer truffles with braised leeks, or shaved hamachi sashimi served with a tomato and peppercorn gelée and citrus *shoyu* (sweet soy sauce). As befits the Four Seasons Resort, this is a restaurant of understated elegance, with tables set with white linen and French china and a decor that emphasizes natural materials. A trio of island musicians and sensational ocean vistas add to the delicious ambience. ✉ *Four Seasons Resort Maui, 3900 Wailea Alanui, Wailea,* ☏ *808/874–8000. AE, D, DC, MC, V. No lunch.*

Hawai'i Regional/Pacific Rim

$$–$$$ ✗ **Hula Moons.** This delightful oceanside spot is full of memorabilia chronicling the island life of Don Blanding, a writer, artist, and poet who became Hawai'i's unofficial ambassador of aloha in the 1930s. The outstanding menu blends locally grown produce with Pacific Rim and European preparations. Try the scallops with Chinese black-bean sauce, charbroiled T-bone steak with pineapple compote and Moloka'i sweet potatoes, or the just-off-the-boat catch of the day. You can dine inside, poolside, or outside on the terrace while you choose your vintage from an extensive wine list. ✉ *Aston Wailea Resort, 3700 Wailea Alanui, Wailea,* ☎ *808/879–1922. AE, D, DC, MC, V.*

$$–$$$ ✗ **A Pacific Cafe.** Hawai'i regional cuisine began with a few innovative island chefs, including Jean-Marie Josselin. With the assistance of corporate chef George Gomes, Jr., who was born and raised in the Islands, Josselin now serves this innovative cuisine in five island locations, two on Maui. Flavorful combinations include pan-seared *mahimahi* (mild-flavored dolphinfish) with a garlic sesame crust and ginger-lime sauce; Chinese roasted duck with baked sour-cherry *manapua* (dough wrapped around diced pork), charred baby eggplant, and *liliko'i*–star anise sauce ("liliko'i" is Hawaiian for passion fruit); and "the original" tiger-eye 'ahi sushi tempura with pear tomato salad and Chinese mustard sauce. The restaurant's tropical, whimsical decor has been described as "the Flintstones meet the Jetsons." ✉ *Azeka Place II Shopping Center, 1279 S. Kīhei Rd., Kīhei,* ☎ *808/879–0069;* ✉ *3350 Lower Honoapi'ilani Rd., Lahaina,* ☎ *808/669–2724. AE, D, DC, MC, V. No lunch.*

Italian

$$ ✗ **Bella Luna Ristorante.** Best sunset view on the island—who could dare to claim such a title? Bella Luna does, and deservedly so. This is a small place (40 seats), where you dine looking out over a golf course and the open sea at the very quiet, off-the-beaten-path Diamond Resort. It's an informal and friendly place, with seafood, Italian dishes, and a wine list with decent, affordable selections. It's a great place for a date. The owners also serve three meals a day out of the Wailea Blue Clubhouse just down the street. ✉ *Diamond Resort, 555 Kaukahi St., Wailea,* ☎ *808/879–8255. AE, DC, MC, V. No lunch.*

Seafood

$$–$$$$ ✗ **Mā'alaea Waterfront Restaurant.** At this harborside establishment fresh fish is prepared in a host of sumptuous ways: baked in buttered parchment paper; imprisoned in ribbons of angel-hair potato; or topped with tomato salsa, smoked chili pepper, and avocado. The varied menu also offers outstanding rack of lamb and veal scallopini. Tourists come early to dine at sunset on the outdoor patio. Enter Mā'alaea at the Maui Ocean Center and then follow the blue WATERFRONT RESTAURANT signs to the third condominium. ✉ *50 Hau'oli St., Mā'alaea,* ☎ *808/244–9028. AE, D, DC, MC, V.*

East Maui

Hawai'i Regional/Pacific Rim

$$–$$$ ✗ **Hāli'imaile General Store.** What do you do with a lofty wooden building that used to be a camp store in the 1920s and is surrounded by a tiny town in the middle of sugarcane and pineapple fields? If you're Bev and Joe Gannon, you turn it into a legendary restaurant. The Szechuan barbecued salmon and rack of lamb Hunan style are classics. For a filling and innovative appetizer, try the sashimi napoleon: a tower of crispy wonton layered with smoked salmon. The outstanding house salad is topped with Maui onions, mandarin oranges, walnuts, and crumbled blue cheese on request. ✉ *900 Hāliʻimaile Rd., left at exit off Hwy. 37, 5 mi from Hāna Hwy., Hāliʻimaile,* ☎ *808/572–2666. MC, V.*

Italian

$$–$$$ ✗ **Casanova Italian Restaurant & Deli.** This is a good Italian dinner house in an out-of-the-way location—Makawao. The pizzas are skimpy, but they're baked in a brick, wood-burning oven imported from Italy. Casanova is also known for its daytime deli and, at night, for its extra-large dance floor and entertainment by well-known island and mainland musicians (☞ Bars and Clubs *in* Chapter 4). ✉ *1188 Makawao Ave., Makawao,* ☎ *808/572–0220. D, DC, MC, V.*

$$–$$$ ★ ✗ **Trattoria Haʻikū.** Here the rural hills of Tuscany and the leafy gulches of Haʻikū not only look alike but also taste alike. The house itself is a renovated 1920s mess hall, built for workers at the adjacent pineapple cannery. With a little understated drama—white linens and splashing fountains—it does a wonderful job of interpreting the classic Italian trattoria. Fresh local ingredients are used whenever possible (they make the marinara from vine-ripened Maui tomatoes), as are specialty products imported from Italy. ✉ *Olde Haʻikū Cannery, Haʻikū and Kokomo Rds., Haʻikū,* ☎ *808/575–2820. MC, V.*

Mexican

$–$$ ★ ✗ **Polli's.** This Mexican restaurant in the paniolo town of Makawao not only has a wide selection of such delicious taste treats as seafood enchiladas, chimichangas, quesadillas, and fajitas, but also offers to prepare any item on the menu with seasoned tofu or vegetarian taco mix instead of meat—and the meatless dishes are just as good. A special treat are the *bunuelos*—light pastries topped with cinnamon, maple syrup, and a scoop of ice cream. The intimate interior is plastered with colorful sombreros and other cantina knickknacks. ✉ *1202 Makawao Ave., Makawao,* ☎ *808/572–7808. AE, D, DC, MC, V.*

Seafood

$$–$$$ ★ ✗ **Mama's Fish House.** As you enjoy the landscaped grounds and ocean views at this cliff-top restaurant, check out the stone path engraved with whimsical Hawaiian geckos. But the real treat here is the fish, prepared in seven mouthwatering ways—baked in a creamy herb sauce, sautéed with macadamia nuts, or grilled with spicy wasabi butter, for example. That's why this thatched-hut restaurant with a Hawaiian nautical theme is packed every evening. The chicken, steak, and kālua pig dishes are worth trying as well. About 1½ mi east of Paʻia on the Hāna Highway, look for Mama's classic '40s-era Ford trucks parked on grassy knolls at both entrances. ✉ *799 Poho Pl., Kūʻau,* ☎ *808/579–8488. Reservations essential. AE, D, DC, MC, V.*

Steak

$$ ✗ **Makawao Steak House.** A restored 1927 house on the slopes of Haleakalā houses this paniolo restaurant that serves consistently good prime rib, rack of lamb, and fresh fish. Three fireplaces, friendly service, and an intimate lounge create a cozy, welcoming atmosphere. ✉ *3612 Baldwin Ave., Makawao,* ☎ *808/572–8711,* FAX *808/572–7103. D, DC, MC, V. No lunch.*

3 LODGING

Maui has it all—from beachside villas to cozy B&Bs. Most of the island's big resorts and hotels are in the west, while lodges and inns are in the east. It takes time to find the perfect home away from home, so be sure to plan ahead.

West Maui

MAUI HAS THE HIGHEST PERCENTAGE of upscale hotel rooms and the highest average accommodation cost of any Hawaiian island. The quality level—and the opulence quotient—are way up there, making this one of the best places in the world to indulge in a first-class resort vacation. But Maui also has the state's highest concentration of condominium units; many are oceanfront and offer the ambience of a hotel suite without the cost.

The county officially sanctions relatively few B&Bs, not wanting to siphon business from the hotels. However, many alternative accommodations offer seclusion and a countryside experience, especially Upcountry and in Hāna. The majority of these are better described as guest cottages—or guest houses—that skip the breakfast part of B&B and offer instead provisions and privacy. Most are a departure from the typical resort-style accommodations associated with the island. Rates for most B&Bs range from $40 to as much as $150 per night.

For price category explanations and further information about Maui B&Bs and condos, see Smart Travel Tips A to Z.

🕮 following the text of a review is your signal that the property has a Web site where you will find details and, usually, images; for a link, visit www.fodors.com/urls.

West Maui

$$$$ 🏨 **Hyatt Regency Maui.** When this trendsetting property was developed in 1980, it set a new standard for luxury resorts: a museum-quality art collection; a seemingly endless swimming pool, with swim-through grottoes and a 130-ft water slide; fantasy landscaping (the builders used 10,000 tons of rock to fabricate the environment) with splashing waterfalls; and a collection of exotic creatures, even penguins. The Hyatt remains Kāʻanapali's premier property. Improved access for people with disabilities and the addition of some new facilities—an outdoor Jacuzzi, a wedding gazebo, and a beachfront bar—have kept this oasis competitive with any resort on the island. ✉ *Kāʻanapali Beach Resort, 200 Nohea Kai Dr., Lahaina 96761,* ☎ *808/661–1234 or 800/233–1234,* FAX *808/667–4499. 815 rooms. 4 restaurants, 6 bars, in-room safes, 12 no-smoking floors, pool, 2 18-hole golf courses, 6 tennis courts, health club, beach, library, children's programs (ages 3–12), chapel. AE, D, DC, MC, V.* 🕮

$$$$ 🏨 **Kāʻanapali Aliʻi.** Yes, this is a condominium, but you'd never know it; the four 11-story buildings are put together so well you still have the feeling of seclusion. Instead of tiny rooms you can choose between one- and two-bedroom apartments. Each features lovely amenities: a chaise in an alcove, a bidet, a sunken living room, a whirlpool, oak kitchen cabinets, and a separate dining room. The Kāʻanapali Aliʻi is maintained like a hotel, with daily maid service, an activities desk, and a 24-hour front desk. ✉ *50 Nohea Kai Dr., Lahaina 96761,* ☎ *808/667–1400 or 800/642–6284,* FAX *808/661–1025. 264 units. 2 pools, sauna, 18-hole golf course, 6 tennis courts, beach. AE, D, DC, MC, V.* 🕮

$$$$ 🏨 **Kapalua Bay Hotel.** Built in 1978 fronting what was once voted America's best beach, at lovely Kapalua Bay, this hotel has a real Maui feel to it. The exterior is understated white and natural wood, and the open lobby, filled with flowering vanda and dendrobium orchids, has a view of the ocean. The plantation-style rooms are decorated in earth tones, and all have views of Lānaʻi and Molokaʻi. A shopping plaza outside the main hotel entrance has some fine restaurants and boutiques. Guests receive preferred rates and tee times at three golf courses in Ka-

Maui Lodging

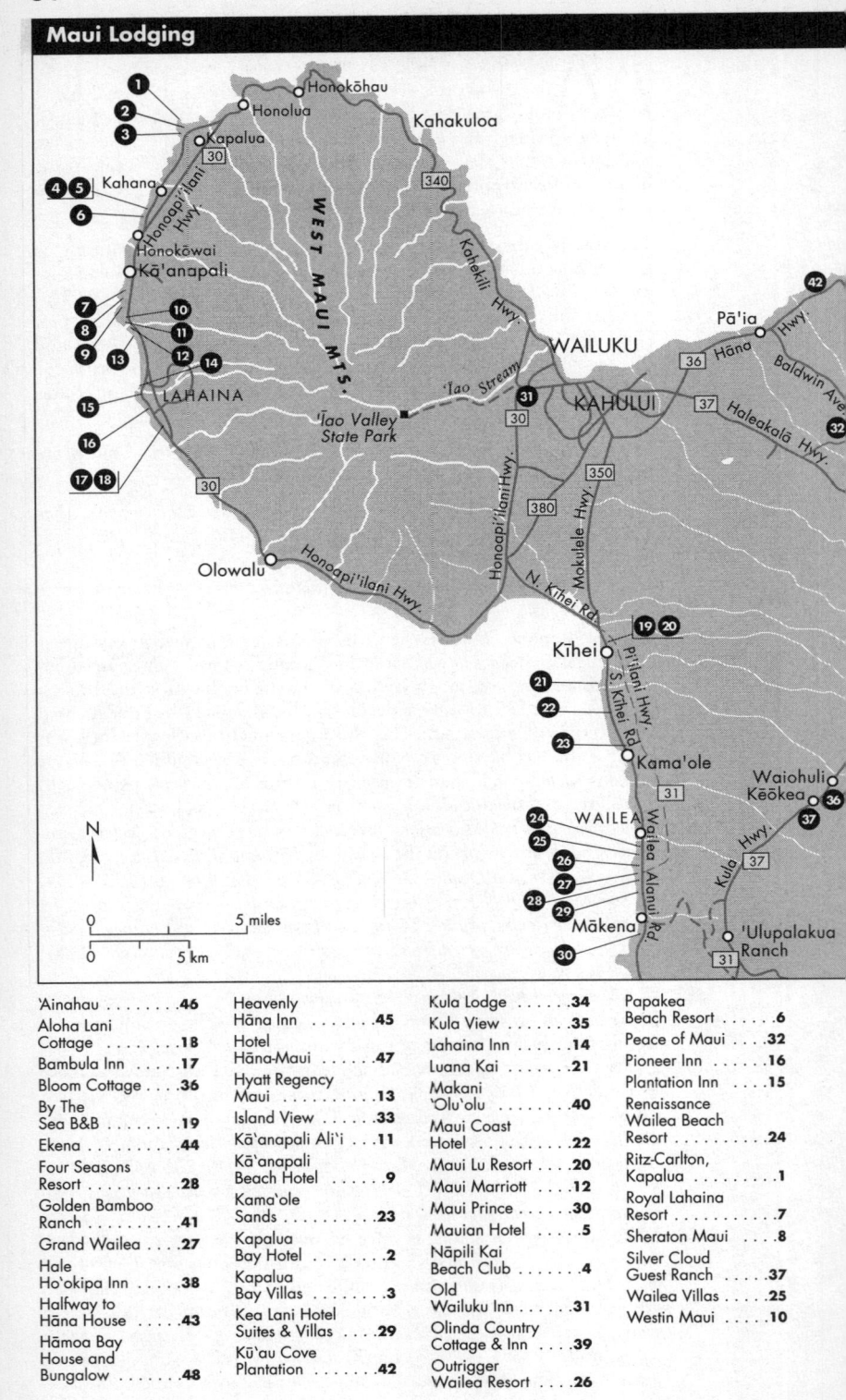

Lodging	#
'Ainahau	46
Aloha Lani Cottage	18
Bambula Inn	17
Bloom Cottage	36
By The Sea B&B	19
Ekena	44
Four Seasons Resort	28
Golden Bamboo Ranch	41
Grand Wailea	27
Hale Ho'okipa Inn	38
Halfway to Hāna House	43
Hāmoa Bay House and Bungalow	48
Heavenly Hāna Inn	45
Hotel Hāna-Maui	47
Hyatt Regency Maui	13
Island View	33
Kā'anapali Ali'i	11
Kā'anapali Beach Hotel	9
Kama'ole Sands	23
Kapalua Bay Hotel	2
Kapalua Bay Villas	3
Kea Lani Hotel Suites & Villas	29
Kū'au Cove Plantation	42
Kula Lodge	34
Kula View	35
Lahaina Inn	14
Luana Kai	21
Makani 'Olu'olu	40
Maui Coast Hotel	22
Maui Lu Resort	20
Maui Marriott	12
Maui Prince	30
Mauian Hotel	5
Nāpili Kai Beach Club	4
Old Wailuku Inn	31
Olinda Country Cottage & Inn	39
Outrigger Wailea Resort	26
Papakea Beach Resort	6
Peace of Maui	32
Pioneer Inn	16
Plantation Inn	15
Renaissance Wailea Beach Resort	24
Ritz-Carlton, Kapalua	1
Royal Lahaina Resort	7
Sheraton Maui	8
Silver Cloud Guest Ranch	37
Wailea Villas	25
Westin Maui	10

55

palua. ⊠ *1 Bay Dr., Kapalua 96761,* ☏ *808/669–5656 or 800/367–8000,* FAX *808/669–4694. 209 rooms. 3 restaurants, 2 pools, 6 tennis courts, beach. AE, DC, MC, V.*

$$$$ ⊡ **Kapalua Bay Villas.** This harmoniously designed complex of two- and three-story buildings seems to cascade down the cliffs to the sea. Privately owned and individually decorated one- and two-bedroom units may be rented through the Kapalua Bay Hotel (☞ *above*). Condos are assigned to one of five luxury categories and regularly inspected to ensure that standards are maintained. The ocean views are great, with the island of Moloka'i in the distance and humpback whales (in season) passing close to shore. Renters enjoy a free shuttle to the hotel and guest rates for golf, tennis, and other hotel amenities. ⊠ *1 Bay Dr., Kapalua 96761,* ☏ *808/669–5656 or 800/367–8000,* FAX *808/669–4694. 125 units. Golf privileges. AE, D, DC, MC, V.*

$$$$ ⊡ **Maui Marriott.** Rooms here are large and tastefully done in pastel tones and bamboo furnishings, and nearly 90% have ocean views. Besides having access to a beachside massage tent and privileges at two 18-hole golf courses in Kā'anapali, guests can join classes featuring aerobics; hula; Hawaiian arts, crafts, and language; food preparation; and a number of sports. The best thing here, however, is the service: The staff is genuinely friendly and helpful. ⊠ *100 Nohea Kai Dr., Lahaina 96761,* ☏ *808/667–1200 or 800/228–9290,* FAX *808/667–8300. 720 rooms. 4 restaurants, 2 lobby lounges, 2 pools, 2 hot tubs, massage, golf privileges, 5 tennis courts, health club, beach, bicycles, children's programs (ages 5–12). AE, D, DC, MC, V.* ✤

$$$$ ⊡ **Nāpili Kai Beach Club.** These lodgings on 10 beautiful beachfront acres appeal to a loyal following. Hawaiian-style rooms are done in sea-foam green, mauve, and rattan; shoji doors open onto your lānai, with the beach and ocean right outside. The property also includes two 18-hole putting greens, four swimming pools, and an extra-large whirlpool. This is a family-friendly place, with kids' programs as well as free classes in hula and lei-making. Packages that include a car, breakfast, and other extras are available if you stay five nights or longer. ⊠ *5900 Lower Honoapi'ilani Rd., Nāpili Bay 96761,* ☏ *808/669–6271 or 800/367–5030,* FAX *808/669–5740. 162 rooms. Kitchenettes, 4 pools, hot tub, 2 putting greens, beach. AE, MC, V.* ✤

$$$$ ⊡ **Ritz-Carlton, Kapalua.** This beachfront hotel features spacious, com-
★ fortable rooms with oversize marble bathrooms, lānai overlooking the three-level pool, and all the grace, elegance, and service that this hotel chain is known for. Most rooms have ocean views. Guests on the Club floors have a private lounge with complimentary snack and beverage service all day long. All guests have golf privileges at three 18-hole courses in Kapalua. ⊠ *1 Ritz-Carlton Dr., Kapalua 96761,* ☏ *808/669–6200 or 800/262–8440,* FAX *808/665–0026. 548 rooms. 4 restaurants, 5 lobby lounges, pool, beauty salon, golf privileges, 10 tennis courts, health club, beach, children's programs (ages 5–12). AE, D, DC, MC, V.* ✤

$$$$ ⊡ **Royal Lahaina Resort.** The lānai at this Hawaiian Hotels & Resorts property afford stunning ocean or golf-course views. What distinguishes the Royal Lahaina are the two-story cottages, each divided into four units; the bedrooms open to the trade winds on two sides. The upstairs units each have a private lānai, and downstairs units share. The walkway to the courtyard wedding gazebo is lined with stepping stones engraved with the names of past brides and grooms and their wedding dates. ⊠ *2780 Keka'a Dr., Lahaina 96761,* ☏ *808/661–3611 or 800/447–6925,* FAX *808/661–3538. 592 rooms. 3 restaurants, 3 pools, 18-hole golf course, 11 tennis courts, beach. AE, D, DC, MC, V.* ✤

$$$$ ⊡ **Sheraton Maui.** This beautiful resort consists of six buildings, each six stories or fewer, set in lush gardens on Kā'anapali's best stretch of beach. The resort sits next to 80-ft-high Black Rock, from which divers

West Maui

leap in a nightly torch-lighting ritual. One of the two swimming pools looks like a natural lagoon, with rock waterways and wooden bridges. The Sheraton has family appeal—a number of rooms provide two double beds and a Murphy bed, and the hotel offers a free children's programs in the summer. Conveniences include generous room amenities and a "no-hassle" check-in that bypasses the registration desk. ✉ *2605 Kā'anapali Pkwy., Lahaina 97671,* ☏ *808/661–0031 or 800/782–9488,* ℻ *808/661–0458. 510 rooms. 3 restaurants, 3 lobby lounges, in-room safes, refrigerators, pool, 3 tennis courts, health club, beach, children's programs (ages 5–12). AE, D, DC, MC, V.* 🍴

$$$$ 🏨 **Westin Maui.** This is a hotel for active people who like to be out and about and won't spend all their time in their rooms, which are rather small for the price. But compensations are provided—an "aquatic playground" with five heated swimming pools, privileges at two 18-hole golf courses in Kā'anapali, and the central-most position on Kā'anapali Beach. The landscaping is lush. There are abundant waterfalls (15 at last count) and lagoons. A valuable Asian and Pacific art collection is displayed throughout the property. ✉ *2365 Kā'anapali Pkwy., Lahaina 96761,* ☏ *808/667–2525 or 800/228–3000,* ℻ *808/661–5831. 761 rooms. 3 restaurants, 4 lobby lounges, 5 pools, beauty salon, hot tub, golf privileges, health club, beach, baby-sitting, children's programs (ages 12 and under). AE, D, DC, MC, V.* 🍴

$$$–$$$$ 🏨 **Plantation Inn.** Charm and luxury set apart this inn reminiscent of
★ a southern plantation home. Filled with Victorian and Far Eastern furnishings, it's set on a quiet street in the heart of Lahaina. Secluded lānai draped with hanging plants face a central courtyard, pool, and garden pavilion perfect for morning coffee. Each guest room or suite is decorated differently, with hardwood floors, French doors, antiques, four-poster beds, and ceiling fans. Some have kitchenettes and whirlpool baths. A generous breakfast is included in the room rate. One of Hawai'i's best French restaurants, Gerard's (☞ *West Maui in* Chapter 2, *above*), adds to the allure. ✉ *174 Lahainaluna Rd., Lahaina 96761,* ☏ *808/667–9225 or 800/433–6815,* ℻ *808/667–9293. 18 rooms. Restaurant, refrigerators, pool, hot tub. AE, MC, V.* 🍴

$$$ 🏨 **Kā'anapali Beach Hotel.** This attractive, old-fashioned hotel is full
★ of aloha and the good-natured spirit of Maui, and the employees' chorus entertains joyously most afternoons. In addition, this happy place is recognized as one of the best values on the West Side. The vintage-style Mixed Plate restaurant, known locally for its Hawaiian food, is decorated with displays honoring the many cultural traditions represented on the staff. The employees themselves contributed the artifacts. There are complimentary classes in hula, lei-making, and 'ukulele-playing—and guests have privileges at the two 18-hole Kā'anapali golf courses. ✉ *2525 Kā'anapali Pkwy., Lahaina 96761,* ☏ *808/661–0011 or 800/262–8450,* ℻ *808/667–5978. 430 rooms. 2 restaurants, lobby lounge, pool, golf privileges, beach. AE, D, DC, MC, V.* 🍴

$$$ 🏨 **Mauian Hotel.** This quiet place way out in Nāpili is for quiet people. The simple two-story buildings date from 1959, but the current owners have renovated the place for comfort and convenience, including fully equipped kitchens. The rooms, however, have neither televisions nor telephones. Such noisy devices are relegated to the 'Ohana Room, where a Continental breakfast is served daily. Best of all, the two-acre property opens out onto lovely Napili Bay. ✉ *5441 Lower Honoapi'ilani Rd., Nāpili 96761,* ☏ *808/669–6205 or 800/367–5034,* ℻ *808/669–0129. 44 rooms. Pool, shuffleboard, coin laundry. AE, D, MC, V.* 🍴

$$$ 🏨 **Papakea Beach Resort.** This resort is an active place to stay if you consider all the classes held here, such as swimming, snorkeling, and pineapple cutting. In Honokōwai, Papakea has built-in privacy because its units are spread out among 11 low-rise buildings on some 13 acres of land. You aren't really aware that you're sharing the property with 364 other units. Bamboo-lined walkways between buildings and fish-stocked ponds create a serene mood. There's a two-day minimum stay. Despite its name, there is no beach on the premises, although there are several nearby. ✉ *3543 Honoapi'ilani Hwy., Lahaina 96761,* ☎ *808/669–4848 or 800/367–5637,* FAX *808/669–0751. 36 studios; 224 1-bedroom and 104 2-bedroom units. 2 pools, hot tub, saunas, putting green, 4 tennis courts. AE, MC, V.*

$$–$$$ ★ **Lahaina Inn.** This antique jewel is classic Lahaina—a two-story wooden building that will transport you back to the turn of the last century. The nine small rooms and three suites shine with authentic period restoration and furnishings, including quilted bedcovers, antique lamps, and Oriental carpets—no televisions. You can sit in a wicker chair on your balcony right in the heart of town. An excellent Continental breakfast is left in the parlor for your convenience. ✉ *127 Lahainaluna Rd., Lahaina 96761,* ☎ *808/661–0577 or 800/669–3444,* FAX *808/667–9480. 12 rooms. AE, D, MC, V.*

$$–$$$ **Pioneer Inn.** Known officially as the Best Western Pioneer Inn–Maui, this historic building has occupied its ringside seat on Lahaina's action since 1901. Its dockside ambience capitalizes on Lahaina's 19th-century whaling days. All rooms are air-conditioned, and New England–style mahogany furnishings recapture Lahaina's missionary era. It's often possible to stay in one of the small rooms for under $100 a night. You might not want to spend your entire vacation here, as the area can be a bit noisy in the evening, but for a night or two of bargain-price historic atmosphere, the place can't be beat. ✉ *658 Wharf St., Lahaina 96761,* ☎ *808/661–3636 or 800/457–5457,* FAX *808/667–5708. 34 rooms. 3 restaurants. AE, D, DC, MC, V.*

The South Shore

$$$$ ★ **Four Seasons Resort.** This is a Maui favorite, partially because of its location, on one of the Valley Isle's finest beaches with all the amenities of the well-groomed Wailea Resort. Access to three 18-hole golf courses and "Wimbledon West," with 11 championship tennis courts, is included. The property itself has great appeal, with terraces, courtyards, gardens, waterfalls, and fountains. Nearly all the rooms have an ocean view and combine traditional style with tropical touches. You'll find terry robes and whole-bean coffee grinders in each room. ✉ *3900 Wailea Alanui, Wailea 96753,* ☎ *808/874–8000 or 800/334–6284,* FAX *808/874–6449. 380 rooms. 3 restaurants, 2 bars, pool, 2 tennis courts, golf privileges, health club, beach. AE, D, DC, MC, V.*

$$$$ ★ **Grand Wailea.** Sunny opulence is everywhere at this 40-acre resort. Elaborate water features include a 2,000-ft multilevel "canyon river-pool" with slides and grottoes. The Spa Grande cossets guests with rejuvenating offerings, from aerobics classes to exotic water-and-massage therapies. Luxury pervades the spacious ocean-view rooms, beautifully outfitted with such amenities as an overstuffed chaise longue, a comfortable writing desk, and an oversize tub and separate shower. Guests have access to three 18-hole golf courses, and tennis privileges are available. ✉ *3850 Wailea Alanui Dr., Wailea 96753,* ☎ *808/875–1234 or 800/888–6100,* FAX *808/874–2442. 779 rooms. 5 restaurants, 6 bars, 3 pools, golf privileges, health club, beach, children's programs (ages 5–12), chapel. AE, D, DC, MC, V.*

$$$$ **Kama'ole Sands.** This is a huge property for Kīhei—11 four-story buildings wrap around a grassy slope on which are clustered swimming and wading pools, a small waterfall, whirlpool baths, and barbecues. All units have kitchens, laundries, and private lānai. Managed by Castle Resorts & Hotels, this condominium property has a 24-hour front

The South Shore

desk and an activities desk, and it is across the road from Kīhei Beach. ✉ 2695 S. Kīhei Rd., Kīhei 96753, ☎ 808/874-8700 or 800/367-5004, FAX 808/879-3273. *11 studios; 211 1-bedroom, 83 2-bedroom, and 4 3-bedroom units. Restaurant, pool, wading pool, 4 tennis courts. AE, D, DC, MC, V.*

$$$$ ☒ **Kea Lani Hotel Suites & Villas.** This Moorish-domed, all-suite resort offers seclusion and privacy in oceanside two- and three-bedroom villas, each with its own small pool and within easy reach of attractions in Wailea and West Maui. Accommodations in the main hotel are spacious one-bedroom suites with dining lānai and marble bathrooms. Guests have access to three 18-hole golf courses, and tennis privileges are available. ✉ 4100 Wailea Alanui, Wailea 96753, ☎ 808/875-4100 or 800/882-4100, FAX 808/875-1200. *413 suites, 37 villas. 3 restaurants, deli, 2 lobby lounges, in-room VCRs, refrigerators, 3 pools, beauty salon, 2 hot tubs, golf privileges, health club, beach, shops, children's programs (ages 5–12). AE, D, DC, MC, V.*

$$$$ ☒ **Maui Prince.** The attention to service, style, and presentation is apparent from the minute you walk into the delightful open-air lobby of this hotel. Rooms on three levels surround the courtyard, which is home to a Japanese garden with a bubbling stream. Each evening a small ensemble performs chamber music in the courtyard. Room decoration is understated, in tones of mauve and beige. Unfortunately, there's an earth berm between the hotel and the beach—part of the agreement the hotel had to make with the zoning commission and local residents—so an ocean view isn't possible from the first floor. ✉ 5400 Mākena Alanui Rd., Mākena 96753, ☎ 808/874-1111 or 800/321-6284, FAX 808/879-8763. *290 rooms. 4 restaurants, pool, 2 18-hole golf courses, 6 tennis courts, beach. AE, DC, MC, V.*

$$$$ ☒ **Outrigger Wailea Resort.** The tropical lobby and interior spaces showcase a remarkable collection of Hawaiian and Pacific Rim artifacts. All of the spacious rooms have private lānai and are styled with a tropical theme. The grounds are beautiful, with walks along paths accented with palm, banana, and torch ginger. There are golf privileges at three nearby courses, as well as tennis privileges at the Wailea Tennis Club. The resort also offers a game bar, two Jacuzzis, children's programs, and a Hawaiian cultural program. ✉ 3700 Wailea Alanui Dr., Wailea 96753, ☎ 808/879-1922 or 800/922-7866, FAX 808/874-8331. *516 rooms. 2 restaurants, 3 pools, 2 hot tubs, beach, children's programs (ages 5–12). AE, D, DC, MC, V.*

$$$-$$$$ ☒ **Maui Coast Hotel.** This is a classy seven-story hotel that you would never notice because it's set back off the street. The standard rooms are fine—very clean and modern—but the best deal is to pay a little more for one of the suites. In these you'll get an enjoyable amount of space and jet nozzles in the bathtub. And the suites adapt well to families. You can lounge by the large pool and order food and drinks from neighboring Jameson's Grill & Bar. Or walk across the street to Kama'ole Beach. There's an activities desk, too, to help you plan your time. ✉ 2259 S. Kīhei Rd., Kīhei, 96753, ☎ 808/874-6284, 800/895-6284, or 800/426-0670, FAX 808/875-4731. *265 rooms, 114 suites. Restaurant, in-room safes, refrigerators, pool, dry cleaning, laundry service. AE, D, DC, MC, V.*

$$$-$$$$ ☒ **Renaissance Wailea Beach Resort.** Most of this hotel's rooms, positioned on fantastic Mōkapu Beach, are contained in a seven-story, T-shape building. Tapestries and gorgeous carpets enhance the public areas. Outside, you'll find exotic gardens, waterfalls, and reflecting ponds. The VIP Mōkapu Beach Club building houses 26 luxury accommodations and has its own concierge, pool, and beach cabanas. Guest rooms are decorated in shades of cream and each has a lānai. Guests have access to the nearby golf and tennis facilities. ✉ 3550 Wailea Alanui Dr.,

Wailea 96753, ☎ 808/879–4900 or 800/992–4532, FAX 808/874–6128. 345 rooms. 4 restaurants, lobby lounge, refrigerators, 2 pools, hot tub, basketball, health club, Ping-Pong, shuffleboard, beach, children's programs. AE, D, DC, MC, V.

$$$–$$$$ **⊞ Wailea Villas.** The Wailea Resort has three fine condominiums, calling them, appropriately, Wailea ʻEkahi, Wailea ʻElua, and Wailea ʻEkolu (Wailea One, Two, and Three). Since then, Wailea has added the Grand Champions Villas, and the adjoining Mākena Resort has built Mākena Surf and Polo Beach Club. All have beautifully landscaped grounds, large units with exceptional views, and access to five of the island's best beaches. The Wailea ʻElua Village, Polo Beach Club, and Mākena Surf are the more luxurious properties, with rates to match. The three original villas are an expansive property, with all the amenities of the fine Wailea Resort, including daily maid service and a concierge. ✉ 3750 Wailea Alanui Dr., Wailea 96753, ☎ 808/879–1595 or 800/367–5246, FAX 808/874–3554. 9 studios; 94 1-bedroom, 157 2-bedroom, and 10 3-bedroom apartments. 6 pools. AE, MC, V.

$$–$$$ **⊞ Luana Kai.** Here's a prime example of the condominium-by-the-sea, perfect for setting up household for at least four days (the required minimum). There are three different room plans, suited for couples, families, or friends traveling together. Each one comes with everything you need to move in and make yourself at home—a fully stocked kitchen, dishwasher, laundry, television, and video and stereo equipment. The pool's a social place, with five gas grills, a full outdoor kitchen, and saunas for men and women. There's no beach on site—for that, you have to go down the road a ways—but the place adjoins a grassy county park with tennis courts. ✉ 940 S. Kīhei Rd., Kīhei 96753, ☎ 808/879–1268 or 800/669–1127, FAX 808/879–1455. 113 units. Pool, sauna, putting green, 4 tennis courts, shuffleboard. AE, DC, MC, V.

$$ **⊞ Maui Lu Resort.** The first hotel in Kīhei and now operated by Aston Resorts, this place is reminiscent of a rustic lodge. The main lobby was the summer home of the original owner, a Canadian logger. Over the years the Maui Lu has added numerous wooden buildings and cottages to its 28 acres. Of the 120 rooms, 50 are right on the beach, and some have their own private coves. The rest are across Kīhei Road on the main property. ✉ 575 S. Kīhei Rd., Kīhei 96753, ☎ 808/879–5881 or 800/922–7865, FAX 808/879–4627. 120 rooms. Restaurant, lounge, in-room safes, refrigerators, 2 tennis courts, beach. AE, D, DC, MC, V.

East Maui

$$$$ ★ **⊞ Hotel Hāna-Maui.** One of the best places to stay in Hawaiʻi—and a departure from the usual resort-style accommodations—is this small, secluded hotel in Hāna surrounded by a 7,000-acre ranch. The original hotel buildings have white plaster walls and trellised verandas. Inside, the spacious rooms have bleached-wood floors, furniture upholstered in natural fabrics, and such welcome touches as fine art and orchids. The newer Sea Ranch Cottages across the road surround a state-of-the-art fitness center. A shuttle carries guests to a secluded beach nearby. ✉ Box 9, Hāna 96713, ☎ 808/248–8211 or 800/321–4262, FAX 808/248–7264. 96 units. Restaurant, bar, 2 pools, massage, 2 tennis courts, exercise room, horseback riding, jogging, beach, library. AE, D, DC, MC, V.

$$–$$$ **⊞ Kula Lodge.** This venue isn't typically Hawaiian: the lodge resembles a chalet in the Swiss Alps, and two of its five units have a gas fireplace. Charming and cozy in spite of the nontropical ambience, this is a perfect spot for a romantic stay. Units are in two wooden cabins; four have lofts in addition to the ample bed space downstairs, but none have phones or TVs. On three wooded acres, the lodge has views of the val-

ley and ocean enhanced by the surrounding forest and tropical gardens. The property has a restaurant and lounge, as well as a gift shop and a protea store that will pack flowers for you to take home. ✉ *R.R. 1, Box 475, Kula 96790,* ☎ *808/878–2517 or 800/233–1535,* FAX *808/878–2518. 5 units. Restaurant. AE, MC, V.*

$$ **Heavenly Hāna Inn.** An impressive Japanese gate marks the entrance to this small upscale inn. The three suites, one a two-bedroom unit, all have TVs. Decor is spare, with Japanese overtones. The furniture was built by Hāna residents. ✉ *Box 790, Hāna 96713,* ☎ *808/248–8442. 3 suites. AE, D, MC, V.*

Guest Houses and Bed-and-Breakfasts

Despite the traditional name bed-and-breakfast, many of these small-scale accommodations (both rooms and cottages) choose not to interrupt your privacy with breakfast. Instead they'll provide you with lush Upcountry or tropical surroundings that will enchant you and a kitchen that will let you do your own thing.

$$$–$$$$ **Ekena.** This idyllic setting (Ekena means Garden of Eden in Hawaiian) is full of tropical fruit trees and exotic flowers, and it sits on a hillside near the town of Hāna with a commanding view of sea and land. There are two houses, each with a fully equipped kitchen and all necessities. Jasmine, the smaller of the two, is suited to parties of two or four. The main house, Sea Breeze, is huge (2,600 square ft), with two large master suites, but the owners restrict its occupancy to a maximum of four people. In order to ensure privacy, they also rent to only one party at a time. There's a minimum stay of three days, and children are not allowed. ✉ *Box 728, Hāna 96713,* ☎ FAX *808/248–7047. 2 houses. No credit cards.*

$$$ ★ **'Ainahau.** Hidden away next to Hāna Bay, this cottage looks so-so till you get inside and start looking around. The place is ingeniously and lovingly crafted and furnished with works of art. The kitchen is set up with all the details of home, including a loaded spice rack and a coffee grinder, and the cottage is equipped with cable TV and a CD player. Nature at its most benign lies around you, and the bed is both theatrical and sensuous. Hāna Settings manages this and several other getaways, provides gourmet catered meals at your order, and organizes custom Hāna weddings. ✉ *Box 970, Hāna 96713,* ☎ *808/248–7849,* FAX *808/248–8267. 1 room. Kitchenette, in-room VCR. AE, MC, V.*

$$$ ★ **Hāmoa Bay House & Bungalow.** This Balinese-inspired property is sensuous and secluded, a private sanctuary in a fragrant jungle. There are two buildings. The main house is 1,300 square ft and contains two bedrooms, one of them a suite set apart by a breezeway; there's a screened veranda with ocean view and also an outdoor lava-rock shower. The 600-square-ft bungalow is a treetop perch with a giant bamboo bed and a hot tub on the veranda. Both accommodations come with complete kitchen and laundry and VCRs. Hāmoa Beach is a short walk away. ✉ *Box 773, Hāna 96713,* ☎ *808/248–7884,* FAX *808/248–7047. 2 rooms, 1 bungalow. No credit cards.*

$$–$$$ **Bloom Cottage.** The name comes from the abundance of roses and other flowers that surround this well-run, classic bed-and-breakfast. This is life in the slow lane, with privacy and quiet and a fireplace when the evenings are nippy. The furnishings are very Ralph Lauren with a cowhide flourish suited to this ranch-country locale 6 mi from Tedeschi Winery. The house, a 1906 antique, has three rooms and is good for four to six people willing to share a single bathroom. The cottage is ideal for a couple. ✉ *229 Kula Hwy., Kula 96790,* ☎ *808/878–1425,* FAX *661/393–5015. 3 rooms; 1 cottage. AE, D, MC, V.*

$$–$$$ ★ 🏨 **Old Wailuku Inn.** This historic home, built in 1924, has been lovingly renovated and may be the ultimate Hawaiian bed-and-breakfast. Each room is decorated on the theme of a Hawaiian flower, and the flower motif is worked into the heirloom Hawaiian quilt on each bed. Other features include 10-ft ceilings, floors of native hardwoods, VCRs, and (depending on the room) some delightful bathtubs. The first-floor rooms have private gardens. A hearty breakfast is included. ✉ *2199 Kahoʻokele St., Wailuku 96793,* ☎ *808/244–5897 or 800/305–4899. 7 rooms. In-room VCRs. AE, D, DC, MC, V.*

$$–$$$ 🏨 **Olinda Country Cottage & Inn.** The restored Tudor home and adjacent cottage are so far up Olinda Road above Makawao you'll keep thinking you must have passed it, but keep driving to reach the inn, which sits amid an 8½-acre protea farm surrounded by forest and some wonderful hiking trails. There are three delightful accommodations in the inn: two upstairs bedrooms with private baths; the downstairs Pineapple Sweet with its French doors; and best of all the ultraromantic cottage, which looks like a dollhouse from the outside. It would be easy to settle in for a long winter here, but bring slippers and warm clothes—the mountain air can be chilly. ✉ *536 Olinda Rd., Makawao 96768,* ☎ FAX *808/572–1453 or* ☎ *800/932–3435. 2 rooms with bath, 1 room shares bath, 2 cottages. No credit cards.*

$$–$$$ ★ 🏨 **Silver Cloud Guest Ranch.** Silver Cloud is in cowboy country, on the high mountainside beyond Kula and just five mi before ʻUlupalakua Ranch. The noble "Plantation House," with six rooms, surveys pasture lands and a spellbinding panorama of islands and sea. Silence is a chief attraction in this offbeat but magnificent part of Maui. Besides the main house, the ranch has a separate "Lānai Cottage" and five studios with kitchenettes (good for families) arranged like a bunkhouse in a horseshoe shape. A complete breakfast with fresh fruit and juice is served out of the Plantation House kitchen every morning. ✉ *R.R. 2, Box 201, Kula 96790,* ☎ *800/532–1111 or 808/878–6101,* FAX *808/878–2132. 12 rooms. Horseback riding. AE, D, DC, MC, V.*

$$ 🏨 **Bambula Inn.** This casual sprawling house in a quiet Lahaina residential area has two studio apartments, one attached to the house and one freestanding. No breakfast is served; this is a move-in-and-hang-out beach house. Just across the street is a small beach, and moored just offshore is a sailboat, the *Bambula*—hand-built by the Frenchman who owns the inn. He likes to take his guests out for whale-watching and sunset sails, no charge. He also provides bicycles and snorkel equipment. This is a friendly, easygoing way to visit Lahaina. ✉ *518 Ilikahi St., Lahaina 96761,* ☎ *808/667–6753 or 800/544–5524,* FAX *808/667–0979. 2 studios. Kitchenettes. D, MC, V.*

$$ 🏨 **By the Sea B&B.** If you want to stay in a bed-and-breakfast in Kīhei, this is a pretty one. You'll be amazed at the lushness and romance that the owner has managed to create in a small lot hemmed in by apartments and commercial buildings. The private yard is a cool little Eden with a large pond and waterfall—a good place to hang out in the hammock by day or the hot tub by night. There are three self-contained apartments in the house. The honeymoon-style Palm Room on the second floor has a king bed and its own lānai. All accommodations have separate entrances and designated parking slots, and the owners provide beach equipment, fishing gear, and Continental breakfast. ✉ *20 Wailana Pl., Kīhei 96753,* ☎ *808/879–2700 or 888/879–2700,* FAX *808/879–5540. 3 rooms. Coin laundry. AE, DC, MC, V.*

$$ 🏨 **Golden Bamboo Ranch.** This secluded 7-acre estate lies in the edge-of-the-rain-forest lushness of rural Haʻikū. The owners scrupulously maintain four units—one cottage, a studio, and two suites. Each has a kitchen or kitchenette and unobstructed views across a brilliant green landscape to the sea. ✉ *422 Kaupakalua Rd., Haʻikū 96708,* ☎

800/344-1238 or 808/572-7824, ℻ 808/572-7824. *4 units. Kitchenettes. AE, D, DC, MC, V.*

$$ ☎ **Hale Hoʻokipa Inn.** This handsome 80-year-old Craftsman-style house is right in the heart of Makawao town, a good home base for excursions to the crater or to Hāna. The owner has lovingly renovated the old place and furnished it with antique furniture and fine art. (She's also a certified tour guide who likes to take guests on hikes.) She has divided the house into three single rooms, each prettier than the last, and the "South Wing," which sleeps four and includes the kitchen. All rooms have private bath, and Continental breakfast is served. This inn matches everybody's mythical notion of grandma and grandpa's house. ✉ *32 Pakani Pl., Makawao 96768,* ☏ *808/572–6698,* ℻ *808/572–2580. 3 rooms, 1 2-bedroom suite. No credit cards.*

$$ ☎ **Kūʻau Cove Plantation.** Here's a rare and handy location for a Maui visit—on a secluded cove midway between the town of Pāʻia and Hoʻokipa Beach Park. The home is quite handsome, dating from the late 1930s and lovingly renovated by the current owners. Furnishings emphasize wicker and rattan and have quilted floral bedcovers. In classic bed-and-breakfast style, the owners rent two large bedrooms in the main house, both set apart from the family living area and each with private bath and queen-size beds. They also have two private studio apartments with kitchens. Continental breakfast is served. ✉ *2 Waʻa Pl., Kūʻau, 96779,* ☏ *808/579–8988,* ℻ *808/579–8710. 2 rooms, 2 apartments. MC, V.*

$$ ☎ **Kula View.** This affordable home away from home sits in comfortable, peaceful rural Kula. The 2,000-ft elevation makes for a pleasantly temperate climate and a panorama that takes in the West Maui mountains and the ocean on either side. Guests stay in the entire upper floor of a simple but tastefully decorated house—Laura Ashley fabrics, a breakfast nook full of wicker furnishings, a private entrance, and a deck. The hostess puts an emphasis on hospitality, providing a welcoming "amenity basket," a very popular Continental breakfast, advice on touring, and even beach towels or warm clothes for your crater trip. This is a quiet, refreshing place to return to after a day on the road. ✉ *140 Holopuni Rd., Kula 96790,* ☏ *808/878–6736. 1 room. No credit cards.*

$–$$ ☎ **Island View.** For that warm-sky, Upcountry-ranch feeling, head for this property not far from Pukalani. The owner is a master builder, and this sprawling house has obviously been a labor of love. There are bonuses for animal lovers: you'll have the company of a Dr. Dolittle–inspired assortment of animals, including Ollie, a surfing dog. The property includes two bed-and-breakfast rooms and one beautifully designed vacation "house" (one bedroom and two stories) for stays of four nights or longer. ✉ *692 Naele Rd., Kula 96790,* ☏ *808/878–6739,* ℻ *808/572–2265. 2 rooms, 1 cottage. No credit cards.*

$–$$ ☎ **Peace of Maui.** The small Upcountry community of Haliʻimaile, 2 mi closer to the coast than Makawao and near both Baldwin Avenue and the Haleakalā Highway, is well situated for accessing the rest of the island. This small inn is a good choice for budget-minded travelers who want to be out and active all day. Six rooms in a "lodge" setting have pantries and mini-refrigerators. The kitchen and bathroom are shared. There's also a separate cottage with its own kitchen and facilities. You'll have sweeping views of the north shore and the mountains here. ✉ *1290 Haliʻimaile Rd., Haliʻimaile 96768,* ☏ *888/475–5045 or 808/572–5045. 7 rooms. No credit cards.*

$ ☎ **Aloha Lani Inn.** This accommodation operates rather like the classic European homestay. You share a bathroom with another guest, or perhaps with the home owners, and you're welcome to the kitchen, the lānai, the laundry facilities, the phone, the snorkel gear, the kayak, and so on. It's a casual, friendly, and inexpensive way to visit the West Side. The inn is in a quiet neighborhood within walking distance of Lahaina town. There's a two-night minimum stay. ✉ *13 Kauaula Rd., Lahaina 96761,* ☎ *808/662–0812 or 800/57–ALOHA,* FAX *808/661–8045. 3 rooms. AE, D, MC, V.*

$ 🏠 **Halfway to Hāna House.** A private studio set in the country on Maui's lush rural north coast, this serene retreat comes with surrounding gardens and great ocean views. It's a short walk from here to natural pools and waterfalls, hiking areas, and horseback riding. The room comes with optional Continental breakfast and a well-supplied kitchenette—all the equipment you need to do your own thing. ✉ *Box 675, Ha'ikū 96708,* ☎ *808/572–1176,* FAX *808/572–3609. 1 room. No credit cards.*

$ 🏠 **Makani 'Olu'olu Cottage.** Actually, these folks offer both a cottage and an *'ohana* (an apartment attached to the house). The location is unusual—the heart of lush rural Ha'ikū, where the *makani* (winds) are *'olu'olu* (*pleasant*). Both rentals are suited to one or two people, with queen beds, complete kitchens, and delightful frescoes on the walls depicting tropical scenes—original works by the multitalented landlady. The tiled 'ohana is downstairs, with its own entrance and a lānai that looks over green pastures. The cottage has decoupage shelves and an antique upright piano. ✉ *925 Kaupakalua Rd., Ha'ikū 96708,* ☎ *808/572–8383. 2 rooms. No credit cards.*

4 NIGHTLIFE AND THE ARTS

Watching a sunset from a tropical perch, taking a moonlight stroll along a near-perfect crescent beach, or dining in a meadow are among the best nightlife options on Maui.

NIGHTLIFE ON MAUI MIGHT BE better labeled "evening life." Quiet Maui has little of Waikīkī's after-hours decadence. But before 10 PM there's a lot on offer, from lūʻau shows and dinner cruises to concerts at "The Center." Lahaina still tries to uphold its reputation as a party town, and succeeds wildly every Halloween, when thousands converge on Front Street.

Since it opened in 1994, the **Maui Arts & Cultural Center** (⊠ Maui Central Park, Kahului, ☎ 808/242–2787) has become the venue for more and more of the island's best live entertainment. The complex includes the 1,200-seat Castle Theater, which hosts classical, country, and world-beat concerts by touring musicians; a 4,000-seat amphitheater for large outdoor concerts; and the 350-seat McCoy Theater for plays and recitals. For information on current programs, check the Events Box Office (☎ 808/242–7469) or the daily newspaper, the *Maui News*. Most major credit cards are accepted at the venues listed below.

For nightlife of a different sort, children and astronomy buffs will enjoy stargazing at **Tour of the Stars,** a one-hour program held nightly on the roof of the Hyatt Regency Maui in Kāʻanapali. You can look through giant binoculars and a deep-space telescope. The program is run by an astronomer. Check in at the hotel lobby 15 minutes prior to starting time. ⊠ *Lahaina Tower, Hyatt Regency Maui, 200 Nohea Kai Dr., Kāʻanapali,* ☎ *808/661–1234, ext. 4727.* ➲ *$20.* ☉ *Nightly at 8, 9, and 10.*

Bars and Clubs

Contemporary Music

Kahale's Beach Club. A friendly, informal hangout, Kahale's offers live music (usually Hawaiian), bar drinks, burgers, fries, and artichokes every day from 10 AM till 2 in the morning. ⊠ *36 Keala Pl., Kīhei,* ☎ *808/875–7711.*

Makai Bar. Live Hawaiian and contemporary music nightly, awesome sunset views, and the best *pūpū* (appetizers) on Maui are at this comfortable spot on the Kāʻanapali coast. ⊠ *Lahaina Tower, Hyatt Regency Maui, Kāʻanapali Beach Resort,* ☎ *808/667–1200.*

Molokini Lounge. This is a pleasant bar with an ocean view, and you can even see Molokini Island before the sun goes down. Live music is presented, often Hawaiian in theme. There's a dance floor for late-night revelry. ⊠ *Lahaina Tower, Hyatt Regency Maui, Kāʻanapali Beach Resort,* ☎ *808/667–1200.*

Jazz

Pacific'O. This highly recommended restaurant (☞ West Maui *in* Chapter 2, *above*) is also the most reliable place to hear live jazz on the beach. It's a mellow, pacific sort of jazz—naturally—and it plays from 9 until midnight Thursday through Saturday. Guests musicians—George Benson, for example—often sit in. ⊠ *505 Front St., Lahaina,* ☎ *808/667–4341.*

Rock

Casanova Italian Restaurant & Deli. Casanova, voted "Best Late Night on Maui" in a *Maui News* readers' survey, claims to be the best place on the island for singles to meet. When a DJ is not spinning hits, contemporary musicians rock on with blues, country-western, rock-and-roll, and reggae. Past favorites have included Kool and the Gang, Los Lobos, and Taj Mahal. Expect a cover charge on nights featuring live entertainment. ⊠ *1188 Makawao Ave., Makawao,* ☎ *808/572–0220.*

Cheeseburger in Paradise. This Front Street hangout is known for—what else?—big beefy cheeseburgers (not to mention a great spinach-nut burger). Locals also know it as a great place to tune in to live bands playing rock-and-roll, Top 40, and oldies sounds from 4:30 PM to closing. There's no dance floor, but the second-floor balcony is a good place to watch Lahaina's Front Street action. ✉ *811 Front St., Lahaina,* ☎ *808/661–4855.*

Hapa's Brewhaus & Restaurant. Good food and some fine brews are on the menu here, along with sports TV, rock and funk bands, disco, hula shows, and comedy. These folks have gone all out to create a first-rate club with a large stage, roomy dance floor, state-of-the-art lighting and sound systems, and tier seating so that everyone gets a good view. Even nonsmokers will find the club comfortable: the air-conditioning system removes secondhand smoke. ✉ *Lipoa Center, 41 E. Lipoa St., Kīhei,* ☎ *808/879–9001.*

Hard Rock Cafe. Maui's version of the Hard Rock is popular with young locals as well as visitors who like their music *loud.* ✉ *Lahaina Center, 900 Front St., Lahaina,* ☎ *808/667–740.*

Maui Brews. Live bands serve up Top 40, reggae, salsa, or some kind of rock every night—a DJ on the weekends. This "island bistro and nightclub" is a big hangout place. They do a complete bar menu of appetizers, pastas, burgers, and entrées, and there are 16 kinds of draft beer, 10 specialty martinis, and a menu for kids. ✉ *Lahaina Center, 900 Front St.,* ☎ *808/667–7794.*

Moose McGillycuddy's. The Moose offers no-cover live music on Tuesday and Thursday. Otherwise, it's recorded music, but it's played so loud you'd swear it's live. This entertaining place tends to draw a young crowd that comes to enjoy the burgers and beer, to dance, and to meet one another. Specials include a pound-and-a-half king crab dinner and, on other nights, a 22-ounce porterhouse. ✉ *844 Front St., Lahaina,* ☎ *808/667–7758.*

Tsunami. You can dance to recorded Top 40 hits in this sophisticated, high-tech disco, where laser beams zigzag high above a futuristic dance floor. The music plays from 9 to 2 on Thursday, Friday, and Saturday nights. On other nights, the room is used for private parties. Tsunami has pool tables and a dress code: no beach wear, jeans, or T-shirts. Expect a $5 cover charge. ✉ *Grand Wailea, 3850 Wailea Alanui Dr., Wailea,* ☎ *808/875–1234.*

Dinner and Sunset Cruises

America II Sunset Sail. The star of this two-hour cruise is the craft itself—a 1987 America's Cup 12-m class contender that is exceptionally smooth and steady, thanks to its renowned winged-keel design. ✉ *Lahaina Harbor, Lahaina,* ☎ *808/667–2195.* 🎫 *$25.*

Kaulana Cocktail Cruise. This two-hour sunset cruise (with a bit of whale-watching thrown in, in season) features a pūpū menu, open bar, and live music. ✉ *Lahaina Harbor, Lahaina,* ☎ *808/871–1144.* 🎫 *$39.*

Pride Charters. A 65-ft catamaran built specifically for Maui's waters, the *Pride of Maui* features a large cabin, a large upper sundeck for unobstructed viewing, and a stable, comfortable ride. Breakfast, lunch, and beverages are provided. For later departures, there is an optional barbecue. ✉ *Mā'alaea Harbor, Mā'alaea,* ☎ *808/242–0955.* 🎫 *$40.*

Scotch Mist Charters. A two-hour champagne sunset sail is offered on the 25-passenger Santa Cruz 50 sloop *Scotch Mist II.* ✉ *Lahaina Harbor, Lahaina,* ☎ *808/661–0386.* 🎫 *$38.*

Windjammer Cruises. This cruise includes a prime rib and Alaskan salmon dinner and live entertainment on the 70-ft, 93-passenger *Spirit of Windjammer,* a three-masted schooner. ✉ *283 Wili Ko Pl., Suite 1, Lahaina,* ☎ *808/661–8600.* 🎫 *$69.*

Film

Maui Film Festival. This ongoing celebration offers weekly screenings of quality films that may not show up at the local megaplex. Most screenings are in Maui's most luxurious movie house—Castle Theater at Maui Arts & Cultural Center. On Wednesday night the usual movies are followed by live music and poetry readings in the Candlelight Cafe. But the schedule varies, and the program is expanding. In summer the festival comes to Wailea for cinema under the stars in a program that includes music, hula, and Hawaiian storytelling. For recorded program information call ☎ 808/572–FILM or check the Web site: www.mauifilmfestival.com.

Lū'au and Revues

Maui Myth & Magic Theatre. Maui's newest live theater opened in 1999 with the debut of 'Ulalena, a 75-minute musical extravaganza that is well received by audiences and Hawaiian-culture experts alike. The ensemble cast (20 singer/dancers and a 5-musician orchestra) mixes native rhythms and stories with acrobatic performance and high-tech stage wizardry to give an inspiring introduction to island culture. It's movie-style seating with beer and wine for sale at the popcorn line. They also offer dinner-theater packages in conjunction with top Lahaina restaurants. ✉ 878 Front St., Lahaina, ☎ 808/661–9913 or 877/688–4800, FAX 808/661–5363. Reservations essential. 🍽 $35. ⊙ Tues.–Sat. 6:30 and 9.

Nāpili Kai Beach Club Keiki Hula Show. Expect to be charmed as well as entertained when 30 children ages 6 to 17 take you on a dance tour of Hawai'i, New Zealand, Tahiti, Samoa, and other Polynesian islands. The talented youngsters make their own ti-leaf skirts and fresh-flower leis. They give the leis to the audience at the end of the show. This is a nonprofessional but delightfully engaging review, and the 80-seat oceanfront room is usually sold out. ✉ Nāpili Kai Beach Club, 5900 Honoapi'ilani Hwy., Nāpili, ☎ 808/669–6271. 🍽 $35. ⊙ Dinner Fri. at 6, show at 7:30.

★ **Old Lahaina Lū'au.** This is the best lū'au you'll find on Maui. It's small, personal, and authentic. Its new home is an outdoor theater designed specifically for traditional Hawaiian entertainment. It feels like an old seaside village. In addition to fresh fish and grilled steak and chicken, you'll get all-you-can-eat traditional lū'au fare: kālua pig, chicken long rice, *lomilomi* salmon (massaged until tender and served with minced onions and tomatoes), *haupia* (coconut pudding), and other treats. You'll also get all you can drink. Guests sit either on tatami mats or at tables. Then there's the entertainment, featuring a musical journey from old Hawai'i to the present with hula dancing, chanting, and singing. ✉ 1287 Front St., Lahaina (makai of the Lahaina Cannery Mall), ☎ 808/667–1998. 🍽 $65. ⊙ Nightly 5:30–8:30.

The Feast at Lele. "Lele" is an older, more traditional name for Lahaina. This "feast" is redefining the lū'au by crossing it with fine dining island-style in an intimate beach setting. Both the show and the three-course gourmet meal express the spirit of a specific island culture—Hawaiian, Samoan, Tongan, or Tahitian. The wine list and liquor selections are excellent. This may be the trend of the future for would-be Polynesian royalty. ✉ 505 Front St., Lahaina, ☎ 808/667–5353, FAX 808/661–8399. Reservations essential. 🍽 $89. ⊙ Tues., Thurs., and Sat. (more often in high season), 5:30 in winter and 6:30 in summer.

Warren & Annabelle's. Magician Warren Gibson entices his guests into a swank nightclub setting with red carpets and a gleaming mahogany bar, then plies them with appetizers (coconut shrimp, crab cakes), desserts (rum cake, crème brûlée), and "smoking cocktails." Then he

Close-Up
HULA, THE DANCE OF HAWAI`I

Legends immortalize Laka as the goddess of hula, portraying her as a gentle deity who journeyed from island to island, sharing the dance with all who were willing to learn. Laka's graceful movements, spiritual and layered with meaning, brought to life the history, the traditions, and the genealogy of the islanders. Ultimately taught by parents to children and by *kumu* (teachers) to students, the hula preserved without a written language the culture of these ancient peoples.

Some legends trace the origins of hula to Moloka`i, where a family named La`ila`i was said to have established the dance at Ka`ana. Eventually the youngest sister of the fifth generation of La`ila`i was given the name Laka, and she carried the dance to all the Islands in the Hawaiian chain.

Another legend credits Hi`iaka, the volcano goddess Pele's youngest sister, as having danced the first hula in the hala groves of Puna on the Big Island. Hi`iaka and possibly even Pele were thought to have learned the dance from Hōpoe, a mortal and a poet also credited as the originator of the dance.

In any case, hula thrived until the arrival of puritanical New England missionaries, who with the support of Queen Ka`ahumanu, an early Christian convert, attempted to ban the dance as an immoral activity throughout the 19th century.

Though hula may not have been publicly performed, it remained a spiritual and poetic art form, as well as a lively celebration of life presented during special celebrations in many Hawaiian homes. David Kalākaua, the popular "Merrie Monarch" who was king from 1874 to 1891, revived the hula. Dancers were called to perform at official functions. In 1906, Nathaniel Emerson wrote about hula, "Its view of life was idyllic, and it gave itself to the celebration of those mythical times when gods and goddesses moved on earth as men and women, and when men and women were as gods."

Gradually, ancient hula, called *kahiko*, was replaced with a lively, updated form of dance called `auana (modern). Modern costumes of fresh ti-leaf or raffia skirts replaced the voluminous *pa`u* skirts made of *kapa* (cloth made of beaten bark), and the music became more melodic, as opposed to earlier chanted routines accompanied by *pahu* (drums), `ili `ili (rocks used as castanets), and other percussion instruments. Such tunes as "Lovely Hula Hands," "Little Grass Shack," and the "Hawaiian Wedding Song" are considered hula `auana. Dancers might wear graceful *holomu`u* with short trains, or ti-leaf skirts with coconut bra tops.

In 1963 the Merrie Monarch Festival was established in Hilo on the Big Island and has since become the most prestigious hula competition in the state. It's staged annually the weekend after Easter, and contestants of various *halau* (hula schools) from Hawai`i and the mainland compete in the categories of Miss Aloha Hula, hula kahiko (ancient), and hula `auana (modern). For more information, contact the **Merrie Monarch Hula Festival** (✉ Hawai`i Naniloa Resort, 93 Banyan Dr., Hilo 96720, ☎ 808/935-9168).

Moloka`i stages its own Ka Hula Piko festival to celebrate the birth of hula every May. Singers, musicians, and dancers perform in a shaded glen at Papohaku Beach State Park, and nearby, islanders sell food and Hawaiian crafts. During the week preceding the festival, John Kaimikaua, the founder, and his halau present hula demonstrations, lectures, and storytelling at various Moloka`i sites.

For more information, contact the **Moloka`i Visitors Association** (✉ Box 960, Kaunakakai 96748, ☎ 808/553-3876 or 800/800-6367).

performs table-side magic while his ghostly assistant, Annabelle, tickles the ivories. The show is fun, and all the better for being not too slick. Note that this is a nightclub, so no one under 21 is allowed. ✉ *Lahaina Center, 900 Front St.,* ☎ *808/667–6244. Reservations essential.* 🎟 *$36.* ⊙ *Mon.–Sat., 7 and 8:30.*

Music

Maui Philharmonic Society. The Society has presented such prestigious performers as Ballet Hispanico, the Shostakovich String Quartet, and the New Age pianist-composer Philip Glass. Performances take place in various spots around the island. ✉ *J. Walter Cameron Center, 95 Mahalani St., Wailuku 96793,* ☎ *808/244–3771.*

Maui Symphony Orchestra (☎ 808/244–5439). The symphony orchestra usually performs at the Maui Arts & Cultural Center (✉ Maui Central Park, Kahului, ☎ 808/242–2787; box office 808/242–7469), offering five seasonal concerts and a few special musical sensations as well. The regular season includes a Christmas concert, an opera gala, a classical concert, and two pops concerts outdoors.

Theater

Baldwin Theatre Guild. Dramas, comedies, and musicals are presented by this group about eight times a year. The guild has staged such favorites as *The Glass Menagerie, Brigadoon,* and *The Miser.* Musicals are held in the Community Auditorium, which seats 1,200. All other plays are presented in the Baldwin High School Mini Theatre. ✉ *1650 Ka'ahumanu Ave., Kahului,* ☎ *808/984–5673.* 🎟 *$8.*

Maui Academy of Performing Arts. For a quarter-century this group has offered fine performances as well as dance and drama classes for children and adults. It has presented such plays as *Peter Pan, Jesus Christ Superstar,* and *The Nutcracker.* MAPA has secured a new home in Wailuku at the old National Dollar Store building. They hope to occupy the new theater and two dance studios in mid 2001. *Main and Market Sts., Wailuku,* ☎ *808/244–8760.* 🎟 *$10–$12.*

Maui Community Theatre. Now staging about six plays a year, this is the oldest dramatic group on the island, started in the early 1900s. Each July the group also holds a fund-raising variety show, which can be a hoot. ✉ *'Iao Theatre, 68 N. Market St., Wailuku,* ☎ *808/242–6969.* 🎟 *Musicals $10–$15, nonmusicals $8–$13.*

Seabury Hall Performance Studio. This college-preparatory school above Makawao town offers a season of often supercharged shows in its satisfying small theater and two dance studios. The school's formula is to mix talented kids with seasoned adults and innovative, even offbeat, concepts. Dance concerts are always a hit. ✉ *480 Olinda Rd., 1 mi north of Makawao crossroads,* ☎ *808/573–1257.* 🎟 *$7–$12.*

5 OUTDOOR ACTIVITIES, BEACHES, AND SPORTS

Visiting Maui's miles and miles of beaches is not the only activity on the island. You might hang glide, fish, sail, snorkel, surf, or waterski. And though it surprises visitors to this tropical paradise, the *paniolo* (cowboy) culture of Upcountry makes horseback riding only natural here.

Beaches

All of Hawai'i's beaches are free and open to the public—even those that grace the front yards of fancy hotels—so you can make yourself at home on any one of them. Blue beach-access signs indicate rights-of-way through condominium and resort properties.

Although they don't appear often, be sure to pay attention to any signs or warning flags on the beaches. Warnings of high surf or rough currents should be taken seriously. Before you seek shade under a coconut palm, be aware that the trade winds are strong enough to knock fruit off the trees and onto your head. Drinking alcoholic beverages on beaches in Hawai'i isn't allowed.

West Maui

"Slaughterhouse" Beach. The island's northernmost beach is part of the Honolua-Mokuleia Marine Life Conservation District. "Slaughterhouse" is the surfers' nickname for what is officially Mokuleia. When the weather permits, this is a great place for bodysurfing and sunbathing. Concrete steps and a green-painted railing help you get down the sheer cliff to the sand. The next bay over, Honolua, has no beach but offers one of the best surf breaks in Hawai'i. Often you'll see competitions happening there, with cars pulled off the road and parked in the pineapple field. There are no facilities at this wild area. ✉ *Mile Marker 32 on the road past Kapalua.*

D. T. Fleming Beach. This charming, mile-long sandy cove is better for sunbathing than for swimming because the current can be quite strong. Still it's one of the island's most popular, and there are rest rooms, showers, picnic tables, grills, and paved parking. Part of the beach runs along the front of the Ritz-Carlton, Kapalua. ✉ *Hwy. 30, 1 mi north of Kapalua Resort.*

Kapalua Beach. On the northern side of Nāpili Bay is small, pristine Kapalua Beach. You may have to share sand space with a number of other beachgoers, however, because the area is quite popular for lazing, swimming, and snorkeling. There are showers, rest rooms, and a paved parking lot. ✉ *Past Bay Club restaurant off Lower Honoapi'ilani Hwy., before Kapalua Bay Hotel.*

★ **Nāpili Beach.** This sparkling white crescent makes a perfect cove for strolling and sunbathing. It's right outside the Nāpili Kai Beach Club, a popular little resort for honeymooners, but despite this and other condominiums and development around the bay, the facilities here are minimal. There are showers at the far right end of the beach and a tap by the beach-access entrance, where you can wash the sand off your feet, and you're only a few miles south of Kapalua. ✉ *5900 Lower Honoapi'ilani Hwy.; from upper highway follow cutoff road closest to Kapalua Resort and look for Nāpili Pl. or Hui Dr.*

★ **Kā'anapali Beach.** This is not the beach if you're looking for peace and quiet, but if you want lots of action, lay out your towel here. It fronts the big hotels at Kā'anapali and is one of Maui's best people-watching spots: cruises, windsurfers, and parasailers head out from here while the beautiful people take in the scenery. Although no facilities are available, the nearby hotels have rest rooms and some, like the Marriott, have outdoor showers. You're also close to plenty of shops and concessions. ✉ *Follow any of 3 Kā'anapali exits from Honoapi'ilani Hwy. and park at any of the hotels.*

The South Shore

Kīhei has excellent beaches right in town, including three beach parks called **Kama'ole I, II,** and **III,** which have showers, rest rooms, picnic

tables, and barbecues. Good snorkeling can be done along the rocky borders of the parks. If Kīhei is excellent, though, Wailea is better. Look for a little road and parking lot between the first two big resorts—the Renaissance and the Outrigger. This gets you to **Mokapu** and **Ulua**
★ **beaches.** A similar road just after the Grand Wailea gets you to **Wailea Beach.** Then, after the Kea Lani, you find **Polo Beach.** Each beach is a pocket-size beauty with wonderful snorkeling, also showers and rest rooms.

★ **Mākena.** Just south of Wailea is the state park at Mākena, with two good beaches. Big Beach is 3,000 ft long and 100 ft wide. The water off Big Beach is fine for swimming and snorkeling, and you'll find showers, rest rooms, and paved parking here. If you walk over the cinder cone at Big Beach, you'll reach Little Beach, which is clothing-optional by popular practice. Officially, nude sunbathing is illegal in Hawai'i, but several bathers who've pushed their arrests through the courts have found their cases dismissed. Understand, though, that you take your chances if you decide to indulge in this favorite local practice at Little Mākena.

The North Shore
Kanahā Beach. Local folk and windsurfers like this long golden strip of sand bordered by a wide grassy area. This is a popular Kahului spot for joggers and picnicking Maui families. Kanahā Beach has toilets, showers, picnic tables, and grills. ✉ *Drive through airport and back out to car-rental road (Koeheke), turn right, and keep going.*

★ **Baldwin Beach.** Another local favorite, just west of Pā'ia town, this beach is a big body of comfortable sand. There's not much wave action for bodysurfing, but this is good place to stretch out and swim or jog. The county park at the right side of the beach has picnic areas, rest rooms, showers, and sometimes even a lifeguard. ✉ *Hāna Rd., 1 mi west of Baldwin Ave.*

★ **Ho'okipa Beach.** If you want to see some of the world's finest windsurfers, stop at this beach along on the Hāna Highway. The sport has become an art—and a career, to some—and its popularity was largely developed right at Ho'okipa. It's also one of Maui's hottest surfing spots, with waves as high as 15 ft. This is not a good swimming beach, nor the place to learn windsurfing yourself, but plenty of picnic tables and barbecue grills are available for hanging out. ✉ *Hwy. 36, 1 mi past Pā'ia.*

Hāna
Kōkī Beach. This beach in Hāna offers unusually good bodysurfing because the sandy bottom stays shallow for a long way out. On the down side, there are no facilities here. But this is a wild place rich in Hawaiian lore. Watch conditions, because the riptides here can be mean. Just down the road is the beach James Michener called the best in the Pacific—crescent-shape Hāmoa Beach. Park on the roadside and walk down either one of the steep paths. Hotel Hāna-Maui keeps facilities here for its guests but has politely included a shower and rest room for the public. ✉ *Haneo'o Loop Rd., 2 mi east of Hāna town.*

Participant Sports

Biking
Maui County has designated hundreds of miles of bikeways on Maui's roads, making biking safer and more convenient than in the past. Painted bike lanes make it possible for a rider to travel all the way from Mākena to Kapalua, and you'll see dozens of hardy souls pedaling under the hot Maui sun. Some visitors rent a bike just to ride around the resort where

they're staying. Whatever your preference, you have several rental choices, including **Island Biker** (✉ 415 Dairy Rd., Kahului, ☏ 808/877-7744), **Maui Sports and Cycle** (✉ Long's Center, Kīhei, ☏ 808/875-8448, **South Maui Bicycles** (✉ Island Surf building, Kīhei, ☏ 808/874-0068), and **West Maui Cycles** (✉ 840 Waine'e St., Lahaina, ☏ 808/661-9005). Bikes rent for $10 to $20 a day. Several companies offer downhill bike tours from the top of Haleakalā all the way to the coast (☞ Smart Travel Tips A to Z).

Camping and Hiking

Let's start with the best—hiking **Haleakalā Crater.** The recommended way to explore the crater is to leave your car at the head of Halemau'u Trail and hitchhike the last few miles up to the summit, or else go in two cars and ferry yourselves back and forth. This way, you can hike from the summit down Sliding Sands Trail, cross the crater floor, investigate the Bottomless Pit and Pele's Paint Pot, then climb out on the switchback trail (Halemau'u). When you emerge, the shelter of your waiting car will be very welcome. Give yourself eight hours for the hike; wear jogging-type shoes and take a backpack with lunch, water, and a reliable jacket for the beginning and end of the hike. This is a demanding trip, but you will never regret or forget it.

If you want to stay longer than a day, plan to shelter in one of the national park's three cabins or two campgrounds. The cabins are equipped with bunk beds, wood-burning stoves, fake logs, and kitchen gear. To reserve a cabin you have to think at least three months in advance and hope the lottery system is kind to you. Contact the National Park Service (✉ Box 369, Makawao 96768, ☏ 808/572-9306). The tent campsites are easy to reserve on a first-come, first-served basis. Just make sure to stop at park headquarters to register on your way in.

Just as you enter the national park, **Hosmer Grove** offers an hour-long loop trail into the "cloud forest" that will give you insight into Hawai'i's fragile ecology. You can pick up a map at the trailhead. Park rangers offer guided hikes on a changing schedule. There are six campsites (no permit needed), pit toilets, drinking water, and cooking shelters.

Another good hiking spot—and something totally unexpected on a tropical island—is **Polipoli Forest.** During the Great Depression, the government began a program to reforest the mountain, and soon cedar, pine, cypress, and even redwood took hold. It's cold here and foggy, often wet or at least misty. To reach the forest, take Highway 37 all the way out to the far end of Kula. Then turn left at Highway 377. In about half a mile, turn right at Waipoli Road. Then up you go. First it's switchbacks. Then it's just plain bad—but passable. There are wonderful trails, also a small campground and a cabin that you can rent from the Division of State Parks. Write far in advance for the cabin (✉ Box 1049, Wailuku 96793, ☏ 808/244-4354); for the campground, you can wait until you arrive in Wailuku and visit the State Parks office (✉ 54 High St.).

Past Hāna you contact the national park again at **'Ohe'o Gulch.** This is the starting point of one of the best hikes on Maui—the 2-mi trek upstream to 400-ft **Waimoku Falls.** Along the way you can take side trips and swim in the stream's basalt-lined pools. Then the trail bridges a sensational gorge and passes onto a boardwalk through a clonking, mystifying forest of giant bamboo. Down at the grassy sea cliffs, you can camp, no permit required, although you can stay only three nights. Toilets, grills, and tables are available here, but no water and no open fires.

In 'Iao Valley, the **Hawai'i Nature Center** (✉ 875 'Iao Valley Rd., Wailuku, 96793, ☏ 808/244-6500) leads interpretive hikes for children and their families.

Participant Sports

Fitness Centers

Most fitness centers on Maui are in hotels. If your hotel does not have a facility, ask if privileges are available at other hotels. Outside the resorts, the most convenient and best equipped are **24 Hour Fitness** (✉ 150 Hāna Hwy., Kahului, ☎ 808/877–7474) and **World Gym** (✉ Kīhei Commercial Center, 300 Ohukai Rd., G-112, Kīhei, ☎ 808/879–1326), both of which have complete fitness facilities. Or contact the **Maui Family YMCA** (✉ 250 Kanaloa Ave., Kahului, ☎ 808/242–9007).

Golf

How do you keep your mind on the game in a place like Maui? It's very hard, because you can't ignore the view, but Maui has become one of the world's premier golf-vacation destinations. The island's major resorts all have golf courses, each of them stunning. They're all open to the public, and most lower their greens fees after 2:30 on weekday afternoons.

Elleair Golf Course. Formerly Silversword Golf Course, this privately owned course independent of the resorts was designed by Bill Newis to take advantage of its lofty location above Kīhei town. You'll get panoramic views not only out to sea but also across Haleakalā. ✉ *1345 Pi'ilani Hwy., Kīhei,* ☎ *808/874–0777.* ⛳ *Greens fee $75, including cart.*

Kā'anapali Golf Courses. Two of Maui's most famous courses are here. The layout consists of the North Course, designed by Robert Trent Jones, Sr., and the South Course, laid out by Arthur Jack Snyder. ✉ *Kā'anapali Beach Resort, Kā'anapali,* ☎ *808/661–3691.* ⛳ *Greens fee $100 guests, $120 nonguests, including cart.*

Kapalua Golf Club. The club has three 18-holers—the Village Course and the Bay Course, both designed by Arnold Palmer, and the Plantation Course, designed by Ben Crenshaw. Kapalua is well-known to television-sports watchers. ✉ *300 Kapalua Dr., Kapalua,* ☎ *808/669–8044.* ⛳ *Greens fee $95–$100 guests, $140–$150 nonguests, including cart; club rental $30–$40.*

Mākena Golf Course. There are two lovely 18-hole courses here, North and South, designed by Robert Trent Jones, Jr. Of all the resort courses, this one is the most remote. At one point, golfers must cross a main road, but there are so few cars that this poses no problem. ✉ *5415 Mākena Alanui Rd., Kīhei,* ☎ *808/879–3344.* ⛳ *Greens fee $80 guests, $140 nonguests, including cart.*

Sandalwood Golf Course. Sandalwood offers a unique location on the slopes of the West Maui mountains just south of Wailuku, with elevated views of Haleakalā. ✉ *2500 Honoapi'ilani Hwy., Wailuku,* ☎ *808/242–4653.* ⛳ *Greens fee $75, including cart.*

Wailea Golf Club. The club has three courses: the Gold and the Blue, which were designed by Arthur Jack Snyder, and the newer Emerald, designed by Robert Trent Jones, Jr. In his design, Snyder incorporated ancient lava-rock walls to create an unusual golfing experience. ✉ *100 Wailea Golf Club Dr., Wailea,* ☎ *808/875–5111.* ⛳ *Greens fee $110 guests, $140 nonguests, including cart.*

Maui also has municipal courses, where the fees are lower. Be forewarned, however, that the weather can be cool and wet, and the locations may not be convenient. The **Waiehu Municipal Golf Course** is on the northeast coast of Maui a few miles past Wailuku. ✉ *Off Hwy. 340, West Maui,* ☎ *808/244–5934.* ⛳ *Greens fee $25 weekdays, $30 weekends; cart $15.*

Hang Gliding

USHGA instructor Armin Engert of **Hang Gliding Maui** (☎ 808/572–6557,✉) will teach you the basics of weight-shift control while he takes you on a tandem hang-gliding experience from the top of Haleakalā to the green pastures of Kula. He has a 100% safety record. The soundless, practically effortless flight lasts anywhere from 30 to 90 minutes, depending on the thermal activity. There's a weight limit of 200 pounds for this trip, which costs $300 and includes 24 snapshots of your adventure taken by a wing-mounted camera.

Parasailing

If you have a yen to be floating in the sky like a bird but lack the derring-do of a barnstormer, parasailing is the perfect alternative to skydiving (you gently rise several hundred feet from the ground instead of leaping out of an aircraft at 10,000 ft) or hang gliding (the safety rope holds you in your flight pattern). This is an easy and fun way to earn your wings: just strap on a harness attached to a parachute and a power boat pulls you up and over the ocean from a launching dock or from a boat's platform. To reduce interference with whales, no "thrill craft"—including parasails—are allowed in Maui waters from December 15 to April 15.

Several companies on Maui will take you for a ride that usually lasts about 10 minutes and costs $30 to $50. For safety reasons, **West Maui Para-Sail** (☎ 808/661–4060) requires that passengers weigh more than 100 pounds, or two must be strapped together in tandem. **Lahaina Para-Sail** (☎ 808/661–4887) lays claim to the only parasail vessel on Maui that is Coast Guard certified for 25 passengers and has bathroom facilities on board. The group will be glad to let you experience a "toe dip" or "freefall" if you request it, and the minimum weight to fly alone is 75 pounds.

Sporting Clays

Skillfully designed to fit inside the crater of a large cinder cone, **Papaka Sporting Clays** (✉ 1325 S. Kīhei Rd., ☎ 808/879–5649) is an outdoor arcade dedicated to the art of shotgun shooting. The 40 stations include "Springing Teal," "High Pheasant," and "Busting Bunnies" (no real bunnies involved; the targets are clay disks). Certified instructors outfit you with a vest, earplugs, eye protection, a shotgun, and instruction. They pick you up in the Kīhei–Wailea area or at ʻUlupalakua Ranch by appointment any morning or afternoon. The cost is $95 for 75 targets. Spectators can come along for free.

Tennis

There are other facilities around the island besides those listed below, usually one or two courts in smaller hotels or condos. Most of them, however, are open only to their guests. The best free courts are the five at the **Lahaina Civic Center** (✉ 1840 Honoapiʻilani Hwy., Lahaina, ☎ 808/661–4685), near Wahikuli State Park. They're available on a first-come, first-served basis.

Hyatt Regency Maui. The Hyatt has six courts, with rentals and instruction. All-day passes cost $15 for guests, $20 for nonguests. ✉ 200 Nohea Kai Dr., Kāʻanapali, ☎ 808/661–1234 ext. 3174.

Kapalua Tennis Garden. This complex serves the Kapalua Resort with 10 courts and a pro shop. You'll pay $10 an hour if you're a guest, $12 if you're not, and you're welcome to stay longer for free if there is no one waiting. ✉ 100 Kapalua Dr., Kapalua, ☎ 808/669–5677.

Mākena Tennis Club. This club at the Mākena Resort, just south of Wailea, has six courts. Rates are $16 per court hour for guests, $18

Participant Sports

for nonguests. After an hour, if there's space available, there's no charge. ✉ 5400 Mākena Alanui Rd., Kīhei, ☎ 808/879–8777.

Maui Beach & Tennis Club. The Maui Marriott's club has five Plexipave courts, with three lighted for night play, and a pro shop. Daily rates are $10 for guests and $12 for nonguests. ✉ 100 Nohea Kai Dr., Kā'anapali, ☎ 808/667–1200, ext. 8689.

Royal Lahaina Tennis Ranch. In the Kā'anapali Beach Resort on West Maui, the Royal Lahaina offers 11 recently resurfaced courts and a pro shop. Rates are a flat $10 per person per day whether you are a guest or not. ✉ 2780 Keka'a Dr., ☎ 808/661–3611 ext. 2296.

Wailea Tennis Club. These are the state's finest tennis facilities, often called "Wimbledon West" because of the two grass courts. There are also 11 Plexipave courts and a pro shop. You'll pay $25 an hour per person for the hard courts. The grass courts are by well-in-advance reservation only. On weekday mornings clinics are given to help you improve your ground strokes, serve, volley, or doubles strategy. ✉ 131 Wailea Ike Pl., Kīhei, ☎ 808/879–1958 or 800/332–1614.

Water Sports

Note that to reduce interference with whales, no "thrill craft"—specifically parasails and Jet Skis—are allowed in Maui waters from December 15 to April 15.

DEEP-SEA FISHING

If fishing is your sport, Maui is the place for it. You'll be able to throw in hook and bait for fish like *'ahi*, *aku* (skipjack tuna), barracuda, bonefish, *kawakawa* (bonito), mahimahi, Pacific blue marlin, *ono* (wahoo), and *ulua* (jack crevalle). On Maui you can fish throughout the year, and you don't need a license.

Plenty of fishing boats run out of Lahaina and Mā'alaea harbors. If you charter a boat by yourself, expect to spend in the neighborhood of $600 a day. But you can share the boat with others who are interested in fishing the same day for about $100 each. Although there are at least 10 companies running boats on a regular basis, these are the most reliable: **Finest Kind Inc.** (✉ Lahaina Harbor, Slip 7, Box 10481, Lahaina 96767, ☎ 808/661–0338), **Hinatea Sportfishing** (✉ Lahaina Harbor, Slip 27, Lahaina 96761, ☎ 808/667–7548), and **Lucky Strike Charters** (✉ Box 1502, Lahaina 96767, ☎ 808/661–4606). **Ocean Activities Center** (✉ 1847 S. Kīhei Rd., Suite 203A, Kīhei 96753, ☎ 808/879–4485 or 800/798–0652) can arrange fishing charters as well. You're responsible for finding your own transportation to the harbor.

KAYAKING

The sport has been gaining popularity on the island. Kayaking off the coast of Maui can be a leisurely paddle or it can be a challenge. This depends on your location, your inclination, and the weather of the day. The company to contact is **Maui Sea Kayaking** (☎ 808/572–6299, FAX 808/572–6151, ✉). They take small parties to secret spots. They like the idea of customizing their outings. For example, the guides accommodate kayakers with disabilities as well as senior kayakers, and they also offer kid-size gear. They're also into kayak surfing. And they offer a honeymoon/vow-renewal experience that could make Tarzan rekindle his appreciation for Jane.

RAFTING

These high-speed inflatable craft are nothing like the raft that Huck Finn used to drift down the Mississippi. While passengers grip straps, these rafts fly, skimming and bouncing, across the top of the sea. Because they're so maneuverable, they go where the big boats can't—secret coves, sea caves, and unvisited beaches. **Blue Water Rafting** (✉ Box 1865, Kīhei 96753, ☎ 808/661–4743 or 800/874–2666) leaves from the Kīhei boat ramp and explores the rugged coast beyond La Pérouse Bay. **Ocean Riders** (✉ Lahaina 96767, ☎ 808/661–3586), in Lahaina, takes people all the way around the island of Lāna'i. For snorkeling or gawking, the "back side" of Lāna'i is one of Hawai'i's unsung marvels.

SAILING

Because of its proximity to the smaller islands of Moloka'i, Lāna'i, Kaho'olawe, and Molokini, Maui can provide some of Hawai'i's best sailing experiences. Most sailing operations like to combine their tours with a meal, some throw in snorkeling or whale-watching, and others offer a sunset cruise.

The best and longest-running operation is the Coon family's **Trilogy Excursions** (✉ 180 Lahainaluna Rd., Lahaina 96761, ☎ 808/661–4743 or 800/874–2666). They have six beautiful multihulled sailing craft, and the crews treat passengers with genuine warmth and affection. A full-day catamaran cruise to Lāna'i includes a guided van tour of the island, a barbecue lunch, beach volleyball, and a "Snorkeling 101" class, in which you can test your skills in the waters of Hulopo'e Marine Preserve. (Trilogy has exclusive commercial access.) Snorkeling gear is supplied. It also offers a Molokini snorkel cruise.

Comparable to Trilogy in its service, good food, and comfortable catamaran cruise is the **Mahana Na'ia** (✉ Mā'alaea Harbor, ☎ 808/871–8636). This boat specializes in snorkel trips to Molokini. In a slip nearby at Mā'alaea Harbor, you'll find a beautiful monohull luxury yacht called **Cinderella** (☎ 808/244–0009), which is available for charters and for customized tours. Another sleek yacht that offers the exhilaration of fast sailing is the 65-ft cutter-rigged **World Class** (☎ 808/667–7733), which picks up passengers on the sand at Kā'anapali.

Other companies offering cruises include **Maui–Moloka'i Sea Cruises** (✉ 831 Eha St., Suite 101, Wailuku 96793, ☎ 808/242–8777), **Sail Hawai'i** (☎ 808/879–2201), **Scotch Mist Charters** (☎ 808/661–0386), and the Hyatt Regency Maui's **Kiele V** (✉ 200 Nohea Kai Dr., Lahaina, ☎ 808/661–1234).

SCUBA DIVING

Maui is just as scenic underwater as it is above. In fact, some of the finest diving spots in Hawai'i lie along the Valley Isle's western and southwestern shores. If you're a certified diver, you can rent gear at any Maui dive shop simply by showing your PADI or NAUI card. Unless you're familiar with the area, however, it's probably best to hook up with a dive shop for an underwater tour.

Maui has no lodging facilities tailored to divers, but there are many dive shops that sell and rent equipment and give lessons and certification. Before signing on with any of these outfitters, however, it's a good idea to ask a few pointed questions.

Some popular outfitters include **Ed Robinson's Diving Adventures** (✉ Kīhei, ☎ 808/879–3584 or 800/635–1273), **Happy Divers** (✉ 840 Waine'e St., Suite 106, Lahaina, ☎ 808/669–0123), **Lahaina Divers** (✉ 143 Dickenson St., Lahaina, ☎ 808/667–7496), **Maui Dive Shop** (✉ Honokōwai Marketplace, ☎ 808/661–0268; ✉ 1455 S. Kīhei Rd Kīhei, ☎ 808/879–0843), and **Pacific Dive Shop** (✉ 150 Dickenson St., Lahaina, ☎ 808/667–5331). All provide equipment with proof of certification, as well as introductory dives for those who aren't certified. Introductory boat dives generally run about $80.

Participant Sports

DIVE SITES

Honolua Bay. In West Maui, this marine preserve is alive with many varieties of coral and tame tropical fish, including large ulua, *kāhala*, barracuda, and manta rays. With depths of 20 ft to 50 ft, this is a popular spot for introductory dives. Dives are generally made only during the summer months.

Molokini Crater. At 'Alalākeiki Channel, this is a crescent-shape islet formed by the top of a volcano. This marine preserve's depth range (10 ft to 80 ft), combined with the attraction of the numerous tame fish dwelling here that can be fed by hand, makes it a popular introductory dive site.

SNORKELING

If you want a personal introduction to Maui's undersea universe, the undisputable authority is **Ann Fielding's Snorkel Maui.** A marine biologist, Fielding—formerly with University of Hawai'i, Waikīkī Aquarium, and the Bishop Museum and the author of several guides to island sealife—is the Carl Sagan of Hawai'i's reef cosmos. She'll not only show you fish, but she'll also introduce you to *individual* fish. This is a good first experience for dry-behind-the-ears types. Snorkel trips include lunch. ✉ *Box 1107, Makawao 96768,* ☎ *808/572–8437.* $75 adults, $65 children.

Of course the same dive companies that take scuba aficionados on tours will take snorkelers as well. One of Maui's most popular snorkeling spots can be reached only by boat: Molokini Crater, that little bowl of land off the coast of Wailea. For about $55, you can spend half a day at Molokini, with meals provided.

Ocean Activities Center (✉ 1847 S. Kīhei Rd., Suite 203A, Kīhei, ☎ 808/879–4485) does a great job, although other companies also offer a Molokini snorkel tour.

You can find some good snorkeling spots on your own. If you need gear, **Snorkel Bob's** (✉ Nāpili Village Hotel, 5425 Lower Honoapi'ilani Rd., Nāpili, ☎ 808/669–9603; ✉ 34 Keala Pl., Kīhei, ☎ 808/879–7449; ✉ 161 Lahainaluna Rd., Lahaina, ☎ 808/661–4421) will rent you a mask, fins, and snorkel and throw in a carrying bag, map, and snorkel tips for as little as $5 per day.

Secluded **Windmill Beach** (✉ Take Hwy. 30 3½ mi north of Kapalua; then turn onto the dirt road to the left) has a superb reef for snorkeling. A little more than 2 mi south, another dirt road leads to **Honolua Bay.** The coral formations on the right side of the bay are particularly dramatic. You'll find **Nāpili Bay,** one beach south of the Kapalua Resort, also quite good for snorkeling.

Almost the entire coastline from Kā'anapali south to Olowalu offers fine snorkeling. Favorite sites include the area just out from the cemetery north of Wahikuli State Park, near the lava cone called **Black Rock,** on which Kā'anapali's Sheraton Maui Hotel is built, and the shallow coral reef south of Olowalu General Store.

The coastline from Wailea to Mākena is also generally good for snorkeling. The best is found near the rocky fringes of Wailea's **Mōkapu, Ulua, Wailea,** and **Polo** beaches.

Between Polo Beach and Mākena Beach (turn right on Mākena Road just past Mākena Surf Condo) lies **Five Caves,** where you'll find a maze of underwater grottoes below offshore rocks. This spot is recommended for experienced snorkelers only, since the tides can get rough. At Mākena, the waters around the **Pu'u Ōla'i** cinder cone provide great snorkeling.

SURFING

Although on land it may not look as if there are seasons on Maui, the tides tell another story. In winter the surf is up on the northern shores of the Hawaiian Islands, and summer brings big swells to the southern side. Near-perfect winter waves on Maui can be found at **Honolua Bay,** on the northern tip of West Maui. To get there, continue 2 mi north of D. T. Fleming Park on Highway 30 and take a left onto the dirt road next to a pineapple field; a path takes you down the cliff to the beach.

Next best for surfing is **Ho'okipa Beach Park** (⊠ Off Hwy. 36, a short distance east of Pā'ia), where the modern-day sport began on Maui. This is the easiest place to watch surfing, because there are paved parking areas and picnic pavilions in the park. A word of warning: the surfers who come here are pros, and if you're not, they may not take kindly to your getting in their way.

Pushing the envelope of big-wave surfing has reached a new level here in the channel waters off Maui, where surfers get pulled out to sea and then whipped into the big waves. At Ho'okipa Beach Park, viewers with a good pair of binoculars might be able to see out past the windsurfers to view an example of tow-in surfing: Jet Ski pilots pull state-of-the-art big-wave surfers out to the 1-mi marker, where the waves can average 30 ft to 40 ft during winter swells. Amazing grace!

You can rent surfboards and boogie boards at many surf shops, such as **Second Wind** (⊠ 111 Hāna Hwy., Kahului, ☎ 808/877–7467), **Lightning Bolt Maui** (⊠ 55 Ka'ahumanu Ave., Kahului, ☎ 808/877–3484), and **Ole Surfboards** (⊠ 277 Wili Ko Pl., Lahaina, ☎ 808/661–3459).

WINDSURFING

It's been about 20 years since Ho'okipa Bay was discovered by boardsailors, who gave this windy beach 10 mi east of Kahului an international reputation. The spot is blessed with optimal wave-sailing wind and sea conditions and, for experienced windsurfers, can offer the ultimate experience. Other locations around Maui are good for windsurfing as well—Honolua Bay, for example—but Ho'okipa is absolutely unrivaled.

Even if you're a windsurfing aficionado, chances are good you didn't bring your equipment. You can rent it—or get lessons—from these shops: **Maui Ocean Activities** (⊠ Whalers Village, Kā'anapali, ☎ 808/667–1964), **Maui Windsurf Company** (⊠ 22 Hāna Hwy., Kahului, ☎ 808/877–4816), **Ocean Activities Center** (⊠ 1847 S. Kīhei Rd., Suite 203A, Kīhei, ☎ 808/879–4485), and **Maui Windsurfari** (⊠ 425 Koloa St., Kahului, ☎ 808/871–7766 or 800/736–6284). Lessons range from $30 to $60 and can last anywhere from one to three hours. Equipment rental also varies—from no charge with lessons to $20 an hour. For the latest prices and special deals, it's best to call around once you've arrived.

Spectator Sports

Golf

Maui has a number of golf tournaments, most of which are of professional caliber and worth watching. Many are also televised nationally. One of those attention-getters is the **Mercedes Championships** (☎ 808/669–2440), formerly called the Lincoln-Mercury Kapalua International, held now in January. This is the first official PGA tour event, held on Kapalua's Plantation Course. The Aloha Section of the Professional Golfers Association of America hosts the **GTE Hawaiian Tel Hall of Fame** (☎ 808/669–8877) championship at the Plantation Course in May and a clambake feast on the beach tops off the **Kapalua Clambake Pro-Am** (☎ 808/669–8812) in July.

ONE LAST TRAVEL TIP:

Pack an easy way to reach the world.

Wherever you travel, the MCI WorldCom Card℠ is the easiest way to stay in touch. You can use it to call to and from more than 125 countries worldwide. And you can earn bonus miles every time you use your card. So go ahead, travel the world. MCI WorldCom℠ makes it even more rewarding. For additional access codes, visit **www.wcom.com/worldphone**.

MCI WORLDCOM.

EASY TO CALL WORLDWIDE

1. Just dial the WorldPhone® access number of the country you're calling from.
2. Dial or give the operator your MCI WorldCom Card number.
3. Dial or give the number you're calling.

Aruba (A) ✛	800-888-8
Australia ◆	1-800-881-100
Bahamas ✛	1-800-888-8000
Barbados (A) ✛	1-800-888-8000
Bermuda ✛	1-800-888-8000
British Virgin Islands (A) ✛	1-800-888-8000
Canada	1-800-888-8000
Costa Rica (A) ◆	0800-012-2222
New Zealand	000-912
Puerto Rico	1-800-888-8000
United States	1-800-888-8000
U.S. Virgin Islands	1-800-888-8000

(A) Calls back to U.S. only.   ✛ Limited availability.   ◆ Public phones may require deposit of coin or phone card for dial tone.

EARN FREQUENT FLIER MILES

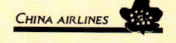

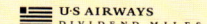

American Airlines AAdvantage®

CHINA AIRLINES

▲ Delta Air Lines SkyMiles®

TWA®

UNITED Mileage Plus®

US AIRWAYS DIVIDEND MILES

Limit of one bonus program per customer. All airline program rules and conditions apply. © 2000 WorldCom, Inc. All Rights Reserved. The names, logos, and taglines identifying WorldCom's products and services are proprietary marks of WorldCom, Inc. or its subsidiaries. All third party marks are the proprietary marks of their respective owners.

© 2000 Visa U.S.A. Inc.

Paris, France.

Paris, Texas.

When it Comes to Getting Cash at an ATM, Same Thing.

Whether you're in Yosemite or Yemen, using your Visa® card or ATM card with the PLUS symbol is the easiest and most convenient way to get cash. Even if your bank is in Minneapolis and you're in Miami, Visa/PLUS ATMs make getting cash so easy, you'll feel right at home. After all, Visa/PLUS ATMs are open 24 hours a day, 7 days a week, rain or shine. And if you need help finding one of Visa's 627,000 ATMs in 127 countries worldwide, visit **visa.com/pd/atm**. We'll make finding an ATM as easy as finding the Eiffel Tower, the Pyramids or even the Grand Canyon.

PLUS

VISA
It's Everywhere You Want To Be®

Close-Up

WHALE-WATCHING

Appealing to both children and adults, whale-watching is one of the most exciting activities in the United States. During the right time of year on Maui—between November and April—you can see whales breaching and blowing just offshore. The humpback whales' attraction to Maui is legendary. More than half the North Pacific's humpback population winters in Hawai'i, as they've been doing for years. At one time there were thousands of the huge mammals, but the world population has dwindled to about 1,500. In 1966 they were put on the endangered species list, which restricts boats and airplanes from getting too close.

Experts believe the humpbacks keep returning to Hawaiian waters because of the warmth. Winter is calving time for the behemoths, and the young whales, born with little blubber, probably couldn't survive in the frigid Alaskan waters. No one has ever seen a whale give birth, but the experts studying whales off Maui know that calving is their main winter activity, since the 1- and 2-ton youngsters suddenly appear while the whales are in residence.

Quite a few operations run whale-watching excursions off the coast of Maui, with many boats departing from the wharves at Lahaina and Mā'alaea each day. **Pacific Whale Foundation** (✉ Kealia Beach Plaza, 101 N. Kīhei Rd., Kīhei 96753, ☎ 808/879-8811) pioneered whale-watching back in 1979 and now runs four boats, plus sea kayaks and special trips to encounter turtles and dolphins. During humpback season (Dec. 15–May 1), PWF has a marine naturalist stationed at McGregor Point Lookout (on the cliffs heading into Lahaina) and also weekdays at 12:15 on the observation deck of its Kīhei office.

Also offering whale-watching in season are **Ocean Activities Center** (✉ 1847 S. Kīhei Rd., Suite 203A, Kīhei 96753, ☎ 808/879-4485); **Island Marine** (✉ 113 Prison St., Lahaina 96761, ☎ 808/661-8397); and **Pride Charters** (✉ 208 Kenolio Rd., Kīhei, ☎ 808/874-8835), whose two-hour whale-watch cruise is narrated by a naturalist from Whales Alive and Keiko (Free Willie) Foundation. Ticket prices average $22–$35.

At Kāʻanapali the **EMC Maui Kāʻanapali Classic SENIOR PGA Golf Tournament** pits veteran professionals in a battle for a $1 million purse each October.

Over in Wailea, in June, on the longest day of the year, self-proclaimed "lunatic" golfers start out at first light to play 100 holes of golf in the annual **Ka Lima O Maui,** a fund-raiser for local charities. In January, 2001, the Wailea resort is adding the **Senior Skins** game, a nationally televised competition that pits four of the most respected Senior PGA players against one another.

Outrigger-Canoe Races

Polynesians first traveled to Hawaiʻi by outrigger canoe, and racing the traditional craft has always been a favorite pastime in the Islands. Canoes were revered in old Hawaiʻi, and no voyage could begin without a blessing, ceremonial chanting, and a hula performance to ensure a safe journey. At Whalers Village in May, the two-day launch festivities for the **Hoʻomanaʻo Challenge Outrigger Sailing Canoe World Championship** (☎ 808/661-3271) also include a torch-lighting ceremony, arts-and-crafts demonstrations, and a chance to observe how the vessels are rigged—as well as the start of the race.

Polo

Polo is popular with Mauians. From April to June Haleakalā Ranch hosts "indoor" contests on a field flanked by side boards. The field is on Highway 377, 1 mi from Highway 37. During the "outdoor" polo season, mid-August to the end of October, matches are held at Olinda Field, 1 mi above Makawao on Olinda Road. There is a $3 admission charge for most games, which start at 1 PM on Sunday. The sport has two special events. One is the **Oskie Rice Memorial Tournament** on Memorial Day. The other—the **High Goal Benefit,** held on the last Sunday in October—draws challengers from Argentina, England, South Africa, New Zealand, and Australia. For information, contact Emiliano (☎ 808/572-4915).

Rodeos

With dozens of working cattle ranches throughout the Islands, many youngsters learn to ride a horse before they can drive a car. Mauians love their rodeos and put on several for students at local high schools throughout the year. Paniolos get in on the act, too, at three major annual events: the **Oskie Rice Memorial Rodeo,** usually staged the weekend after Labor Day; the **Cancer Benefit Rodeo** in April, held at an arena 3 mi east of Pāʻia; and Maui's biggest event, drawing competitors from all islands as well as the U.S. mainland, the **4th of July Rodeo,** which comes with a full-on parade and other festivities that last for days. Spectator admission fees to the competitions vary from free to $7. Cowboys are a tough bunch to tie down to a phone, but you can try calling the **Maui Roping Club** (☎ 808/572-2076) for information.

Surfing and Windsurfing

Not many places can lay claim to as many windsurfing tournaments as Maui. The Valley Isle is generally thought to be the world's preeminent windsurfing location and draws boardsailing experts from around the globe who want to compete on its waves. In March the **Hawaiian Pro Am Windsurfing** competition gets under way. In April the **Da Kine Hawaiian Pro Am** lures top windsurfers, and the **Aloha Classic World Wave Sailing Championships** takes place in October. All are held at Hoʻokipa Bay, right outside the town of Pāʻia, near Kahului. For competitions featuring amateurs as well as professionals, check out the **Maui Race Series** (☎ 808/877-2111), six events held at Kanahā Beach in Kahului in summer when winds are the strongest and lack of big waves

Spectator Sports

makes conditions excellent for the slalom (speed-racing) course. Competitors maneuver their boards close to shore, and the huge beach provides plenty of seating and viewing space. Hoʻokipa Bay's large waves are also prime territory for surfers. The **Local Motion Surfing** competition heats up the action in May, and in January the **Maui Rusty Pro,** held jointly at Honolua Bay, invites professionals to compete for a $40,000 purse.

Tennis

At the **Kapalua Jr. Vet/Sr. Tennis Championships** in May, where the minimum age is 30, players have been competing in singles and doubles events since 1979. On Labor Day, the **Wilson Kapalua Open Tennis Tournament,** Maui's grand prix of tennis, calls Hawaiʻi's hottest hitters to volley for a $12,000 purse at Kapalua's Tennis Garden and Village Tennis Center. Also at the Tennis Center, Women's International Tennis Association professionals rally with avid amateurs in a week of pro-am and pro-doubles competition during the **Kapalua Betsy Nagelsen Tennis Invitational** in December. All events are put on by the **Kapalua Tennis Club** (☎ 808/669–5677).

In East Maui, 2000 marks the 16th year for the Wailea Open Tennis Championship, held in July on the Plexipave courts at the **Wailea Tennis Club** (☎ 808/879–1958).

6 SHOPPING

You'll enjoy browsing in the shops that line Front Street in Lahaina or the boutiques that are packed into the major resorts. Kanului and Lahaina also have some good-size shopping malls.

Shopping

WHETHER YOU HEAD FOR one of the malls or opt for the boutiques hidden around the Valley Isle, one thing you should have no problem finding is clothing made in Hawai'i. The Hawaiian garment industry is now the state's third-largest economic sector, after tourism and agriculture.

Maui has an abundance of locally made art and crafts in a range of prices. A group that calls itself Made on Maui exists solely to promote the products of its members—items that range from pottery and paintings to Hawaiian teas and macadamia caramel corn. You can identify the group by its distinctive Haleakalā logo.

Business hours for individual shops on the island are usually 9–5, seven days a week. Shopping centers tend to stay open later (until 9 or 10 at least one night of the week).

Shopping Centers

Azeka Place Shopping Center (⊠ 1280 S. Kīhei Rd.). Kīhei offers this large and bustling place. Azeka I is the older half, on the makai side of the street. Azeka II, on the mauka side, has a **Long's Drugs** and several good lunch stops. Residents, however, favor the locally owned shops at the small Kama'ole Shopping Center (⊠ 2463 S. Kīhei Rd.). Another place to rub elbows with Kīhei locals is Rainbow Mall (⊠ 2439 S. Kīhei Rd.).

Ka'ahumanu Center (⊠ 275 Ka'ahumanu Ave., Kahului, ☎ 808/877-3369). An expansion turned this into Maui's largest mall and a showplace with more than 75 stores and a gorgeous glass-enclosed atrium entrance topped by an umbrella-shaded food court. Stop at Camellia Seed Shop for what the locals call "crack seed," a delicacy made from dried fruits, nuts, and sugar. Other interesting stops here include Shirokiya, a popular Japanese retailer; Maui Hands, purveyor of prints, paintings, woodwork, and jewelry by some of the island's finest artists; and such mall standards as Foot Locker, Mrs. Field's Cookies, and Kinney Shoes.

Lahaina Cannery Mall (⊠ 1221 Honoapi'ilani Hwy., Lahaina, ☎ 808/661-5304). The 50 shops here are set in a building reminiscent of an old pineapple cannery. Unlike many other shopping centers in Hawai'i, the Lahaina Cannery isn't open-air, but it is air-conditioned. Recommended stops include Hawaiian Island Gems, featuring striking Hawaiian heirloom jewelry and pearls; Superwhale, with a good selection of children's tropical wear; and Kite Fantasy, one of the best kite shops on Maui.

Lahaina Center (⊠ 900 Front St., Lahaina, ☎ 808/667-9216). Island department store Hilo Hattie anchors the center and puts on a free hula show at 2 PM every Wednesday and Friday. An additional 10,000 square ft of parking lot space here have been transformed into an ancient Hawaiian village complete with three full-size thatch huts built with 10,000 linear ft of 'ōhi'a wood from the Big Island, 20 tons of *pili* grass, and more than 4 mi of handwoven coconut *senit* (twine). Indoor entertainment is found at a four-screen cinema. The roster of shops and restaurants includes World Cafe and the Hard Rock Cafe for eats and Banana Republic and Waterwear for clothing.

Maui Mall (⊠ 70 Ka'ahumanu Ave., Kahului, ☎ 808/877-7559). Perhaps spurred by new competition from Ka'ahumanu Center, this place has given itself a face-lift and added a whimsically designed 12-screen megaplex, and these improvements have started attracting new tenants. The anchor stores are still Long's Drugs and Star Market, and they've kept a good Japanese diner named Restaurant Matsu (☞ Central Maui *in* Chapter 2, *above*). The Tasaka Guri Guri Shop is an oddity.

It's been around a hundred years, selling an ice cream–like confection called *"guri guri"* that you will find nowhere else in the world.

Maui Marketplace (✉ 270 Dairy Rd., Kahului, ☎ 808/873–0400). At this 20-acre complex, several outlet stores and big retailers, such as Eagle Hardware, Sports Authority, and Borders Books & Music, have made their first expansion to a Neighbor Island. The center couldn't have a more convenient location. It's at the busy intersection of Hāna Highway and Dairy Road, close to Kahului Airport.

The Shops at Wailea (✉ Between the Aston Wailea Resort and the Grand Wailea). The Wailea resort has taken a couple of years to completely re-create its shopping. The place has an Old World piazza design that covers 150,000 square ft and includes a central stage for shows. Tenants include Louis Vuitton, Tiffany & Co., several art galleries, and a new Longhi's restaurant.

Whalers Village (✉ 2435 Kā'anapali Pkwy., Kā'anapali, ☎ 808/661–4567). Chic and trendy, Whalers Village has grown into a major West Maui shopping center, with a whaling museum and more than 50 restaurants and shops. Upscale haunts include Louis Vuitton, Prada, Ferragamo, Hunting World, and Chanel Boutique. The complex also offers some interesting diversions: Hawaiian artisans display their crafts daily, hula dancers perform on an outdoor stage weeknights from 7 to 8, and a free slide show spotlighting whales and other marine life takes place at the Whale Center of the Pacific on Tuesday and Thursday at 7.

Grocery Stores

If you need groceries to take back to your condo, the following are conveniently located and offer good selections and extended hours.

Foodland (✉ 1881 S. Kīhei Rd., Kīhei, ☎ 808/879–9350). In Kīhei town center, this is the most convenient supermarket for visitors staying in Wailea. It's open around the clock.

Lahaina Square Shopping Center Foodland (✉ 840 Waine'e St., Lahaina, ☎ 808/661–0975). This Foodland serves West Maui and is open daily from 6 AM to midnight.

Safeway (✉ Lahaina Cannery Mall, Honoapi'ilani Hwy., Lahaina, ☎ 808/667–4392; ✉ 170 E. Kamehameha Ave., Kahului, ☎ 808/877–3377). Safeway has two stores on the island open 24 hours daily. The one in Lahaina serves West Maui, and the one in Kahului provides a convenient stop for visitors shopping at Ka'ahumanu Center or touring the historic sites of Central Maui before returning to Wailea lodgings.

Specialty Stores

Art

Maui has more art per square mile than any other Hawaiian island—maybe more than any other U.S. county. There are artists' guilds and co-ops and galleries galore all over the island. Art shows are held throughout the year at the Maui Arts & Cultural Center. Marine sculptors and painters showcase their work during **Celebration of Whales** at the Four Seasons Resort Wailea in January. The Lahaina Arts Society presents **Art in the Park** under the town's historic banyan tree every Friday and Saturday from 9 to 5. Moreover, the town of Lahaina hosts **Art Night** every Friday from 7 to 10. Galleries open their doors (some serve refreshments) and musicians stroll the streets.

Hot Island Glassblowing Studio & Gallery (✉ 3620 Baldwin Ave., Makawao, ☎ 808/572–4527). This is an exciting place to visit, with the glass-melting furnaces glowing bright orange and the shop loaded with mesmerizing sculptures and functional pieces. Set back from

Specialty Stores

Makawao's main street in "The Courtyard," the working studio is owned by a family of award-winning glassblowers.

Hui No'eau Visual Arts Center (✉ 2841 Baldwin Ave., Makawao, ☎ 808/572–6560). The center presents juried and nonjuried exhibits by local artists.

Lahaina Galleries (✉ 728 Front St., Lahaina, ☎ 808/667–2152; ✉ Kapalua Resort, ☎ 808/669–0202). The gallery has two locations in West Maui offering a mixed collection of the works of both national and international artists.

Martin Lawrence Galleries (✉ Lahaina Market Place, Front St. and Lahainaluna Rd., Lahaina, ☎ 808/661–1788). Martin Lawrence represents noted mainland artists, including Andy Warhol and Keith Haring, in a bright and friendly gallery open since 1991.

Maui Crafts Guild (✉ 43 Hāna Hwy., Pā'ia, ☎ 808/579–9697). This is one of the most interesting galleries on Maui. Set in a two-story wooden building alongside the highway, the Guild is crammed with work by local artists. The best pieces are the pottery and sculpture. Upstairs, antique kimonos, hand-painted silks, and batik fabric are on display.

Maui Hands (✉ 3620 Baldwin Ave., Makawao, ☎ 808/572–5194; ✉ Ka'ahumanu Center, Kahului, ☎ 808/877–0368). This gallery shows work by dozens of local artists, including paniolo-theme lithographs by Sharon Shigekawa, who knows whereof she paints: she rides each year in the Kaupō Roundup. The shop is in the town's old theater.

Viewpoints (✉ 3620 Baldwin Ave., Makawao, ☎ 808/572–5979). Viewpoints calls itself Maui's only fine-arts collective; it is a cooperative venture of about two dozen Maui painters and sculptors, representing a wide variety of styles.

Village Gallery (✉ 120 Dickenson St., Lahaina, ☎ 808/661–4402; ✉ Ritz-Carlton, 1 Ritz-Carlton Dr., Kapalua, ☎ 808/669–1800). This gallery, with two locations on the island, features such popular local artists as Betty Hay Freeland, Wailehua Gray, Margaret Bedell, George Allen, Joyce Clark, Pamela Andelin, Stephen Burr, and Macario Pascual.

Clothing

ISLAND WEAR

Hilo Hattie (✉ Lahaina Center, Lahaina, ☎ 808/661–8457). Hawai'i's largest manufacturer of aloha shirts and mu'umu'u. They also carry brightly colored blouses, skirts, and children's clothing.

Liberty House. Liberty House has the kind of island wear—colorful shirts and mu'umu'u as well as other graceful styles—worn by people who live year-round on Maui. The store has several branches on the island, including shops at the Hyatt Regency and at the Four Seasons Wailea, but the largest is the one at Ka'ahumanu Center in Kahului (☎ 808/877–3361).

Reyn's (✉ Kapalua Bay Hotel, Kapalua, ☎ 808/669–5260; ✉ Hyatt Regency Maui, Kā'anapali, ☎ 808/661–0215; ✉ Whalers Village, Kā'anapali, ☎ 808/661–9032). This is the place to go for high-quality aloha shirts in the subtler shades that local men favor for business attire.

RESORT WEAR

Not all of Maui's casual clothing is floral. You can find island-worthy sportswear in shops all over the Valley Isle, including most of the stores that sell island wear, as well as these:

Honolua Surf Company (✉ 845 Front St., Lahaina, ☎ 808/661–8848; ✉ Whalers Village, Kā'anapali, ☎ 808/661–5455; ✉ Lahaina Cannery Mall, Lahaina, ☎ 808/661–5777; ✉ 2411 S. Kīhei Rd., Kīhei, ☎ 808/874–0999). This chain is popular with young women for casual clothing and sportswear.

SGT Leisure (✉ 855B Front St., Lahaina, ☎ 808/667–0661; ✉ Whalers Village, Kāʻanapali, ☎ 808/667–9433). These shops carry resort wear by Tori Richards and other designers. Primarily, though, they sell their own line of informal apparel—sweatshirts, T-shirts, and accessories such as beach bags and hats—bearing their big fish logo.

Tropical Tantrum Outlet Store (✉ Azeka Place Shopping Center, Kīhei, ☎ 808/874–3835; ✉ Kaʻahumanu Center, Kahului, ☎ 808/871–8088; ✉ Kamaʻole Shopping Center, Kīhei, ☎ 808/875–4433). This well-known outfitter has three retail stores on Maui, but here at the outlets you'll find a wide selection of stylish resort wear, aloha shirts, and muʻumuʻu for 50% less than at the company's retail stores.

Flea Market

Maui Swap Meet. This Saturday flea market is the biggest bargain on Maui, with crafts, gifts, souvenirs, fruit, flowers, jewelry, antiques, art, shells, and lots more. ✉ *Hwy. 350, off S. Puʻunēnē Ave., Kahului.* 💰 *50¢.* ⊙ *Sat. 5:30–noon.*

Food

Many visitors to Hawaiʻi opt to take home some of the local produce: pineapples, papayas, coconuts, or Maui onions. You can find jams and jellies—some of them "Made on Maui" products—in a wide variety of tropical flavors. Cook Kwee's Maui Cookies have gained quite a following, as have Maui Potato Chips. Both are available in most Valley Isle grocery stores. Coffee sellers now have Maui-grown and -roasted beans alongside the better-known Kona varieties.

Remember that fresh fruit must be inspected by the U.S. Department of Agriculture before it can leave the state, so it's safer to buy a box that has already passed muster.

Airport Flower & Fruit Co. (☎ 808/243–9367 or 800/922–9352). Ready-to-ship pineapples, Maui onions, papayas, and fresh coconuts are available by phone.

Take Home Maui (✉ 121 Dickenson St., Lahaina, ☎ 808/661–8067 or 800/545–6284). These folks will supply, pack, and deliver produce free to the airport or your hotel.

Gifts

Lahaina Printsellers Ltd. (✉ Lahaina Cannery Mall, 1221 Honoapiʻilani Hwy., Lahaina, ☎ 808/667–7843). Hawaiʻi's largest selection of antique maps and prints pertaining to Hawaiʻi and the Pacific are available here. They also sell museum-quality reproductions and original oil paintings from the Pacific Artists Guild. Two smaller shops are also at Whalers Village in Kāʻanapali and at the Grand Wailea Resort in Wailea.

Maui's Best (✉ Kaʻahumanu Center, Kahului, ☎ 808/877–7959; ✉ Azeka Place Shopping Center, Kīhei, ☎ 808/874–9216). This a good stop for a wide selection of gifts from Maui and around the world.

Ola's Makawao (✉ 1156 Makawao Ave., Makawao, ☎ 808/573–1334). Ola's has a delightful assortment of whimsical gifts and affordable, functional contemporary art made by artists from Hawaiʻi and the U.S. mainland. It is also the exclusive western-U.S. distributor for chocolates by JoMart Candies.

Hawaiian Crafts

The arts and crafts native to Hawaiʻi are first on the list for many visiting shoppers. Such woods as koa and milo grow only in certain parts of the world, and because of their increasing scarcity, prices are rising. Artisans turn the woods into bowls, trays, and jewelry boxes that will last for years. Look for them in galleries and museum shops.

Specialty Stores

Hāna Cultural Center (✉ Ukea St., Hāna, ☎ 808/248–8622). The culture center sells distinctive island quilts and other Hawaiian crafts.
Kīhei Kalama Village Marketplace (✉ 1941 S. Kīhei Rd., Kīhei, ☎ 808/879–6610). This is a fun place to investigate. A shaded collection of outdoor stalls sells everything from printed and hand-painted T-shirts and sundresses to jewelry, pottery, wood carvings, fruit, and gaudily painted coconut husks—all made by local craftspeople.
Quilters Corner (✉ 1000 Limahana Pl., Lahaina, ☎ 808/661–0944). Here you'll find a huge selection of Hawaiian quilts and needlepoint, as well as plenty of tropical-print fabrics, silver jewelry, and other local crafts and gift items.

Jewelry

Haimoff & Haimoff Creations in Gold (✉ Kapalua Resort, ☎ 808/669–5213). This shop features the original work of several jewelry designers, including the award-winning Harry Haimoff.
Jessica's Gems (✉ Whalers Village, Kā'anapali, ☎ 808/661–4223; ✉ 858 Front St., Lahaina, ☎ 808/661–9200). Jessica's has a good selection of Hawaiian heirloom jewelry, and its Lahaina store specializes in black pearls.
Lahaina Scrimshaw (✉ 845A Front St., Lahaina, ☎ 808/661–8820; ✉ Whalers Village, Kā'anapali, ☎ 808/661–4034). Here you can buy brooches, rings, pendants, cuff links, tie tacks, and collector's items adorned with this intricately carved sailors' art.
Master Touch Gallery (✉ 3655 Baldwin Ave., Makawao, ☎ 808/572–6000). The exterior of this shop is as rustic as all the old buildings of Makawao, so there's no way to prepare yourself for the elegance and sensuousness of the handcrafted jewelry displayed within. Owner David Sacco truly has the "master touch."
Maui Divers (✉ 640 Front St., Lahaina, ☎ 808/661–0988). This company has been crafting gold and coral into jewelry for more than 20 years.

7 SIDE TRIP TO LĀNAʻI

Lānaʻi's only population center is Lānaʻi City, smack in the middle of the island. The town is surrounded by natural wonders: Garden of the Gods, strewn with colorful boulders, to the northwest; breathtaking Hulopoʻe Beach to the south; and Lānaʻihale, the highest point on the island, to the east.

Side Trip to Lāna'i

By Marty Wentzel

Updated by Sophia Schweitzer

FOR DECADES, LĀNA'I WAS KNOWN as "the Pineapple Island," with hundreds of acres of fields filled with the golden fruit. Today this 141-square-mi island has been renamed "Hawai'i's Most Secluded Island," and the pineapple fields have given way to sophisticated hotels and guest activities. In 1990, Dole Foods Inc.—now Castle & Cooke, Inc.—which owns 98% of the island, opened the luxurious 102-room Lodge at Kō'ele, and, the following year, the 250-room Mānele Bay Hotel, plus two championship golf courses. Despite these new additions, Lāna'i remains the most remote and intimate visitor destination in Hawai'i.

Most of the island's population is centered in Lāna'i City, an old plantation town of 2,800 residents, whose tiny houses have colorful façades, tin roofs, and tidy gardens. Although the weather across much of the island is hot and dry, the tall Cook pines that line Lāna'i City's streets create a cool refuge. Here you'll encounter descendants of those who in the 1920s came from the Philippines, Korea, China, and Japan to work in Lāna'i's pineapple fields. Mainland *haole* (Caucasians) have also moved in. Though Lāna'i City has a few family-run shops and stores, its options are limited. You'll find a couple of diner-style eateries; an art center; and the comfy old Hotel Lāna'i, an 11-room hostelry that serves as a gathering place for locals and tourists. The town adds a hint of civilization to a mostly wild island.

Lāna'i City, however, is not the primary reason for visiting the island. Among the unique outdoor attractions is the Garden of the Gods in Kānepu'u, where rocks and boulders are scattered across a crimson landscape as if some divine being had placed them there as a sculpture garden. Adjacent is a self-guided nature trail leading through the Kānepu'u Preserve, a unique dryland forest hosting some 48 native species, including endangered the Hawaiian gardenia. The waters at Hulopo'e Beach are so clear that within a minute of snorkeling you can see fish the colors of turquoise and jade. After hiking or driving to the summit of Lāna'ihale, a 3,370-ft-high windswept perch, you'll find a splendid view of nearly every inhabited Hawaiian island.

Although today it is an island that welcomes visitors with its friendly, rustic charm, Lāna'i has not always been so amiable. The earliest Polynesians believed it to be haunted by evil ghosts who gobbled up unsuspecting visitors. In 1836 a pair of missionaries named Dwight Baldwin and William Richards came and went after failing to convert the locals to their Christian beliefs. In 1854 a group of Mormons tried to create the City of Joseph here, but they were forced to abandon their mission after a drought in 1857.

One of Lāna'i's more successful visitors was a man named Jim Dole (1877–1958). In 1922 Dole bought the island for $1.1 million and began to grow pineapples on it. He built Lāna'i City on the flatlands, where the crater floor is flanked by volcanic slopes. Then he planned the harbor at Kaumālapa'u, from which pineapples would be shipped. Four years later, as he watched the first harvest sail away to Honolulu, this enterprising businessman could safely say that Dole Plantation was a success. But in the late 1980s pineapples ceased to be profitable because of global competition. The solution? The company built two new hotels and developed a tourism industry which is starting to thrive.

Isolated as it may seem, Lāna'i has found a powerful way to connect with the outside world through its hotel-hosted Visiting Artist Program. Pulitzer Prize–winning authors, celebrity chefs, and world-famous actors enliven the island with complimentary performances for guests and residents. You can meet inspirational people such as author Armistead Maupin or jazz guitarist Bucky Pizzarelle.

A visit to Lāna'i can be either simple or elegant. Solitude is easily acquired, though you may encounter the occasional deer on the hillsides, the spirits that linger in the ancient fishing village of Kaunolū, and the playful dolphins of Mānele Bay. On the other hand, you can rub elbows with sophisticated travelers during a game of croquet at the Lodge at Kō'ele or a round of golf. Bring casual clothes because many of your activities will be laid-back, whether you're riding the unpaved roads in a four-wheel-drive vehicle or having a drink on the porch of the Hotel Lāna'i. Come, take your time, and enjoy it before the island changes too much more.

Pleasures and Pastimes

Dining
Lāna'i's has developed its own unique version of Hawai'i regional cuisine. The upscale menus at the two resorts reflect the fresh-flavored products provided by local hunters and fishermen—everything from Mānele *'ahi* (yellowfin tuna) to Lāna'i venison. Lāna'i City's eclectic fare ranges from hamburgers to Cajun dishes and pizzas with organic toppings. Pricing is straightforward: hotel dining rooms are expensive, and family-run eateries are much more affordable.

Golf
Lāna'i's two championship golf courses compete with the finest in the world. The pine-covered fields of the Experience at Kō'ele stretch across rolling hills. At the top-ranking oceanfront Challenge at Mānele, dolphins and whales have been known to distract even the most serious golfer.

Hiking
Only 30 mi of Lanai'i's roads are paved. But red-dirt, four-wheel-drive roads and walking trails will take you to abandoned villages and historic *heiau* (stone platforms that were used as worship sites), isolated beaches and forest preserves. Follow a self-guided walk through Hawai'i's largest native dryland forest or hike the 8 mi of the Munro Trail over Lāna'ihale with views of plunging canyons and all of Hawai'i Nei. Before you go, fill a water bottle and arm yourself with provisions and maps.

Lodging
Lāna'i offers several lodging options on its limited number of properties. The Lodge at Kō'ele and Mānele Bay Hotel are luxury resorts, and their rates reflect this. If you're on a tighter budget, seek out a bed-and-breakfast or consider the Hotel Lāna'i. House rentals, although expensive, give you a taste of what it's like to live here.

Snorkeling and Scuba Diving
With Cathedrals (pinnacle formations) for a dive site and angelfish among the marine life, it's no wonder that snorkeling and scuba-diving buffs call the waters off Lāna'i a religious experience. For the best underwater viewing, try Hulopo'e Beach (☞ Beaches, *below*), a marine-life conservation area, or go on an excursion with Lāna'i Ecoadventure Centre (☞ Contacts and Resources *in* Lāna'i A to Z, *below*).

EXPLORING LĀNA'I

Most of Lāna'i's sights are out of the way. You have to search, but it's worth it. Ask your hotel's concierge for a road and site map, fill up on gas if you have a four-wheel-drive vehicle, and bring along a cooler with drinks and snacks. Admission is free to all sights mentioned.

Exploring Lāna'i

Great Itineraries

Lāna'i is small enough to explore in a couple of days of leisurely travel. Be selective with your time, for it goes by fast here.

Numbers in the text correspond to numbers in the margin and on the Lāna'i map.

IF YOU HAVE 1 DAY

If you can only tear yourself away from your lounge chair for one day of exploring, rent a four-wheel-drive vehicle and get to know the back roads of Lāna'i, where the power of the landscape is immense. If you're staying at the Lodge at Kō'ele or Hotel Lāna'i, allow yourself enough time to see the **Garden of the Gods** ⑦ and the **Kānepu'u Preserve** ⑥ in the morning. After lunch in **Lāna'i City** ⑩, drive down to **Lu'ahiwa Petroglyphs** ② and **Kaunolū** ③, followed by a late-afternoon swim at Hulopo'e Beach (☞ Beaches, *below*). Guests of the Mānele Bay Hotel should reverse the itinerary, with the beach, petroglyphs, and Kaunolū in the morning and Garden of the Gods in the afternoon.

IF YOU HAVE 3 DAYS

Follow the one-day itinerary above. On day two, take an adventurous tour of the undeveloped north and east shores. Pack a picnic and start the day with a drive to **Shipwreck Beach** ⑨ for a morning walk and some sunbathing. Then drive along the bumpy coastal road to **Keōmuku** ⑪, **Kahe'a Heiau** ⑫, **Naha** ⑬, and Lōpā Beach, where you can picnic. After retracing your route, relive the day's adventures over tropical drinks at your hotel's lounge. Start your third day with a cool morning hike atop Lāna'ihale, stopping midway for a picnic. In the afternoon, how about a spa treatment or some time in the swimming pool and hot tub?

IF YOU HAVE 5 DAYS

Follow the three-day itinerary and then dedicate day four to the sport of your choice, be it golf on the championship courses, tennis at the Mānele Bay Hotel or the Lodge at Kō'ele, horseback riding from the Stables at Kō'ele, or sporting clays in the highlands; or sign up for a lesson and learn a new sport. On day five, see the island from the sea by going on a half-day fishing trip or snorkeling–scuba diving expedition. In the afternoon, stroll around Lāna'i City, "talk story" (chat) with the residents and shop owners, and pick up some island souvenirs like hand-carved pine bowls.

When to Tour Lāna'i

The weather on Lāna'i is warm and clear throughout the year. It's sunniest at sea level, while in upcountry Lāna'i City the nights and mornings can feel chilly and the fog can settle in on the tops of the pine trees. As in all of Hawai'i, winter weather is cooler and less predictable. For a taste of local arts, crafts, and entertainment, time your trip with an island event such as autumn's Aloha Festivals.

South and West Lāna'i

Pineapples once blanketed the Pālāwai Basin, the flat area south of Lāna'i City. Today it is used primarily for agriculture and grazing and holds historic and natural treasures worth exploring. In the Islands, the directions *mauka* (toward the mountains) and *makai* (toward the ocean) are often used.

A Good Drive

From Lāna'i City, drive south on Highway 440 a few blocks until you reach a major intersection. Go straight, following the highway west to **Kaumālapa'u Harbor** ①, the island's main seaport. Backtrack to the intersection, turn right, and take Highway 440 south (also called Mānele Road). After about a mile you'll see a dirt road on your left leading to the **Lu'ahiwa Petroglyphs** ② and its ancient rock carvings.

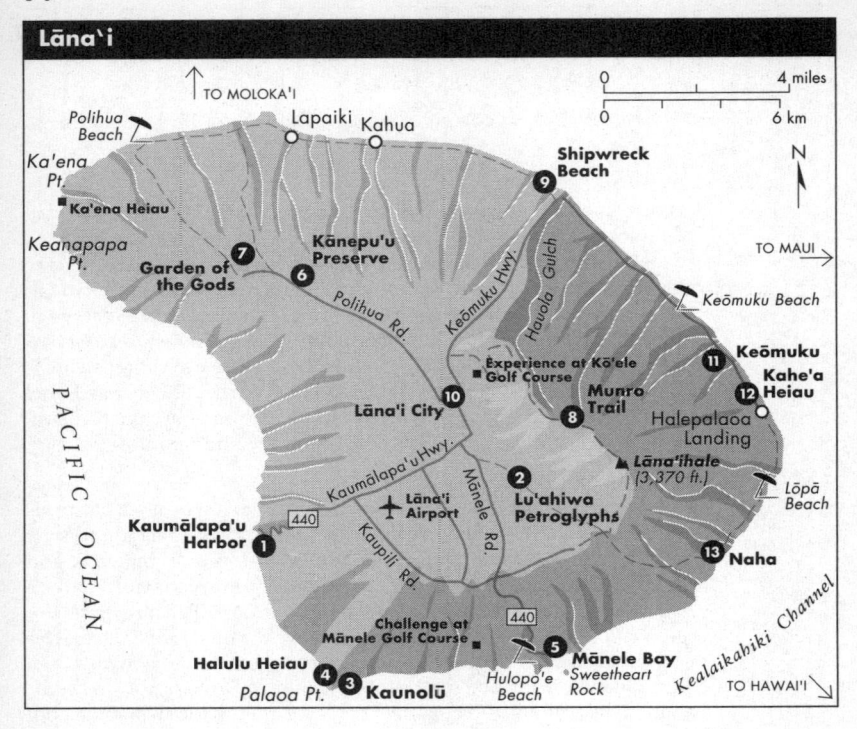

Return to Highway 440 and drive another 2 mi south until the road veers left. Here, go straight on bumpy and unpaved Kaupili Road (you'll need a four-wheel-drive vehicle for this). Then take the fourth left onto another unnamed dirt road. All of this four-wheeling pays off when you reach your destination: the well-preserved archaeological sites of **Kaunolū** ③ and **Halulu Heiau** ④.

Back on Highway 440, drive down the long, steep hill. At the bottom awaits **Mānele Bay** ⑤, with its boat harbor. Take a look at Pu'upehe (Sweetheart Rock) and its sheer 50-ft-high cliffs. The road ends at the island's only true swimming area, Hulopo'e Beach (☞ Beaches, *below*).

TIMING

Although it's a small area, south and west Lāna'i deserves a full day of exploration. If you're a fan of water sports, you'll want to spend half the day at Hulopo'e Beach and use the rest for visiting the other attractions. The south is almost always sunny, clear, and warm, so wear sunscreen and head for shade in the middle of the day.

Sights to See

✍ *following the text of a review is your signal that the property has a Web site where you will find details and, usually, images; for a link, visit www.fodors.com/urls.*

④ **Halulu Heiau.** The carefully excavated remains of an impressive heiau attest to the sacred history of this spot, which was actively used by the earliest residents of Lāna'i. As late as 1810, this hilltop site was also considered a place of refuge for wayward islanders. ✉ *From Lāna'i*

Exploring Lāna'i

City, follow Hwy. 440 (Mānele Rd.) south; when road makes sharp left, continue straight on Kaupili Rd.; turn makai onto fourth dirt road.

① **Kaumālapa'u Harbor.** Built in 1926 by the Hawaiian Pineapple Company, which later became Dole, this is the principal seaport for Lāna'i. The cliffs flanking the western shore are as much as 1,000 ft tall. No water activities are allowed here, but if you are in the area on a Thursday, be sure to witness the arrival of the barge. The Island depends on its weekly deliveries. ✉ *From Lāna'i City, follow Hwy. 440 (Kaumālapa'u Hwy.) west as far as it goes; turn left and drive about 7 mi makai.*

③ **Kaunolū.** Set atop the island's highest sea cliffs, Kaunolū was a prosperous fishing village in precontact times. This important Hawaiian archaeological site includes terraces, stone floors, and platforms where 86 houses and 35 shelters once stood. You'll also see petroglyphs, a series of intricate rock carvings that have been preserved. Kaunolū has additional significance because Hawai'i's King Kamehameha I sometimes lived here. ✉ *From Lāna'i City follow Hwy. 440 (Mānele Rd.) south; when road makes sharp left, continue straight on Kaupili Rd. through pineapple fields; turn makai onto fourth dirt road.*

② **Lu'ahiwa Petroglyphs.** On a steep slope overlooking the Pālāwai Basin, in the flatlands of Lāna'i, are 34 boulders with ancient rock carvings inscribed on them. Drawn in a mixture of ancient and historic styles, the simple stick-figure drawings represent humans, nature, and life on Lāna'i. ✉ *From Lāna'i City, follow Hwy. 440 (Mānele Rd.) south 1 mi to an unmarked dirt road that leads left through pineapple fields; at end of that road, walk up unmarked trail to petroglyphs.*

⑤ **Mānele Bay.** The site of an ancient Hawaiian village dating back to AD 900, Mānele Bay is flanked by lava cliffs that are hundreds of feet high. A Marine Life Conservation District, it is the only public boat harbor on Lāna'i, and it was the location of most post-contact shipping until Kaumālapa'u Harbor was built in 1926. The ferry to and from Maui also pulls in here.

Just offshore you can catch a glimpse of **Pu'upehe.** Often called Sweetheart Rock, the islet is an isolated 50-ft-high formation that carries a sad Hawaiian legend. To make a long story short, a man hid his wife Pehe here, she drowned, and he then buried her on the summit of this rock with the help of the gods. ✉ *From Lāna'i City, follow Hwy. 440 (Mānele Rd.) south to bottom of hill and look for harbor on your left.*

North and East Lāna'i

With a ghost town and heiau to its credit, the north and east section of Lāna'i is wild and untamed. The best way to explore the area's distinctive beauty is by hiking or four-wheel-vehicle driving, since most attractions are accessible only by rugged dirt roads.

A Good Drive

From Lāna'i City, take Keōmuku Highway north. Turn left on the road that runs between the Stables at Kō'ele and tennis courts. This leads you to a dirt road, which cuts through hay fields for a couple of miles. At the crossroad, turn right onto Polihua Road, which heads upward through the dryland forest of **Kānepu'u Preserve** ⑥ and, 1½ mi beyond, to the **Garden of the Gods** ⑦. Red and black lava rocks are scattered across this unique landscape. Beyond is a crystal-blue seascape.

Return to Keōmuku Highway, turn left, and drive toward the top of the hill. If you're in a four-wheel-drive vehicle, make a right onto the only major dirt road in sight, and you're on your way to the **Munro**

Close-Up

HAWAIIAN MUSIC

Ask most visitors about Hawaiian music and they'll likely break into a lighthearted rendition of "Little Grass Shack." When they're done, lead them directly to a stereo.

First, play them a recording of singer Kekuhi Kanahele, whose compositions combine ancient Hawaiian chants with modern melodies. Then ask them to listen to a CD by guitarist Keola Beamer, who loosens his strings and plays slack-key tunings dating back to the 1830s.

Share a recording by falsetto virtuoso Amy Hanaiali'i Gilliom, one of the very few singers perpetuating the upper-register vocal style. Then take them to a concert by Henry Kapono, who writes and sings of the pride—and pain—of being pure Hawaiian.

These artists, like many others, are proving just how multifaceted Hawaiian music has become. They're unearthing their island roots in the form of revered songs and chants, and they're reinterpreting them for today's audiences. It's "chicken-skin" (goose-bumps) stuff, to be sure, and it's made only in Hawai'i.

Granted, "Little Grass Shack" does have its place in the history books. After Hawai'i became a U.S. territory in 1900, the world discovered its music thanks to touring ensembles who turned heads with swaying hips, steel guitars, and pseudo-Hawaiian lyrics. Once radio and movies got into the act, dreams of Hawai'i came with a saccharine Hollywood sound track.

But Hawaiian music is far more complex. It harks back to the sounds of the ancient Islanders who beat rough-hewn drums, blew haunting calls on conch shells, and intoned repetitive chants for their gods. It recalls the voices of 19th-century Christian missionaries who taught Islanders how to sing in four-part harmony, a style that's still popular today.

The music takes on international overtones thanks to gifts from foreign immigrants: the 'ukulele from Portuguese laborers, for instance, and the guitar from Mexican traders. And it's enlivened by a million renderings of "Tiny Bubbles," as mainstream entertainers like Don Ho croon Hawaiian-pop hits for Waikīkī tourists.

Island music came full circle in the late 1960s and '70s, a time termed the Hawaiian Renaissance. While the rest of the world was rocking 'n' rolling, a few dedicated artists began giving voice to a resurgence of interest in Hawaiian culture, history, and traditions.

Today's artistic trailblazers are digging deep to explore their heritage, and their music reflects that thoughtful search. They go one step further by incorporating such time-honored instruments as nose flutes and gourds, helping them keep pace with the past.

Why is Hawaiian music such a well-kept secret? Simply put, it's rarely played outside of the Islands. A handful of local performers are making their mark on the mainland and in Japan. But if you want to experience the true essence of Hawaiian music, you must come to Hawai'i. Check ads and listings in local papers for information on concerts, which take place in indoor and outdoor theaters, hotel ballrooms, and cozy nightclubs. When you hear the sound, you'll know it's Hawaiian because it'll make you feel right at home.

Trail ⑧, an 8-mi route that runs over the top of Lāna'ihale, the mountain that rises above Lāna'i City.

After enjoying the stunning views from the trail, head back to Keōmuku Highway, and follow its long descent to **Shipwreck Beach** ⑨, an 8-mi expanse of sand. Here, stretch your legs and look for glass balls (used as flotation devices for fishing nets) and other washed-up treasures.

Return to **Lāna'i City** ⑩ for an afternoon drink and some browsing in its gift stores. Or if you feel adventurous, head southeast (the opposite direction from Shipwreck Beach, but only if you have a four-wheel-drive vehicle). At the end of the paved road (Keōmuku Highway, which dead-ends at Shipwreck Beach), turn right and follow the very bumpy dirt road. Five miles later you will see dozens of tall coconut trees and a historic church. This is the site of **Keōmuku** ⑪, an abandoned town where 2,000 people once lived. A mile and a half farther down the road, you can see the ruins of a temple called **Kahe'a Heiau** ⑫. The road ends 3 mi later at the remnants of an old Hawaiian fishpond at **Naha** ⑬ and the often-deserted Lōpā Beach. To get back to Keōmuku Highway, retrace your route.

TIMING

Give yourself a day to tour the north and east reaches of the island. You can visit all of the following sights any day of the year, but keep your eye on the sky. It's more apt to rain in the highlands than in Lāna'i City. If you're a hiker, you'll want a day just to enjoy the splendors of Lāna'ihale. Bring a jacket because it gets cool up there. A walk along Shipwreck Beach makes a nice morning outing, with stops for shell-collecting, picture-taking, and picnicking. Since most of the driving is on rugged roads, it takes more time to reach such places as the Garden of the Gods and Keōmuku than it does actually to experience them. Relax. On Lāna'i, getting there is half the fun.

Sights to See

★ ⑦ **Garden of the Gods.** This heavily eroded landscape is scattered with boulders of different sizes, shapes, and colors that seem to have been placed here for some divine purpose. This lunar appearance is unmatched in Hawai'i. Anyone who's a geology buff will want to photograph the area, which presents magnificent views of the Pacific Ocean, Moloka'i, and, on clear days, O'ahu. Stand quietly and you might spot a deer here. ✉ *From Stables at Kō'ele, follow dirt road through hay fields 2 mi; turn right at crossroads and head through ironwood forest 1½ mi.*

⑫ **Kahe'a Heiau.** This ancient temple was once a place of worship for the people of Lāna'i. Today you must look hard to find its stone platforms and walls, for they have succumbed to an overgrowth of weeds and bushes. There are also remnants here of an old wharf used for shipping sugarcane. ✉ *6½ mi southeast from where Keōmuku Hwy. dead-ends at Shipwreck Beach, on dirt road running along north shore.*

⑥ **Kānepu'u Preserve.** The 590 acres of this native dryland forest have been under the stewardship of the Nature Conservancy of Hawai'i since 1991. Kānepu'u is the largest remnant of this unique forest type. More than 45 native species of plants, including the endangered Hawaiian gardenia, grow in the shade of such rare trees as Hawaiian sandalwood, olive, and ebony. A short self-guided loop trail with carefully illustrated signs reveals the beauty of this ecosystem and the challenges it faces today. ✉ *Polihua Rd.,* ☎ *808/537–4508.*

⑪ **Keōmuku.** During the late-19th century, this busy Lāna'i community of some 2,000 residents served as the headquarters of the Maunalei Sugar Company. The company failed, and Keōmuku shut down in 1901.

The land was used for ranching, but by 1954 the area had been abandoned. Its church, built in 1903, making it the oldest on the island, is currently being restored by volunteers. There's an eerie beauty about Keōmuku, with its crumbling stone walls and once-stately homes now reduced to weed-infested ruins. ✉ *5 mi along unpaved road southeast of Shipwreck Beach.*

⑩ **Lāna'i City.** This neat plantation town—Lāna'i's only population center—was built in 1924 by Jim Dole. Remarkably organized, it reflects his wish to create a model plantation village: a tidy grid of roads lined with tall Cook pines and all the basic services a person might need. Visit the **Lāna'i Arts & Culture Center** to get a glimpse of this Island's creative abundance, then relax with a drink at the vintage **Hotel Lāna'i**, built in 1923 for Dole's VIPs.

★ ⑧ **Munro Trail.** This 8-mi path winds through a lush tropical rain forest. It was named after George Munro, ranch manager of the Lāna'i Ranch Co., who began a reforestation program in the 1950s. Use caution if it has been raining, as the roads get very muddy. The trail winds over the top of **Lāna'ihale**, which means "House of Lāna'i" in Hawaiian. At 3,370 ft, it's the highest point of the island and offers spectacular views of nearly all the Hawaiian Islands. ✉ *From Lodge at Kō'ele head north on Keōmuku Hwy. for 1¼ mi, then turn right onto tree-lined dirt road; trailhead is ½ mi past cemetery on right.*

⑬ **Naha.** An ancient rock-walled fishpond can be seen clearly here at low tide, where the sandy shorelines end and the cliffs begin their rise along the south, west, and north shores of the island. Local fishermen come here to fish, but the treacherous tide and currents make this a dangerous place for swimming. ✉ *East side of Lāna'i, at end of dirt road that runs from end of Keōmuku Hwy. along the eastern shore.*

★ ⑨ **Shipwreck Beach.** Beachcombers come for its shells and washed-up treasures, photographers love the spectacular view of Moloka'i across the Kalohi Channel, and walkers enjoy its broad, 8-mi-long stretch of sand—in all, a beach to explore. It's not, however, for swimmers. Have a look at the tanker rusting offshore and you'll see that these are not friendly waters. ✉ *End of Keōmuku Hwy. heading north.*

BEACHES

Only a few beaches on Lāna'i are worth seeking out, and only one has good swimming in protected waters. If you need more information, try **Destination Lāna'i** (✉ 730 Lāna'i Ave., Suite 102, Lāna'i City 96763, ☎ 808/565–7600) or ask at your hotel. The beaches below are listed clockwise from the south.

★ **Hulopo'e Beach.** Lāna'i's only swimming beach, the sparkling crescent of this Marine Life Conservation District beckons with its perennially clear waters, great snorkeling reefs, and views of spinner dolphins at play. Here was once an ancient village dating back to AD 900. The tide pools, like natural aquariums, are fascinating to explore. One of the best beaches in all of Hawai'i, it also has shady trees and grassy expanses perfect for picnics, and there are showers, rest rooms, and changing facilities. It's a five-minute walk from the Mānele Bay Hotel via a short path. ✉ *From Lāna'i City follow Hwy. 440 (Mānele Rd.) south to bottom of hill; road dead-ends at beach's parking lot.*

Polihua Beach. Due to its more obscure location and frequent high winds, this beach is often deserted, except for the turtles that nest here. That makes it all the more spectacular, with its long white-sand strand and glorious views of Moloka'i. Because of strong currents, swimming is

Dining 99

dangerous. To get here you need a four-wheel-drive vehicle. ✉ *Northwest shore, 11 mi from Lāna'i City, past Garden of the Gods.*

Shipwreck Beach. A nice beach for walking but not swimming, Shipwreck is an 8-mi stretch of sand on the 9-mi wide Kalohi Channel between Lāna'i and Moloka'i. The beach has no lifeguards, no changing rooms, and no outdoor showers. ✉ *North shore, 10 mi north of Lāna'i City at end of Keōmuku Hwy.*

DINING

Although Lāna'i's restaurant choices are limited, the menus are wide-ranging. If you dine at the Lodge at Kō'ele or Mānele Bay Hotel, you'll be treated to unique preparations of ingredients harvested or caught locally and served in upscale surroundings. Dining in Lāna'i City is a different story. Its restaurants have simple fare, homey atmospheres, and nondescript service. For an explanation of price categories, *see* Dining *in* Smart Travel Tips A to Z.

South and West Lāna'i

$$$$ ✗ **'Ihilani.** The Mānele Bay Hotel's (☞ South and West Lāna'i *in*
★ Lodging, *below*) dining room shimmers with crystal, exquisite china, and silver. Moonlight filters through the glass ceiling of its open-air terrace. Executive chef Edwin Goto uses fresh island ingredients to create a cuisine he calls "Mediterranean gourmet." The changing menu may include such dishes as grilled filet mignon with seared foie gras and a sauce of wild mushrooms, port, and truffles. You can opt for a five-course food-and-wine pairing menu. The dessert menu features such taste explosions as a white chocolate and pistachio dome with *liliko'i* (passion fruit) sauce. ✉ *Mānele Bay Hotel, Lāna'i City,* ☎ *808/565-7700. Reservations essential. AE, DC, MC, V. No lunch.*

North and East Lāna'i

$$$$ ✗ **Formal Dining Room.** Reflecting the elegant country atmosphere of
★ the Lodge at Kō'ele (☞ North and East Lāna'i *in* Lodging, *below*), this romantic octagonal-shape restaurant offers intimate tables close to a roaring fireplace. The walls are hand-stenciled by local artists. The chef expands on the concept of Hawai'i regional cuisine with a changing menu that includes specialties such as roasted Lāna'i venison loin with pineapple-cider sauce or potato-wrapped Hawaiian *moi,* a fish that in ancient times was savored only by chiefs. The wine list has selections from small, unique wineries. ✉ *Lodge at Kō'ele,* ☎ *808/565-7300. Reservations essential. Jacket required. AE, DC, MC, V. No lunch.*

$$-$$$ ✗ **Henry Clay's Rotisserie.** Don't overlook this popular spot at the Hotel Lāna'i (☞ North and East Lāna'i *in* Lodging, *below*). Louisiana-style ribs, Cajun-style dishes, and seafood jalapeño over fettuccine add up to what Chef Henry Clay Richardson calls "American country," but he brings it back home with such fresh local ingredients as venison, Hawaiian-caught seafood, and island produce. A redbrick fireplace and the paintings of a local artist add to the country ambience. ✉ *Hotel Lāna'i, 828 Lāna'i Ave.,* ☎ *808/565-7211. MC, V.*

$ ✗ **Blue Ginger Cafe.** This small, no-frills eatery may look run-down with its bare floor and plastic tablecloths, but the menu is diverse and the wonderful owner, Georgia Abilay, has turned this place into the town's most popular hangout. At breakfast enjoy a three-egg omelet with rice or a big plate of French toast. Blue Ginger also has fresh pastries each morning. Lunchtime selections include burgers, chef's salad, pizza, and saimin. Try the stir-fry fish or some Mexican fare for dinner. ✉ *409 7th Ave.,* ☎ *808/565-6363. No credit cards.*

$ ✕ **Pele's Other Garden.** Call it a juice bar, a deli, or a pizzeria. By any name, this white building with blue trim adds a healthy twist to the Lāna'i City dining scene with mile-high sandwiches, vegetarian dishes, and fresh-baked breads. The signature 16-inch whole wheat–crust pizza is a great reward after an arduous hike. You can also order tantalizing picnic lunches, which come with your choice of salad, dessert, and juice—all in a convenient cooler bag. There are just four tables in the cramped space inside, so it's better to have a seat on the porch or on the new terrace, or to order carryout. ✉ *811 Houston St.,* ☎ *808/ 565–9628. Reservations not accepted. AE, D, DC, MC, V.*

LODGING

In years past the only accommodation on the island was the no-fuss Hotel Lāna'i in Lāna'i City. Today you can choose from among two classy resorts, pleasant bed-and-breakfasts, and a few house rentals. For an explanation of price categories, *see* Lodging in Smart Travel Tips A to Z.

South and West Lāna'i

$$$$ 🏨 **Mānele Bay Hotel.** This elaborate beachfront property on historic
★ land has spectacular views of Lāna'i's dramatic coastline and beyond. Open arcades, breezeways, and bridges connect guest-room buildings with the main entrance, and five courtyard gardens are lavishly landscaped in different themes. The design combines elements both Mediterranean and traditionally Hawaiian. Asian art as well as work by local artists fills the common areas, and a library is a quiet, inviting escape for guests. For parents with kids, the hotel offers a unique children's program with daily adventures. The crescent of Hulopo'e Bay is just minutes away. ✉ *Box 310, Lāna'i City 96763,* ☎ *808/565–7700 or 800/321–4666,* 🅵🅰🆇 *808/565–3868. 222 rooms, 28 suites. 4 restaurants, bar, minibars, room service, pool, spa, 18-hole golf course, 6 tennis courts, health club, children's programs. AE, DC, MC, V.* 🐢

North and East Lāna'i

$$$$ 🏨 **Captain's Retreat.** Single-room bookings are not available here, but if its rate is split between four couples or a family, this two-story private home turns out to be a reasonably priced lodging alternative. Within walking distance of town, it's the ultimate group getaway, with 3,000 square ft, four bedrooms, a redwood deck, an outside shower, and a roomy kitchen. ✉ *Okamoto Realty, 730 Lāna'i Ave., Lāna'i City 96763,* ☎ *808/565–7519. 1 unit. MC, V.* 🐢

$$$$ 🏨 **Jasmine Garden.** The Hunters, who run the Dreams Come True B&B (☞ *below*), rent out several houses. One of them is this three-bedroom residence in the older section of Lāna'i City. It sleeps six, so three couples can share it. It has a well-equipped kitchen. Weekly and monthly rates are available. Call to find out more about their other properties. They rent four-wheel-drive vehicles as well. ✉ *Jasmine St. at 13th Ave., Lāna'i City 96763,* ☎ *808/565–6961 or 800/566–6961,* 🅵🅰🆇 *808/565– 7056. 1 unit. Car rental. AE, D, MC, V.*

$$$$ 🏨 **Lodge at Kō'ele.** Situated on 21 acres in the highlands on the edge
★ of Lāna'i City, this grand country estate feels like a luxurious private mountain retreat. Secluded by old pines, 1½ mi of pathways meander through theme gardens, along a pond and waterfall, and past an orchid greenhouse. Inside, beamed ceilings, stone fireplaces, a music room, a tea room, and the magnificent Great Hall (where afternoon tea with scones and clotted cream is served) create an Old World ambiance. A generous porch offers views of spectacular sunsets, and unique artworks and artifacts are on display. The Lodge has been

called the most romantic getaway in America, and if you have *keiki* (children) with you, they'll love the children's program. ✉ Box 310, Lāna'i City 96763, ☎ 808/565–7300 or 800/321–4666, ℻ 808/565–3868. 88 rooms, 14 suites. 2 restaurants, bar, lobby lounge, minibars, room service, pool, 18-hole golf course, 3 tennis courts, croquet, health club, horseback riding, children's programs. AE, DC, MC, V.

$$–$$$ 🏨 **Hotel Lāna'i.** Built in 1923 to house visiting plantation executives, this quaint 11-room inn was once the only accommodation on the island. Today, even though two luxury hotels may tempt you, you shouldn't overlook this island institution. The old front porch with the big wicker chairs has long been a meeting place for residents and locals, who gather to read the paper, order a drink, and talk story. The rooms, with country quilts and original plantation-era pictures, make you feel like you're in a country home. A Continental breakfast with fresh-baked breads is included in the rate. ✉ 828 Lāna'i Ave., Lāna'i City 96763, ☎ 808/565–7211 or 800/795–7211, ℻ 808/565–6450. 11 rooms. Restaurant. AE, MC, V.

$$ 🏨 **Blue Ginger Vacation Rental.** Georgia Abilay, of Blue Ginger Cafe (☞ North and East Lāna'i *in* Dining, *above*) fame, owns this vacation home in a newer neighborhood of Lāna'i City. Grounds are landscaped with tropical plants and roses, and room decor is modern. One of the bedrooms has a double bed, the other has twin beds, and the living room's overstuffed couch converts to a bed. Breakfast can be arranged courtesy of the café. ✉ 421 Lama St., Lāna'i City 96763, ☎ 808/565–6363 or 808/565–6666. 1 unit. No credit cards.

$$ 🏨 **Dreams Come True.** Michael and Susan Hunter's bed-and-breakfast in the heart of Lāna'i City has canopy beds, antique furnishings, and memorabilia from their many years in Asia and on Lāna'i. Fresh fruit from their own trees enhances the big morning meal. Susan is a trained massage therapist and provides in-house massage for $35 an hour. Vehicle rental is also available. ✉ 547 12th St., Lāna'i City 96763, ☎ 808/565–6961 or 800/566–6961, ℻ 808/565–7056. 3 rooms. Massage. AE, D, MC, V.

NIGHTLIFE AND THE ARTS

Locals entertain themselves by gathering on the front porch of the **Hotel Lāna'i** (✉ 828 Lāna'i Ave., Lāna'i City, ☎ 808/565–7211) for drinks and conversation. The classy lounge at the **Mānele Bay Hotel** (✉ Lāna'i City, ☎ 808/565–7700), Hale Aheahe (House of Gentle Breezes), offers entertainment every evening. The cozy cocktail lounge at the **Lodge at Kō'ele** (✉ Lāna'i City, ☎ 808/565–7300) stays open until 11 PM. The lodge also features music in its Great Hall. The 153-seat **Lāna'i Theater and Playhouse** (☎ 808/565–7500), a '30s landmark, presents first-run movies. Lāna'i's **Visiting Artist Program** brings world-renowned authors and musicians to the island once a month for free, informal presentations. Past visitors have included author Armistead Maupin, the Irish folk music band Gaelic Storm, and jazz guitarist Bucky Pizzarelle. These events take place at either the Lodge at Kō'ele or the Mānele Bay Hotel.

OUTDOOR ACTIVITIES AND SPORTS

Participant Sports

Golf

Cavendish Golf Course. This nine-hole course in the pines is free, but a donation for upkeep is requested. Call the Lodge at Kō'ele concierge (☎ 808/565–7300) for information and directions. Bring your own clubs.

Challenge at Mānele. This 18-hole world-class course was designed by Jack Nicklaus. The clubhouse here serves lunch. ✉ *Mānele Bay Hotel,* ☎ 808/565–2222 or 800/321–4666. 🖃 *Greens fee $125 for guests of the Lodge at Kō'ele or Mānele Bay Hotel, $150 nonguests; cart included.*

Experience at Kō'ele. The Lodge at Kō'ele has this 18-hole championship course designed by Greg Norman. There's also an 18-hole executive putting course, free to guests but not accessible to nonguests. The clubhouse serves lunch. ✉ *Lodge at Kō'ele,* ☎ 808/565–4653. 🖃 *Greens fee $125 guests, $150 nonguests; cart included.*

Hiking and Camping

Lāna'i is a hiker's paradise, with trails roaming through unique forests, over rugged grasslands, and along splendid shores. The most popular Lāna'i hike is the **Munro Trail,** a strenuous 9-mi trek that takes about eight hours. There is an elevation gain of 1,400 ft, leading you to the lookout at Lāna'i's highest point, Lāna'ihale.

The remote 8-mi trail along **Shipwreck Beach** is an adventure for beachcombers.

There are lesser known treks with whimsical names, such as **Eucalyptus Ladder, Old Cowboy Trail,** and **Ancient Graveyard.** It's a good idea to get one of the guidebooks described below, and a good map. Also make sure—especially if you want to camp—to call the folks at Destination Lāna'i (☎ 808/565–7600 or 800/947–4774, ✍) or to stop by at the **Lāna'i Ecoadventure Centre** (☞ Contacts and Resources *in* Lāna'i A to Z, *below*) in town, where you can rent camping gear as well.

Horseback Riding

The **Stables at Kō'ele** (☎ 808/565–4424) take you to scenic high-country trails. They have a corral full of well-groomed horses for riders of all ages and skill levels. Group rides cost $40 for one hour, $65 for two hours. Lessons start at $30. Private rides start at $70 for the first hour. Customized rides, with lunch, can be arranged as well.

Mountain Biking

The **Lodge at Kō'ele** (☎ 808/565–7300) rents mountain bikes only to guests of the lodge and of the Mānele Bay Hotel for $8 per hour or $40 per day. John and Kris, the friendly couple at **Lāna'i Ecoadventure Centre** (☞ Contacts and Resources *in* Lāna'i A to Z, *below*), rent out mountain bikes starting at $19.95 per day.

Sporting Clays

Lāna'i Pine Sporting Clays Range is the only target course of its kind in Hawai'i. The rustic, 14-station course is in a pine-wood valley overlooking the sea. A single shooter can complete the course in an hour. Cost is $125 for 100 targets and $65 for 50 targets. Beginners can start with an introductory lesson—25 targets—for $55. Each October, celebrities—Arnold Schwarzenegger and Tom Selleck have been among them—host the cash-winning Open Play Target Shoot. You have to arrange to play the course through your hotel.

Water Sports

DEEP-SEA FISHING

Spinning Dolphin Fishing Charters (☎ 808/565–6613) handles both heavy and light tackle fishing on its 28-ft diesel-powered Omega sport fisher. The half-day ($400) and full-day ($800) charters are private, with a six-person maximum. Bring your own lunch. Juice and ice are provided.

SCUBA DIVING

Trilogy Excursions (☎ 808/667–7721 or 888/628–4800, ✍) offers introductory and one-tank dives for $55. Scuba diving is also available on Trilogy's daily snorkel sail (☞ Snorkeling, *below*). There's a free diving session for novices at the Mānele Bay Hotel pool. It's best to book this through your hotel concierge.

The dive site **Cathedrals,** off the south shore, gets its name from the spacious caverns created by numerous pinnacles that rise from depths of 60 ft to just below the water's surface. In these beautiful chambers lurk spotted moray eels, lobster, and ghost shrimp.

Sergeant Major Reef, on the south shore, is made up of three parallel lava ridges, a cave, and an archway, with rippled sand valleys between the ridges. It's home to several large schools of sergeant major fish. Depths range from 15 to 50 ft. Other nearby sites include Lobster Rock, Menpachi Cave, Grand Canyon, Sharkfin Rock, and Monolith.

SNORKELING

Hulopo'e Beach (☞ Beaches, *above*) is one of Hawai'i's outstanding snorkeling destinations. It attracts brilliantly colored fish to its protected cove, in which you can also marvel at underwater coral and lava formations. Ask at your hotel about renting equipment. The companies also offer snorkeling tours.

Spinning Dolphin Fishing Charters (☞ Deep-Sea Fishing, *above*) offers private snorkel and sightseeing tours. When the whales are here (December through April), three-hour whale-watching tours are also available.

Trilogy Excursions (☞ Deep-Sea Fishing, *above*) presents a daily 4-hour morning snorkel sail on a 51-ft catamaran for $95. Continental breakfast, lessons, equipment, and lunch are included. Make arrangements with the concierge at the Mānele Bay Hotel (☎ 808/565–7700) in Lāna'i City.

SHOPPING

Except for the boutiques at the Lodge at Kō'ele and Mānele Bay Hotel, Lāna'i City is the island's only place to buy what you need. Its main streets, 7th and 8th avenues, have a scattering of shops straight out of the '20s. In the most literal sense, the main businesses in town are what you would call general stores. They do offer personal service and congenial charm. Stores open their doors Monday through Saturday between 8 and 9 and close between 5 and 6. Some shops are closed on Sunday and between noon and 1:30 on weekdays.

General Stores

International Food and Clothing Center. You may not find everything the name implies, but this old-fashioned emporium does stock many items for your everyday needs. ✉ 833 'Ilima Ave., ☎ 808/565–6433.

Lāna'i City Service. In addition to being a gas station, taxi company, and car-rental operation, this outfit sells fast food and sodas, sundries, T-shirts, and island crafts. ✉ 1036 Lāna'i Ave., ☎ 808/565–7227.

Pine Isle Market. You can get everything from cosmetics to canned vegetables here at one of Lāna'i City's two supermarkets. It's a great place to buy fresh fish. ✉ 356 8th Ave., ☎ 808/565–6488.

Richard's Shopping Center. Richard Tamashiro founded this place in 1946, and the Tamashiro clan continues to run the place. Along with groceries, the store has a fun selection of Lāna'i T-shirts. ✉ 434 8th Ave., ☎ 808/565–6047.

Crafts

Akamai Trading. Akamai Trading sells such unique Lāna'i crafts as pine-tree bowls and flower-dyed gourds alongside its island posters, T-shirts, and tropical jellies and jams. It's also the only place in town that serves cappuccino and espresso. ✉ *408 8th Ave.*, ☎ *808/565-6587*.

Gifts With Aloha. In addition to a tasteful selection of gift items and casual resort wear, the work of Lāna'i and Hawai'i artists here includes ceramic ware, raku (Japanese-style lead-glazed pottery), fine hand-blown glass, and watercolor prints. ✉ *811-B Houston St.*, ☎ *808/565-6589*.

Lāna'i Art Studio. This is the home of the Lāna'i Art Program, which offers art classes to residents and visitors. Its gift shop sells unique Lāna'i handicrafts, from painted silk scarves to beaded jewelry. ✉ *339 7th Ave.*, ☎ *808/565-7503*.

Hotel Shops

The **Lodge at Kō'ele** (☎ 808/565-7300) and the **Mānele Bay Hotel** (☎ 808/565-7700) have sundries shops that are handy for guests who need to stock up on suntan lotion, aspirin, and other vacation necessities. It also carries classy logo wear, resort clothing, books, and jewelry.

LĀNA'I A TO Z

Arriving and Departing

By Ferry

Expeditions (☎ 808/661-3756 or 800/695-2624) crosses the channel five times daily departing from Lahaina on Maui and Mānele Bay Harbor on Lāna'i. The crossing takes 45 minutes and costs $25.

By Plane

The small **Lāna'i Airport** (☎ 808/565-6757) is centrally located in the southwest area of the island. There is a gift shop, food concession, plenty of parking, and a federal agricultural inspection station so that departing guests can check luggage directly to the mainland.

In order to reach Lāna'i from the mainland United States, you must first stop at O'ahu's Honolulu International Airport or at Maui's Kahului Airport. From there it takes about a half hour to fly to Lāna'i. **Hawaiian Airlines** (☎ 800/882-8811) offers two round-trip flights daily between Honolulu and Lāna'i. A round trip on one of its DC-9 jets costs $194. **Island Air** (☎ 808/484-2222 or 800/323-3345) offers about 12 flights daily on its 18-passenger Dash-6's and 37-seat Dash-8's, also at a cost of $194.

BETWEEN THE AIRPORT AND HOTELS

Lāna'i Airport is a 10-minute drive from Lāna'i City. If you're staying at the Hotel Lāna'i, the Lodge at Kō'ele, or the Mānele Bay Hotel, you will be met by a complimentary shuttle. Don't expect to see any public buses at the airport, because there aren't any on the island.

By Car. With public transportation virtually nonexistent and attractions so far apart, you'll want to rent a car while on Lāna'i. Make your reservation for a car or four-wheel-drive-vehicle way in advance of your trip, because Lāna'i's fleet of vehicles is limited (☞ Car and Four-Wheel-Drive-Vehicle Rentals *in* Contacts and Resources, *below*).

By Taxi. Taxi transfers between Lāna'i City and the airport are handled by **Lāna'i City Service,** a subsidiary of Dollar Rent-A-Car (☎ 808/565-7227 or 800/533-7808). One-way charges are $5 per person for the Lodge at Kō'ele and $15 for Mānele Bay Hotel.

Getting Around

Private transportation is advised on Lāna'i, unless you plan to stay in one place during your entire visit. Avoid that urge, because the island has natural splendors from one end to the other.

By Car

Driving around Lāna'i isn't as easy as on other islands. Secondary roads aren't marked. But renting a car can be fun (☞ Car and Four-Wheel-Drive Vehicle Rentals *in* Contacts and Resources, *below*). From town, the streets extend outward as paved roads with two-way traffic. Keōmuku Highway runs north to Shipwreck Beach, and Highway 440 leads south down to Mānele Bay and Hulopo'e Beach and west to Kaumālapa'u Harbor. The rest of your driving takes place on bumpy, muddy roads best navigated by a four-wheel-drive vehicle or van.

The island doesn't have traffic lights, and you'll never find yourself in a traffic jam. However, heed these words of caution: before heading out on your explorations, ask at your hotel desk for a road and site map, and ask for confirmation that you're headed in the right direction. Some attractions don't have signs, and it's easy to get lost.

By Taxi

It costs $5 to $15 per person for a cab ride from Lāna'i City to almost any point on the paved roads of the island. Call **Lāna'i City Service** (☎ 808/565–7227 or 800/533–7808).

Contacts and Resources

Car and Four-Wheel-Drive-Vehicle Rentals

Two companies on Lāna'i rent vehicles. **Lāna'i City Service** (✉ Lāna'i Ave. at 11th St., Lāna'i City, ☎ 808/565–7227 or 800/533–7808) is the Dollar Rent-a-Car affiliate on the island. Fees are $60 a day for a compact car, $80 a day for a midsize vehicle, $129 a day for a seven-passenger minivan or a four-wheel-drive Jeep Wrangler, and $145 a day for a four-wheel-drive Cherokee. There's an additional charge if you want to pick your car up or drop it off at the airport. **Lāna'i Ecoadventure Centre** (☞ Guided Tours, *below*) also has a fleet of reliable jeeps.

Emergencies

Police, fire, or **ambulance** (☎ 911).

HOSPITAL

The **Lāna'i Community Hospital** (✉ 628 7th Ave., Lāna'i City, ☎ 808/565–6411) is the health-care center for the island. It has 24-hour ambulance service and a pharmacy.

Guided Tours

Lāna'i Ecoadventure Centre (✉ 8th Ave., next to the police station, ☎ 808/565–7737 or 808/565–7373, ✉) takes all the worries about getting lost or stuck in the mud away with its popular 4x4 Trek. They'll stop where and when you want as they take you to Lāna'i's most scenic places. Guides talk story about island history and the unique plants and animals. They even provide binoculars, snorkel gear, snacks, and drinks. Call John or Kris for costs.

Tours of the island's two major hotels and properties are free to the public upon request. Contact the concierge at **Mānele Bay Hotel** (☎ 808/565–7700) or the **Lodge at Kō'ele** (☎ 808/565–7300).

Visitor Information

Your best contact for complementary and general information, and for brochures and maps, is Lāna'i's visitors bureau, **Destination Lāna'i** (✉

730 Lāna'i Ave., Suite 102, Lāna'i City 96763, ☎ 808/565–7600, ✉); feel free to stop in (although it has erratic opening hours), or e-mail or write ahead of time. The **Maui Visitors Bureau** (✉ 1727 Wili Pa Loop, Wailuku, Maui 96793, ☎ 808/244–3530, FAX 808/244–1337, ✉) has some information about Lāna'i as well as Maui. Once you're on the island, the **information desks** of the two major hotels—the Lodge at Kō'ele and the Mānele Bay Hotel—are useful sources if you are a guest at either of these properties.

8 BACKGROUND AND ESSENTIALS

Portraits of Maui

Books and Videos

Chronology

Smart Travel Tips A to Z

Hawaiian Vocabulary

Menu Guide

WELCOME TO THE VALLEY ISLE

Portraits

Maui, say the locals, *nō ka 'oi*. It's the best, the most, the top of the heap. To those who know Maui well, there's good reason for the superlatives. Maui magic weaves a spell over the 2.2 million people who visit its shores each year and leaves them wanting more. Often visitors decide to return for good.

In many ways Maui, the second-largest island in the Hawaiian chain, comes by its admirable reputation honestly. The island's 729 square mi contain Haleakalā, a 10,023-ft dormant volcano whose misty summit beckons the adventurous; several villages where Hawaiian is still spoken; more millionaires per capita than nearly anywhere else in the world; three major resort destinations that have set new standards for luxury; Lahaina, an old whaling port that still serves as one of the island's commercial crossroads; and more than 80,000 residents who work, play, and live on what they fondly call the Valley Isle.

Maui residents have had a bit to do with their island's success story. In the mid-1970s, savvy marketers saw a way to improve the island's economy through tourism and started advertising and promoting their "Valley Isle" separately from the rest of the state. They nicknamed West Maui "the Golf Coast," luring heavyweight tournaments that, in turn, brought more visitors. They went after the upscale tourist—hotels were renovated to accommodate a clientele that would pay more for the best. Condominiums on Maui were also refurbished—the word condo no longer meant second-best accommodations. Maui's visitor count swelled, putting it far ahead of that of the other Neighbor Islands.

That quick growth has led to its share of problems. During the busy seasons—from Christmas to Easter and then again during the summer—West Maui can be overly crowded. Although the County of Maui has successfully widened the two-lane road that connects Lahaina and Kā'anapali, the stop-and-go traffic during rush hour reminds some visitors of what they left at home. It's not that residents aren't trying to do something about it—the Kapalua-West Maui Airport, with its free shuttle to and from Kā'anapali, has alleviated some of the heavy traffic between Kahului and Lahaina.

The explosion of visitors seeking out the Valley Isle has also created a large number of businesses looking to make a fast buck from the high-spending vacationers. Lahaina could easily be called the T-shirt capital of the Pacific (in close competition with Waikīkī), and the island has nearly as many art galleries and cruise-boat companies as T-shirts. As in other popular travel destinations, the opportunity to make money from visitors has produced its fair share of schlock.

But then consider Maui's natural resources. Geologists claim that Maui was created between 1 and 2 million years ago by the eruption of two volcanoes, Pu'u kukui and Haleakalā, the former extinct and the latter now dormant; a low central isthmus formed between them and joined them into West and East Maui. The resulting depression between the two is what gives Maui its nickname, the Valley Isle. West Maui's 5,788-ft Pu'u kukui was the first volcano to form, a distinction that gives the area's mountainous topography a more weathered look. Rainbows seem to grow wild over this terrain as gentle mists move quietly from one end of the long mountain chain to the other. Sugarcane gives the rocky region its life, with its green stalks moving in the trade winds born near the summit.

The Valley Isle's second volcano is the 10,023-ft Haleakalā, a mountain so enormous that its lava filled in the gap between the two volcanoes. You can't miss Haleakalā, whose name means House of the Sun, a spectacle that rises to the east, often hiding in the clouds that cover its peak. To Hawaiians, Haleakalā is holy, and it's easy to see why. It's a mammoth mountain, and if you hike its slopes or peer into one of its craters, you'll witness an impressive variety of nature: desertlike terrain butted up against tropical forests; dew-dripping ferns a few steps from the surface of the moon; spiked, alien plants poking their heads out of the soil right near the most elegant and fragrant flowers.

In fact, the island's volcanic history gives Maui much of its beauty. Rich red soil lines the roads around the island—*becoming* the roads in some parts. That same earth has provided fertile sowing grounds for the sugarcane that has for years covered the island's hills. As the deep blue of ocean and sky mingle with the red and green of Maui's land, it looks as if an artist has been busy painting the scenery. Indeed, visual artists love Maui. Maybe it's the natural inspiration; maybe it's the slower pace, so conducive to creativity.

Farmers also appreciate the Valley Isle. On the slopes of Haleakalā, the volcanic miracle has wrought agricultural wonders, luring those with a penchant for peat moss to plant and watch the lush results. Sweetly scented flowers bloom large and healthy, destined to adorn a happy brow or become a lovely lei. Grapes cultivated on Haleakalā's slopes ripen evenly and deliciously, and are then pressed for wine and champagne. Horses graze languidly on rolling meadows of the best Upcountry grasses, while jacaranda trees dot the hillsides with spurts of luscious lavender. On the eastern slopes of the volcano, lavish rains turn the soil into a jungle.

Maui had no indigenous plants or animals because of its volcanic origins. Birds brought some of the life that would inhabit Maui, as did the waves that washed upon its newly formed shores. Then in about AD 800, Polynesians began to arrive on Maui's shores. They had journeyed from the Marquesas and Society Islands, braving rough waters in their canoes as they navigated by the stars across thousands of miles. These first residents brought animals, such as pigs and chickens, as well as plants, such as breadfruit, yams, coconuts, and bananas.

Not until 1778, when Captain James Cook made his second voyage to the Hawaiian Islands, did the Mauians receive their first visitor. Months earlier, Cook had landed on Kaua'i and Ni'ihau; he had made friends with the Polynesians and left behind bartered goods, as well as dread white man's diseases. When he got to Maui, Cook was surprised to find that the venereal disease running rampant on his ships had preceded him there. Shortly afterward, Cook pushed on to the Big Island.

Before leaving, however, Cook anchored his ship off the northeast coast of Maui while he hosted Kalani'ōpu'u, the aging chief of the Big Island, who spent a night on the Englishman's HMS *Resolution*. At the time, the Hawaiian Islands were rife with divided kingdoms waging war one against another, and the elderly Kalani'ōpu'u was certainly plotting against Maui's principal chief, Kahekili. How much Cook figured into these strategy sessions is unknown, but the records show that Kalani'ōpu'u was accompanied by his young warrior nephew, Kamehameha.

Perhaps it was the experience off Maui's coast that eventually fired Kamehameha's ambition to rule more than a tiny section of one island. Kamehameha witnessed that Cook was master of his destiny, and the callow youth, no doubt, wanted the same thing. Years of battle followed as the young chief fought for the right to dominate the Islands. Finally, in 1794, Kamehameha defeated Maui's chief, thereby gaining the Valley Isle as well as its smaller neighboring islands of Moloka'i and Lāna'i. The following year he con-

Portraits

quered the Big Island and Oʻahu. Kauaʻi wouldn't knuckle under, but in 1810 it was won over diplomatically. Kamehameha had earned the right to be king of all the islands. He was called Kamehameha I, or Kamehameha the Great, and the kingdom's headquarters were in Lahaina, on Maui. The site of the king's Lahaina palace is between the Pioneer Inn and the ocean; the palace itself is long gone, however.

The great king had 21 wives during his lifetime, and the two most notable hailed from Maui. Queen Keōpūolani was Kamehameha's "sacred" wife, the daughter of a traditional brother-sister union that was considered so powerful that Keōpūolani was assured of producing honorable heirs for her husband. Historians believe she was the first Christian convert; she was extremely supportive of the missionaries who came to Hawaiʻi. Preceded in death by her royal spouse, Queen Keōpūolani is buried in the Waineʻe/Waiola Cemetery (on Waineʻe Street in Lahaina), next to her second husband, Hawaiian chief Hoapili, who was governor of Maui.

Kamehameha's favorite wife, Kaʻahumanu, also came from Maui. She was tall, statuesque, and politically astute. In fact, after her husband's death in 1819, Queen Kaʻahumanu named herself Hawaiʻi's first regent when Keōpūolani's eldest son, Liholiho, took the throne; she even continued that role when Liholiho's brother Kauʻikeaʻōuli succeeded him. Kaʻahumanu was so powerful that she was instrumental in banning the *kapu* system, the Hawaiian set of rules and standards that had been in force for generations. It was she who insisted that the king move from the Brick Palace in Lahaina to another home in Honolulu.

Not long after Captain Cook landed on Maui, others arrived to take up residence. Missionaries who came from the eastern United States thought Mauians were heathens who needed to be saved, and they diligently tried to convert the residents. The missionaries' job was made even more challenging by the almost simultaneous arrival of whalers from New England. Soon Lahaina developed into the area's most important whaling port, and with the new industry came a lusty lifestyle that included more diseases, wild revelry, and additional motivation for the missionaries to continue their quest.

In 1840 Kauʻikeaʻōuli, as King Kamehameha III, moved his court to Honolulu, but Lahaina continued to be an important city for trade, education, and hearty living. Many of the buildings used during this era still exist in Lahaina and are open to visitors. The Spring House, now located in the Wharf Shopping Center on Front Street, once protected a freshwater source for the missionaries, while the Seamen's Hospital, also on Front Street, was converted by the U.S. government from a royal party residence to a medical facility for sailors.

Along with missionaries and whalers, other new settlers began to come to Maui. The most notable arrivals were businessmen, who viewed the Islands as a place to buy cheap land—or, better yet, to get it for free by befriending a member of the royal family. To the most astute entrepreneurs, sugar, which grew wild on Maui, looked like a good bet for cultivation, and when the Civil War knocked out sugar supplies in the South, the Hawaiian plantations boomed. By the late 1800s, "King Sugar" had become the new ruler in the Islands.

Some of the most prominent leaders in the sugar industry were the grown children of missionaries. On Maui two of the most important businessmen were Samuel Alexander and Henry Baldwin, who joined forces in a sugar dynasty eventually called Alexander & Baldwin. A&B, as it came to be known, was a charter member of Hawaiʻi's Big Five—the five giant corporations that controlled the Islands economically and politically well into the 20th century. Although the power and influence of the Big Five have waned dramatically in the past few years with the increase of takeovers and buyouts, Alexander &

Baldwin remains both Maui's largest private landholder and its largest private employer. The company developed the sunny Wailea Resort and owned it until 1990, as well as all of the island's sugar operations and macadamia-nut farms.

It wasn't until the early 1960s—only a few years after Hawai'i became a state in 1959—that tourism took root on Maui in a major way. That was when Amfac Inc., the largest of the Big Five, opened its major resort destination in West Maui, calling it Kā'anapali. It soon became Hawai'i's second most popular resort area after Waikīkī and was the first to have a master plan. The Royal Lahaina, which opened in 1962, was the first lodging to break ground in the Kā'anapali Resort, which now contains six deluxe hotels and at least a dozen condominiums.

North of Kā'anapali, Maui Land & Pineapple entered into the tourism arena in the mid-1970s when it broke ground for the Kapalua Resort with its 194-room Kapalua Bay Hotel, joined in 1992 by the Ritz-Carlton's 550-room showplace.

Tourism now accounts for about half of all jobs on the Valley Isle. Beginning in the mid-1800s, the dwindling indigenous population—those Hawaiians whose descendants came from the Marquesas and the Society Islands—were reinforced by labor from Japan, China, Portugal, and the Philippines, so that today's Maui has become a heady stew of ethnicity and culture.

The Valley Isle is full of people ready to share the friendly aloha spirit. If you take the drive to Hāna, around dozens of hairpin curves, across bridges, and past waterfalls, you'll find plenty of folks who still speak the Hawaiian language. Or if you relax on the wharf in historic Lahaina, you can watch transplanted Californians have a great time surfing; most of them find West Maui the best place in the world for working and living. All these residents love their island and will gladly help you have a good time.

By all means, make the effort to meet some locals. Although a fantastic time can be had simply by relaxing on the silky-soft, white-sand beaches, the wonder of Maui is that much, much more awaits your discovery. Don't be surprised if quite a few of your fantasies are actually fulfilled. The Valley Isle hates to let anyone down.

THESE VOLCANIC ISLES

Dawn at the crater on horseback. It's cold at 10,023 ft above the warm Pacific—maybe 45°F. The horses' breath condenses into a smoky cloud, and the riders cling against their saddles. It's eerily quiet except for the creak of straining leather and the crunch of volcanic cinders under foot, sounds that are absurdly magnified in the vast empty space that yawns below.

This is Haleakalā, the "House of the Sun." It's the crown of east Maui and the largest dormant volcano crater in the world. Every year thousands of visitors shake themselves awake at three in the morning to board vans that take them from their comfortable hotels and up the world's most steeply ascending auto route to the summit of Haleakalā National Park. Sunrise is extraordinary here. Colors from the palest pink to the most fiery red slowly spread across the lip of the summit. Mark Twain called it "the sublimest spectacle" he had ever witnessed.

But sunrise is only the beginning. The park encompasses 28,665 acres, and the valley itself is 21 mi in circumference and 19 square mi in area. At its deepest, it measures 3,000 ft from the summit. The two towers of Manhattan's World Trade Center could be placed one atop the other and still not reach the top. While Haleakalā is dormant, the vast, wondrous valley here isn't a single crater created by some devastating explosion. Misnamed by the first European explorers, Haleakalā's huge depression would be more properly called an "erosional valley," the result of eons of wind and rain wearing down what was likely a small crater at the mountain's original summit. The small hills within the valley are volcanic cinder cones, each the site of an eruption.

More than anything, entering Haleakalā is like descending to the moon. Trails for hiking and horseback riding crisscross the crater for some 32 mi. The way is strewn with volcanic rubble, crater cones, frozen lava flows, vents, and lava tubes. The colors you see on your descent are muted yet dramatic—black, yellow, russet, orange, lavender, brown, and gray, even a pinkish-blue. It seems as if nothing could live here, but in fact this is an ecosystem that sustains, among other, more humble life forms, the surefooted mountain goat, the rare nēnē goose (no webbing between its toes, the better to negotiate this rugged terrain with), and the strange and delicate silversword. The silversword, a spiny, metallic-leaf plant, once grew abundantly on Haleakalā's slopes. Today it survives in small numbers at Haleakalā and at high elevations on the Big Island of Hawai'i. The plants live up to 20 years, bloom only once, scatter their seeds, and die.

The valley's starkness is overwhelming. Even shadows cast in the thin mountain air are flinty and spare. It's easy to understand why in the early days of this nation's space program moon-bound astronauts trained in this desolate place.

It is also not difficult to see this place as a bubbling, sulfurous cauldron, a direct connection not to the heavens but to the core of the earth. Haleakalā's last—and probably final—eruption occurred in 1790, a few years after a Frenchman named La Perouse became the first European to set foot on Maui. That fiery outburst was only one of many in Hawai'i over the millennia, just as Maui and its now-cold crater are just one facet of the volcanic variety of the Aloha State.

Large and small, awake or sleeping, volcanoes are Hawai'i's history and its heritage. Behind their beauty is the story of the flames that created this ethereal island chain. The tale began some 25 million years ago, yet it is still unfinished.

The islands in the Hawaiian archipelago are really only the very crests of immense mountains rising from the bottom of the sea. Formed by molten rock known as magma, the islands were slowly pushed up from the earth's volatile, uneasy mantle, forced through cracks in the thin crust that is the ocean floor. The first ancient eruptions cooled and formed pools on the Pacific bottom. Then, as more and more magma spilled from the vents over millions of years, the pools became ridges and grew into crests. The latter built upon themselves over the eons, until finally, miles high, they towered above the surface of the sea.

As the islands cooled in the Pacific waters, the stark lava slopes slowly bloomed, over centuries, with colorful flora—exotic, jewellike species endemic only to these islands, with their generous washings of tropical rain and abundant sunshine. Gradually, as seeds, spores, or eggs of living creatures were carried by the winds and currents to these isolated volcanic isles more than 2,000 mi from the closest continental land mass, the bare and rocky atolls became a paradise of greenery.

This type of volcano, with its slowly formed, gently sloping sides, is known as a shield volcano, and each of the Hawaiian isles is composed of them. As long as the underwater vents spew the lifeblood lava out from the earth's core and into the heart of the mountain, a shield volcano will continue to grow.

The Hawaiian Islands rest on an area called the Pacific Plate, and this vast shelf of land is making its way slowly to the northwest, creeping perhaps 2–3 inches every year. The result is that contact between the submarine vents and the volcanoes' conduits for magma is gradually disrupted and closed off. Slowly, the mountains stop growing, one by one. Surface eruptions slow down and finally halt completely, and these volcanoes ultimately become extinct.

That, at least, is one explanation. Another—centuries older and still revered in Hawaiian art and song—centers upon Pele, the beautiful and tempestuous daughter of Haumea, the Earth Mother, and Wakea, the Sky Father. Pele is the Hawaiian goddess of fire, the maker of mountains, melter of rocks, eater of forests, and burner of land—both creator and destroyer. Legend has it that Pele came to the Islands long ago to flee from her cruel older sister, Na Maka o Kahai, goddess of the sea. Pele ran first to the small island of Ni'ihau, making a crater home there with her digging stick. But Na Maka found her and destroyed her hideaway, so Pele again had to flee. On Kaua'i she delved deeper, but Na Maka chased her from that home as well. Pele ran on—from O'ahu to Moloka'i, Lana'i to Kaho'olawe, Molokini to Maui—but always and ever Na Maka pursued her.

Pele came at last to Halema'uma'u, the vast firepit crater of Ki'lauea, and there, on the Big Island, she dug deepest of all. There she is said to remain, all-powerful, quick to rage, and often unpredictable; the mountain is her impenetrable fortress and domain—a safe refuge, at least for a time, from Na Maka o Kahai.

Interestingly, the chronology of the old tales of Pele's flight from isle to isle closely matches the reckonings of modern volcanologists regarding the ages of the various craters. Today, the Big Island's Ki'lauea and Mauna Loa retain the closest links with the earth's superheated core and are active and volatile, though three other volcanoes that shaped the island are not. The remainder of the Hawaiian volcanoes have been carried beyond their magma supply by the movement of the Pacific Plate. Those farthest to the northwest in the island chain are completely extinct. Those at the southeasterly end of the island chain—Haleakalā, Mauna Kea, and Hualālai—are dormant and slipping away, so that the implacable process of volcanic death has begun.

Eventually, experts say, in another age or so, the same cooling and slow demise will overtake all of the burning rocks that are the Hawaiian Islands. Eventually, the sea will claim their bodies and, to Pele's rage, Na Maka o Kahai will win in the end. Or will she? Off the Big Island of Hawai'i a new island is forming. It's still ½ mi below the water's surface. Several thousand years more will be required for it to break into the sunlight. But it already has a name: Loihi.

By far the largest island of the archipelago, the Big Island of Hawai'i rises some 13,796 ft above sea level at the summit of Mauna Kea. Mauna Loa is nearly as high at 13,667 ft. From their bases on the ocean floor, these shield volcanoes are the largest mountain masses on the planet. Geologists believe it required more than 3 million years of steady volcanic activity to raise these peaks up above the waters of the Pacific.

Mauna Loa's little sister, Ki'lauea, at about 4,077 ft, is the most active volcano in the world. Between the two of them, they have covered nearly 200,000 acres of land with their red-hot lava flows over the past 200 years or so. In the process, they have ravished trees, fields, meadows, villages, and more than a few unlucky human witnesses. For generations, Ki'lauea, in a continually eruptive state, has pushed molten lava up from the earth's magma at 1,800°F and more. But as active as she and Mauna Loa are, their eruptions are comparatively safe and gentle, producing continuous small and especially liquid lava flows rather than dangerous bursts of fire and ash. The exceptions were two violently explosive displays during recorded history—one in 1790, the other in 1924. During these eruptions, Pele came closest to destroying the Big Island's largest city, Hilo. She also gave residents another scare as recently as 1985.

It is around these major volcanoes that the island's Hawai'i Volcanoes National Park was created. A sprawling natural preserve, the park attracts geology experts, volcanologists, and ordinary wide-eyed visitors from all over the world. They come for the park's unparalleled opportunity to view, up close and in person, the visual wonders of Pele's kingdom of fire and fantasy. They come to study and to improve methods for predicting the times and sites of eruptions. They have done so for a century or more.

Thomas Augustus Jaggar, the preeminent volcanologist and student of Kiʻlauea, built his home on stilts wedged into cracks in the volcanic rock of the crater rim. Harvard-trained and universally respected, he was the driving force behind the establishment of the Hawaiian Volcano Observatory at Kiʻlauea. When he couldn't raise research funds from donations, public and private, he raised pigs to keep the scientific work going. After Jaggar's death, his wife scattered his ashes over the great fiery abyss.

The park is on the Big Island's southeastern flank, about 30 minutes out of Hilo on the aptly named Volcano Highway. Wear sturdy walking shoes and carry a warm sweater. It can be a long hike across the lava flats to see Pele in action, and at 4,000 ft above sea level, temperatures can be brisk, however hot the volcanic activity. So much can be seen at close range along the road circling the crater that Kiʻlauea has been dubbed the "drive-in volcano."

At the park's visitor center sits a large display case. It contains dozens of lava-rock "souvenirs"—removed from Pele's grasp and then returned, accompanied by letters of apology. They are sent back by visitors who say they regret having broken the *kapu* (taboo) against removing even the smallest grain of native volcanic rock from Hawaiʻi. A typical letter might say: "I never thought Pele would miss just one little rock, but she did, and now I've wrecked two cars . . . I lost my job, my health is poor, and I know it's because I took this stone." The letters can be humorous, or poignant and remorseful, requesting Pele's forgiveness.

It is surprisingly safe at the crater's lip. Unlike Japan's Mount Fuji or Washington State's Mount St. Helens, Hawaiʻi's shield volcanoes spew their lava downhill, along the sides of the mountain. Still, the clouds of sulfur gas and fumes produced during volcanic eruptions are noxious and heady and can make breathing unpleasant, if not difficult. It has been pointed out that the chemistry of volcanoes—sulfur, hydrogen, oxygen, carbon dioxide—closely resembles the chemistry of the egg.

It's an 11-mi drive around the Kiʻlauea crater via the Crater Rim Road, and the trip takes about an hour. But it's better to walk a bit. There are at least eight major trails in the park, ranging from short 15-minute strolls to the three-day, 18-mi (one way) Mauna Loa Trail, which is, as you might expect, only for the seasoned hiker. A comfortable walk is Sulfur Banks, with its many vast, steaming vents creating halos of clouds around the rim of Kiʻlauea. The route passes through a seemingly enchanted forest of sandalwood, flowers, and ferns.

Just ahead is the main attraction: the center of Pele's power, Halemaʻumaʻu. This yawning pit of flame and burning rock measures some 3,000 ft wide and is a breathtaking sight. When Pele is in full fury, visitors come here in droves, on foot and by helicopter, to see her crimson expulsions coloring the dark earth and smoky sky. Recently, however, Kiʻlauea's most violent activity has occurred along vents in the mountain's sides instead of at its summit crater. Known as rift zones, they are lateral conduits that often open in shield volcanoes.

Kiʻlauea has two rift zones, one extending from the summit crater toward the southwest, through Kau, the other to the east-northeast through Puna, past Cape Kumakahi, and into the sea. In the last two decades, repeated eruptions in the east rift zone have blocked off 12 mi of coastal road—some under more than 300 ft of rock—and have covered a total of 10,000 acres with lava. Where the flows entered the ocean, roughly 200 acres have been added to the Big Island.

Farther along the Crater Rim Road (about 4 mi from the visitor center) is the Thurston Lava Tube, an example of a strangely beautiful volcanic phenomenon common on the Islands. Lava tubes form when lava flows rapidly downhill. The sides and top of this river of molten rock cool, while the fluid center flows on. Most formations are short and shallow, but some measure 30 ft–50 ft high and hundreds of yards long. Dark, cave-like places, lava tubes were often used to store remains of the ancient Hawaiian royalty—the *aliʻi*. The Thurston Lava Tube sits in a beautiful prehistoric fern forest called Fern Jungle.

Throughout the park, new lava formations are continually being created. Starkly beautiful, these volcanic deposits exhibit the different types of lava produced by Hawaiʻi's volcanoes: *ʻaʻā*, the dark, rough lava that solidifies as cinders of rock; and the more common *pāhoehoe*, the smooth, satiny lava that forms the vast plains of black rock in ropy swirls known as lava flats, which in some areas go on for miles. Other terms that help identify what may be seen in the park include *caldera*, which are the open, bowl-like lips of a volcano summit; *ejecta*, the cinders and ash that float through the air around an eruption; and olivine, the semiprecious chrysolite (greenish in color) found in volcanic ash.

But it isn't all fire and flash, cinders, and devastation in this volcanic landscape. Hawaiʻi Volcanoes National Park is also the home of some of the most beautiful of the state's black-sand beaches; humid forest glens full of lacy butterflies and colorful birds like the dainty flycatcher, called the *ʻelepaio*; and exquisite grottoes sparked with bright wild orchid sprays and crashing waterfalls. Even as the lava cools, still bearing a golden, glassy skin, lush, green native ferns—*amaʻumaʻu,*

kupukupu, and *ʻōkupukupu*—spring up in the midst of Pele's fallout, as if defying her destructiveness or simply confirming the fact that after fire she brings life.

Some 12 centuries ago, in fact, Pele brought humans to her verdant islands: The fiery explosions that lit Kiʻlauea and Mauna Loa like twin beacons in the night probably guided to Pele's side the first stout-hearted explorers to Hawaiʻi from the Marquesas Islands, some 2,400 mi away across the trackless, treacherous ocean.

Once summoned, they worshiped her from a discreet distance. Great numbers of religious *heiau* (outdoor stone platforms) dot the landscapes near the many older and extinct craters scattered throughout Hawaiʻi, demonstrating the great reverence the native islanders have always held for Pele and her creations. But the ruins of only two heiau are to be found near the very active crater at Halemaʻumaʻu. There, at the center of the capricious Pele's power, native Hawaiians caution one even today to "step lightly, for you are on holy ground."

For all the teeming tourism and bustle that are modern Hawaiʻi, no one today steps on the ground that Pele may one day claim for her own. In future ages, when mighty Kiʻlauea is no more, this area will still be a volcanic isle. Beneath the blue Pacific waters, fiery magma flows and new mountains form and grow. Just below the surface, Loihi waits.

— Gary Diedrichs

THE ALOHA SHIRT: A COLORFUL SWATCH OF ISLAND HISTORY

Elvis Presley had an entire wardrobe of them in the '60s films *Blue Hawaii* and *Paradise, Hawaiian Style*. During the '50s, entertainer Arthur Godfrey and bandleader Harry Owens often sported them on television shows. John Wayne

"The Aloha Shirt: A Colorful Swatch of Island History" first appeared in ALOHA *Magazine. Reprinted with permission of Davick Publications.*

loved to lounge around in them. Mick Jagger felt compelled to buy one on a visit to Hawai'i in the 1970s. Dustin Hoffman, Steven Spielberg, and Bill Cosby avidly collect them.

From gaudy to grand, from tawdry to tasteful, aloha shirts are Hawai'i's gift to the world of fashion. It has been more than 50 years since those riotously colored garments made their first appearance as immediately recognizable symbols of the Islands.

The roots of the aloha shirt go back to the early 1930s, when Hawai'i's garment industry was just beginning to develop its own unique style. Although locally made clothes did exist, they were almost exclusively for plantation workers and were constructed of durable palaka or plain cotton material.

Out of this came the first stirrings of fashion: beachboys and schoolchildren started having sport shirts made from colorful Japanese kimono fabric. The favored type of cloth was the kind used for children's kimonos—bright pink and orange floral prints for girls; masculine motifs in browns and blues for boys. In Japan, such flamboyant patterns were considered unsuitable for adult clothing, but in the Islands such rules didn't apply, and it seemed the flashier the shirt, the better—for either sex. Thus, the aloha shirt was born.

It was easy and inexpensive in those days to have garments tailored to order; the next step was moving to mass production and marketing. In June 1935, Honolulu's best-known tailoring establishment, Musa-Shiya, advertised the availability of "Aloha shirts—well tailored, beautiful designs and radiant colors. Ready-made or made to order . . . 95¢ and up." This is the first known printed use of the term that would soon refer to an entire industry. By the following year, several local manufacturers had begun full-scale production of "aloha wear." One of them, Ellery Chun of King-Smith, registered as local trademarks the terms "Aloha Sportswear" and "Aloha Shirt" in 1936 and 1937, respectively.

These early entrepreneurs were the first to create uniquely Hawaiian designs for fabric as well—splashy patterns that would forever symbolize the Islands. A 1939 *Honolulu Advertiser* story described them as a "delightful confusion (of) tropical fish and palm trees, Diamond Head and the Aloha Tower, surfboards and leis, ukuleles and Waikīkī beach scenes."

The aloha wear of the late 1930s was intended for—and mostly worn by—tourists, and interestingly, a great deal of it was exported to the mainland and even Europe and Australia. By the end of the decade, for example, only 5% of the output of one local firm, the Kamehameha Garment Company, was sold in Hawai'i.

World War II brought this trend to a halt, and during the postwar period, aloha wear really came into its own in Hawai'i itself. A strong push to support local industry gradually nudged island garb into the workplace, and kama'āina began to wear the clothing that previously had been seen as attire for visitors.

In 1947, for example, male employees of the City and County of Honolulu were first allowed to wear aloha shirts "in plain shades" during the summer months. Later that year, the first observance of Aloha Week started the tradition of "bankers and bellhops . . . mix(ing) colorfully in multihued and tapa-designed Aloha shirts every day," as a local newspaper's Sunday magazine supplement noted in 1948. By the 1960s, "Aloha Friday," set aside specifically for the wearing of aloha attire, had become a tradition. In the following decade, the suit and tie practically disappeared as work attire in Hawai'i, even for executives.

Most of the Hawaiian-theme fabric used in manufacturing aloha wear was designed in the Islands, then printed on the mainland or in Japan. The glowingly vibrant rayons of the late '40s and early '50s (a period now seen as aloha wear's heyday) were at first printed on the East Coast, but manufacturers there usually required such large orders, local firms eventually found it impossible to continue using them. By 1964, 90% of Hawaiian fabric was being manufactured in Japan—a situation that still exists today.

Fashion trends usually move in cycles, and aloha wear is no exception. By the 1960s, the "chop suey print" with its "tired clichés of Diamond Head, Aloha Tower, outrigger canoes (and) stereotyped leis" was seen as corny and garish, according to an article published in the *Honolulu Star-Bulletin*. But it was just that outdated aspect that began to appeal to the younger crowd, who began searching out old-fashioned aloha shirts at the Salvation Army and Goodwill thrift stores. These shirts were dubbed "silkies," a name by which they're still known, even though most of them were actually made of rayon.

Before long, what had been 50¢ shirts began escalating in price, and a customer who had balked at paying $5 for a shirt that someone had already worn soon found the same item selling for $10—and more. By the late 1970s, aloha-wear designers were copying the prints of yesteryear for their new creations.

The days of bargain silkies are now gone. The few choice aloha shirts from decades past that still remain are offered today by specialized dealers for hundreds of dollars apiece, causing many to look back with chagrin to the time when such treasures were foolishly worn to the beach until they fell apart. The best examples of vintage aloha shirts are now rightly seen as art objects, worthy of preservation for the lovely depictions they offer of Hawai'i's colorful and unique scene.

— DeSoto Brown

THE HOUSE OF THE SUN

There are hosts of people who journey like restless spirits round and about this earth in search of seascapes and landscapes and the wonders and beauties of nature. They overrun Europe in armies; they can be met in droves and herds in Florida and the West Indies, at the pyramids, and on the slopes and summits of the Canadian and American Rockies; but in the House of the Sun they are as rare as live and wriggling dinosaurs. Haleakala is the Hawaiian name for "the House of the Sun." It is a noble dwelling situated on the island of Maui; but so few tourists have ever peeped into it, much less entered it, that their number may be practically reckoned as zero. Yet I venture to state that for natural beauty and wonder the nature lover may see dissimilar things as great as Haleakalā, but no greater, while he will never see elsewhere anything more beautiful or wonderful. Honolulu is six days' steaming from San Francisco; Maui is a night's run on the steamer from Honolulu, and six hours more, if he is in a hurry, can bring the traveler to Kolikoli, which is 10,032 feet above the sea and which stands hard by the entrance portal to the House of the Sun. Yet the tourist comes not, and Haleakalā sleeps on in lonely and unseen grandeur.

Not being tourists, we of the *Snark* went to Haleakala. On the slopes of that monster mountain there is a cattle ranch of some 50,000 acres, where we spent the night at an altitude of 2,000 feet. The next morning it was boots and saddles, and with cowboys and pack horses we climbed to Ukulele, a mountain ranch house, the altitude of which, 5,500 feet, gives a severely temperate climate, compelling blankets at night and a roaring fireplace in the living room. Ukulele, by the way, is the Hawaiian for "jumping flea," as it is also the Hawaiian for a certain musical instrument that may be likened to a young guitar. It is my opinion that the mountain ranch house was named after the young guitar. We were not in a hurry, and we spent the day at Ukulele, learnedly dis-

---

Although it was written in the early 20th century, before Haleakalā became a popular tourist attraction, Jack London's account of camping among the crater's cinder cones is still fascinating to read today.

cussing altitudes and barometers and shaking our particular barometer whenever anyone's argument stood in need of demonstration. Our barometer was the most graciously acquiescent instrument I have ever seen. Also, we gathered mountain raspberries, large as hen's eggs and larger, gazed up the pasture-covered lava slopes to the summit of Haleakala, 4,500 feet above us, and looked down upon a mighty battle of the clouds that was being fought beneath us, ourselves in the bright sunshine.

Every day and every day this unending battle goes on. Ukiukiu is the name of the trade wind that comes raging down out of the northeast and hurls itself upon Haleakala. Now Haleakala is so bulky and tall that it turns the northeast trade wind aside on either hand, so that in the lee of Haleakala no trade wind blows at all. On the contrary, the wind blows in the counter direction, in the teeth of the northeast trade. This wind is called Naulu. And day and night and always Ukiukiu and Naulu strive with each other, advancing, retreating, flanking, curving, curling, and turning and twisting, the conflict made visible by the cloud masses plucked from the heavens and hurled back and forth in squadrons, battalions, armies, and great mountain ranges. Once in a while, Ukiukiu, in mighty gusts, flings immense cloud masses clear over the summit of Haleakala; whereupon Naulu craftily captures them, lines them up in new battle formation, and with them smites back at his ancient and eternal antagonist. Then Ukiukiu sends a great cloud army around the eastern side of the mountain. It is a flanking movement, well executed. But Naulu, from his lair on the leeward side, gathers the flanking army in, pulling and twisting and dragging it, hammering it into shape, and sends it charging back against Ukiukiu around the western side of the mountain. And all the while, above and below the main battlefield, high up the slopes toward the sea, Ukiukiu and Naulu are continually sending out little wisps of cloud, in ragged skirmish line, that creep and crawl over the ground, among the trees and through the canyons, and that spring upon and capture one another in sudden ambuscades and sorties. And sometimes Ukiukiu or Naulu, abruptly sending out a heavy charging column, captures the ragged little skirmishers or drives them skyward, turning over and over, in vertical whirls, thousands of feet in the air.

But it is on the western slopes of Haleakala that the main battle goes on. Here Naulu masses his heaviest formation and wins his greatest victories. Ukiukiu grows weak toward late afternoon, which is the way of all trade winds, and is driven backward by Naulu. Naulu's generalship is excellent. All day he has been gathering and packing away immense reserves. As the afternoon draws on, he welds them into a solid column, sharp-pointed, miles in length, a mile in width, and hundreds of feet thick. This column he slowly thrusts forward into the broad battle front of Ukiukiu, and slowly and surely Ukiukiu, weakening fast, is split asunder. But it is not all bloodless. At times Ukiukiu struggles wildly, and with fresh accessions of strength from the limitless northeast smashes away half a mile at a time at Naulu's column and sweeps it off and away toward West Maui. Sometimes, when the two charging armies meet end-on, a tremendous perpendicular whirl results, the cloud masses, locked together, mounting thousands of feet into the air and turning over and over. A favorite device of Ukiukiu is to send a low, squat formation, densely packed, forward along the ground and under Naulu. When Ukiukiu is under, he proceeds to buck. Naulu's mighty middle gives to the blow and bends upward, but usually he turns the attacking column back upon itself and sets it milling. And all the while the ragged little skirmishers, stray and detached, sneak through the trees and canyons, crawl along and through the grass, and surprise one another with unexpected leaps and rushes; while above, far above, serene and lonely in the rays of the setting sun, Haleakala looks down upon the conflict. And so, the night. But in the morning, after the fashion of trade winds, Ukiukiu gathers strength and sends the hosts of Naulu rolling back in confusion and rout. And one day is like another day in the battle of the clouds, where Ukiukiu and Naulu strive eternally on the slopes of Haleakala.

Again in the morning, it was boots and saddles, cowboys and pack horses, and the climb to the top began. One pack horse carried 20 gallons of water, slung in five-gallon bags on either side; for water is precious and rare in the crater itself, in spite of the fact that several miles to the north and east of the crater rim more rain comes down than in any other place in the world. The way led upward across countless lava flows, without regard for trails, and never have I seen horses with such perfect footing as that of the 13 that composed our outfit. They climbed or dropped down perpendicular places with the sureness and coolness of mountain goats, and never a horse fell or balked.

There is a familiar and strange illusion experienced by all who climb isolated mountains. The higher one climbs, the more of the earth's surface becomes visible, and the effect of this is that the horizon seems uphill from the observer. This illusion is especially notable on Haleakala, for the old volcano rises directly from the sea, without buttresses or connecting ranges. In consequence, as fast as we climbed up the grim slope of Haleakala, still faster did Haleakala, ourselves, and all about us sink down into the center of what appeared a profound abyss. Everywhere, far above us, towered the horizon. The ocean sloped down from the horizon to us. The higher we climbed, the deeper did we seem to sink down, the farther above us shone the horizon, and the steeper pitched the grade up to that horizontal line where sky and ocean met. It was weird and unreal, and vagrant thoughts of Simm's Hole and of the volcano through which Jules Verne journeyed to the center of the earth flitted through one's mind.

And then, when at last we reached the summit of that monster mountain, which summit was like the bottom of an inverted cone situated in the center of an awful cosmic pit, we found that we were at neither top nor bottom. Far above us was the heaven-towering horizon, and far beneath us, where the top of the mountain should have been, was a deeper deep, the great crater, the House of the Sun. Twenty-three miles around stretched the dizzy walls of the crater. We stood on the edge of the nearly vertical western wall, and the floor of the crater lay nearly half a mile beneath. This floor, broken by lava flows and cinder cones, was as red and fresh and uneroded as if it were but yesterday that the fires went out. The cinder cones, the smallest over 400 feet in height and the largest over 900, seemed no more than puny little sand hills, so mighty was the magnitude of the setting. Two gaps, thousands of feet deep, broke the rim of the crater, and through these Ukiukiu vainly strove to drive his fleecy herds of trade-wind clouds. As fast as they advanced through the gaps, the heat of the crater dissipated them into thin air, and though they advanced always, they got nowhere.

It was a scene of vast bleakness and desolation, stern, forbidding, fascinating. We gazed down upon a place of fire and earthquake. The tie-ribs of earth lay bare before us. It was a workshop of nature still cluttered with the raw beginnings of world-making. Here and there great dikes of primordial rock had thrust themselves up from the bowels of earth, straight through the molten surface ferment that had evidently cooled only the other day. It was all unreal and unbelievable. Looking upward, far above us (in reality beneath us) floated the cloud battle of Ukiukiu and Naulu. And higher up the slope of the seeming abyss, above the cloud battle, in the air and sky, hung the islands of Lanai and Molokai. Across the crater, to the southeast, still apparently looking upward, we saw ascending, first, the turquoise sea, then the white surf line of the shore of Hawaii; above that the belt of trade clouds, and next, 80 miles away, rearing their stupendous bulks out of the azure sky, tipped with snow, wreathed with cloud, trembling like a mirage, the peaks of Mauna Kea and Mauna Loa hung poised on the wall of heaven.

It is told that long ago, one Maui, the son of Hina, lived on what is now known as West Maui. His mother, Hina, employed her time in the making of kapas. She must have made them at night, for her days were occupied in trying to dry the kapas. Each morning, and all morning, she toiled at spreading them out in the sun. But no sooner were they out than she began taking them in, in order to have them all under shelter for the night. For know that the days were shorter then than now. Maui watched his mother's futile toil and felt sorry for her. He decided to do something—oh, no, not to help her hang out and take in the kapas. He was too clever for that. His idea was to make the sun go slower. Perhaps he was the first Hawaiian astronomer. At any rate, he took a series of observations of the sun from various parts of the island. His conclusion was that the sun's path was directly across Haleakala. Unlike Joshua, he stood in no need of divine assistance. He gathered a huge quantity of coconuts, from the fiber of which he braided a stout cord, and in one end of which he made a noose, even as the cowboys of Haleakala do to this day. Next he climbed into the House of the Sun and laid in wait. When the sun came tearing along the path, bent on completing its journey in the shortest time possible, the valiant youth threw his lariat around one of the sun's largest and strongest beams. He made the sun slow down some; also, he broke the beam short off. And he kept on roping and breaking off beams till the sun said it was willing to listen to reason. Maui set forth his terms of peace, which the sun accepted, agreeing to go more slowly thereafter. Wherefore Hina had ample time in which to dry her kapas, and the days are longer than they used to be, which last is quite in accord with the teachings of modern astronomy.

We had a lunch of jerked beef and hard poi in a stone corral, used of old time for the night impounding of cattle being driven across the island. Then we skirted the rim for half a mile and began the descent into the crater. Twenty-five hundred feet beneath lay the floor, and down a steep slope of loose volcanic cinders we dropped, the sure-footed horses slipping and sliding, but always keeping their feet. The black surface of the cinders, when broken by the horses' hoofs, turned to a yellow ocher dust, virulent in appearance and acid of taste, that arose in clouds. There was a gallop across a level stretch to the mouth of a convenient blowhole, and then the descent continued in clouds of volcanic dust, winding in and out among cinder cones, brick-red, old rose, and purplish black of color. Above us, higher and higher, towered the crater walls, while we journeyed on across innumerable lava flows, turning and twisting a devious way among the adamantine billows of a petrified sea. Saw-toothed waves of lava vexed the surface of this weird ocean, while on either hand rose jagged crests and spiracles of fantastic shape. Our way led on past a bottomless pit and along and over the main stream of the latest lava flow for 7 miles.

At the lower end of the crater was our camping spot, in a small grove of olapa and kolea trees, tucked away in a corner of the crater at the base of walls that rose perpendicularly 1,500 feet. Here was pasturage for the horses, but no water, and first we turned aside and picked our way across a mile of lava to a known water hole in a crevice in the crater wall. The water hole was empty. But on climbing 50 feet up the crevice, a pool was found containing half a dozen barrels of water. A pail was carried up, and soon a steady stream of the precious liquid was running down the rock and filling the lower pool, while the cowboys below were busy fighting the horses back, for there was room for one only to drink at a time. Then it was on to camp at the foot of the wall, up which herds of wild goats scrambled and blatted, while the tent rose to the sound of rifle firing. Jerked beef, hard poi, and broiled kid was the menu. Over the crest of the crater, just above our heads, rolled a sea of clouds, driven on by Ukiukiu. Though this sea rolled over the crest unceasingly, it never blotted out nor dimmed the moon, for the heat of the crater dissolved the clouds as fast as they rolled in. Through the moonlight, attracted by the camp fire, came the crater cattle to peer and challenge. They were rolling fat, though they rarely drank water, the morning dew on the grass taking its place. It was because of this dew that the tent made a welcome bedchamber, and we fell asleep to the chanting of hulas by the unwearied Hawaiian cowboys, in whose veins, no doubt, ran the blood of Maui, their valiant forebear.

The camera cannot do justice to the House of the Sun. The sublimated chemistry of photography may not lie, but it certainly does not tell all the truth. The Koolau Gap [may be] faithfully reproduced, just as it impinged on the retina of the camera, yet in the resulting picture the gigantic scale of things is missing. Those walls that seem several hundred feet in height are almost as many thousand; that entering wedge of cloud is a mile and a half wide in the gap itself, while beyond the gap it is a veritable ocean; and that foreground of cinder cone and volcanic ash, mushy and colorless in appearance, is in truth gorgeous-hued in brick-red, terra cotta, rose, yellow, ocher, and purplish black. Also, words are a vain thing and drive to despair. To say that a crater wall is 2,000 feet high is to say just precisely that it is 2,000 feet high; but there is a vast deal more to that crater wall than a mere statistic. The sun is 93 million miles distant, but to mortal conception the adjoining county is farther away. This frailty of the human brain is hard on the sun. It is likewise hard on the House of the Sun. Haleakala has a message of beauty and wonder for the human soul that cannot be delivered by proxy. Kolikoli is six hours from Kahului; Kahului is a night's run from Honolulu; Honolulu is six days from San Francisco; and there you are.

We climbed the crater walls, put the horses over impossible places, rolled stones, and shot wild goats. I did not get any goats. I was too busy rolling stones. One spot in particular I remember, where we started a stone the size of a horse. It began the descent easy enough, rolling over, wobbling, and threatening to stop; but in a few minutes it was soaring through the air 200 feet at a jump. It grew rapidly smaller until it struck a slight slope of volcanic sand, over which it darted like a startled jack rabbit, kicking up behind it a tiny trail of yellow dust. Stone and dust diminished in size, until some of the party said the stone had stopped. That was because they could not see it any longer. It had vanished into the distance beyond their ken. Others saw it rolling farther on—I know I did; and it is my firm conviction that that stone is still rolling.

Our last day in the crater, Ukiukiu gave us a taste of his strength. He smashed Naulu back all along the line, filled the House of the Sun to overflowing with clouds, and drowned us out. Our rain gauge was a pint cup under a tiny hole in the tent. That last night of storm and rain filled the cup, and there was no way of measuring the water that spilled over into the blankets. With the rain gauge out of business there was no longer any reason for remaining; so we broke camp in the wet-gray of dawn and plunged eastward across the lava to the Kaupo Gap. East Maui is nothing more or less than the vast lava stream that flowed long ago through the Kaupo Gap; and down this stream we picked our way from an altitude of 6,500 feet to the sea. This was a day's work in itself for the horses; but never were there such horses. Safe in the bad places, never rushing, never losing their heads, as soon as they found a trail wide and smooth enough to run on, they ran. There was no stopping them until the trail became bad again, and then they stopped of themselves. Continuously, for days, they had performed the hardest kind of work, and fed most of the time on grass foraged by themselves at night while we slept, and yet that day they covered 28 leg-breaking miles and galloped into Hana like a bunch of colts. Also, there were several of them, reared in the dry region on the leeward side of Haleakala, that had never worn shoes in all their lives. Day after day, and all day long, unshod, they had traveled over the sharp lava, with the extra weight of a man on their backs, and their hoofs were in better condition than those of the shod horses.

The scenery between Vieiras's (where the Kaupo Gap empties into the sea) and Hana, which we covered in half a day, is well worth a week or a month; but, wildly beautiful as it is, it becomes pale and small in comparison with the wonderland that lies beyond the rubber plantations between Hana and the Honomanu Gulch. Two days were required to cover this marvelous stretch, which lies on the windward side of Haleakala. The people who dwell there call it "the ditch country," an unprepossessing name, but it has no other. Nobody else ever comes there. Nobody else knows anything about it. With the exception of a handful of men, whom business has brought there, nobody has heard of the ditch country of Maui. Now a ditch is a ditch, assumably muddy, and usually traversing uninteresting and monotonous landscapes. But the Nahiku Ditch is not an ordinary ditch. The windward side of Haleakala is serried by a thousand precipitous gorges, down which rush as many torrents, each torrent of which achieves a score of cascades and waterfalls before it reaches the sea. More rain comes down here than in any other region in the world. In 1904 the year's downpour was 420 inches. Water means sugar, and sugar is the backbone of the territory of Hawaii, wherefore the Nahiku Ditch, which is not a ditch, but a chain of tunnels. The water travels underground, appearing only at intervals to leap a gorge, traveling high in the air on a giddy flume and plunging into and through the opposing mountain. This magnificent waterway is called a "ditch," and with equal appropriateness can Cleopatra's barge be called a boxcar.

There are no carriage roads through the ditch country, and before the ditch was built, or bored, rather, there was no horse trail. Hundreds of inches of rain annually, on fertile soil, under a tropic sun, means a steaming jungle of vegetation. A man, on foot, cutting his way through, might advance a mile a day, but at the end of a week he would be a wreck, and he would have to crawl hastily back if he wanted to get out before the vegetation overran the passageway he had cut. O'Shaughnessy was the daring engineer who conquered the jungle and the gorges, ran the ditch, and made the horse trail. He built enduringly, in concrete and masonry, and made one of the most remarkable water farms in the world. Every little runlet and dribble is harvested and conveyed by subterranean channels to the main ditch. But so heavily does it rain at times that countless spillways let the surplus escape to the sea.

The horse trail is not very wide. Like the engineer who built it, it dares anything. Where the ditch plunges through the mountain, it climbs over; and where the ditch leaps a gorge on a flume, the horse trail takes advantage of the ditch and crosses on top of the flume. That careless trail thinks nothing of traveling up or down the faces of precipices. It gouges its narrow way out of the wall, dodging around waterfalls or passing under them where they thunder down in white fury; while straight overhead the wall rises hundreds of feet, and straight beneath it sinks a thousand. And those marvelous mountain horses are as unconcerned as the trail. They fox-trot along it as a matter of course, though the footing is slippery with rain, and they will gallop with their hind feet slipping over the edge if you let them. I advise only those with steady nerves and cool heads to tackle the Nahiku Ditch trail. One of our cowboys was noted as the strongest and bravest on the big ranch. He had ridden mountain horses all his life on the rugged western slopes of Haleakala. He was first in the horse breaking; and when the others hung back, as a matter of course, he would go in to meet a wild bull in the cattle pen. He had a reputation. But he had never ridden over the Nahiku Ditch. It was there he lost his reputation.

When he faced the first flume, spanning a hair-raising gorge, narrow, without railings, with a bellowing waterfall above, another below, and directly beneath a wild cascade, the air filled with driving spray and rocking to the clamor and rush of sound and motion—well, that cowboy dismounted from his horse, explained briefly that he had a wife and two children, and crossed over on foot, leading the horse behind him.

The only relief from the flumes was the precipices; and the only relief from the precipices was the flumes, except where the ditch was far underground, in which case we crossed one horse and rider at a time, on primitive log bridges that swayed and teetered and threatened to carry away. I confess that at first I rode such places with my feet loose in the stirrups, and that on the sheer walls I saw to it, by a definite, conscious act of will, that the foot in the outside stirrup, overhanging the thousand feet of fall, was exceedingly loose. I say "at first"; for, as in the crater itself we quickly lost our conception of magnitude, so, on the Nahiku Ditch, we quickly lost our apprehension of depth. The ceaseless iteration of height and depth produced a state of consciousness in which height and depth were accepted as the ordinary conditions of existence; and from the horse's back to look sheer down 400 or 500 feet became quite commonplace and nonproductive of thrills. And as carelessly as the trail and the horses, we swung along the dizzy heights and ducked around or through the waterfalls.

And such a ride! Falling water was everywhere. We rode above the clouds, under the clouds, and through the clouds! and every now and then a shaft of sunshine penetrated like a searchlight to the depths yawning beneath us, or flashed upon some pinnacle of the crater rim thousands of feet above. At every turn of the trail a waterfall or a dozen waterfalls, leaping hundreds of feet through the air, burst upon our vision. At our first night's camp, in the Keanae Gulch, we counted 32 waterfalls from a single viewpoint. The vegetation ran riot over that wild land. There were forests of koa and kolea trees, and candlenut trees; and then there were the trees called ohia-ai, which bore red mountain apples, mellow and juicy and most excellent to eat. Wild bananas grew everywhere, clinging to the sides of the gorges, and, overborne by their great bunches of ripe fruit, falling across the trail and blocking the way. And over the forest surged a sea of green life, the climbers of a thousand varieties, some that floated airily, in lacelike filaments, from the tallest branches; others that coiled and wound about the trees like huge serpents; and one, the ie-ie, that was for all the world like a climbing palm, swinging on a thick stem from branch to branch and tree to tree and throttling the supports whereby it climbed. Through the sea of green, lofty tree ferns thrust their great delicate fronds, and the lehua flaunted its scarlet blossoms. Underneath the climbers, in no less profusion, grew the warm-colored, strangely marked plants that in the United States one is accustomed to seeing preciously conserved in hothouses. In fact, the ditch country of Maui is nothing more nor less than a huge conservatory. Every familiar variety of fern flourishes, and more varieties that are unfamiliar, from the tiniest maidenhair to the gross and voracious staghorn, the latter the terror of the woodsmen, interlacing with itself in tangled masses five or six feet deep and covering acres.

Never was there such a ride. For two days it lasted, when we emerged into rolling country, and, along an actual wagon road, came home to the ranch at a gallop. I know it was cruel to gallop the horses after such a long, hard journey; but we blistered our hands in a vain effort to hold them in. That's the sort of horses they grow on Haleakala. At the ranch there was a great festival of cattle driving, branding, and horse breaking. Overhead Ukiukiu and Naulu battled valiantly, and far above, in the sunshine, towered the mighty summit of Haleakala.

— Jack London

WHAT TO READ AND WATCH BEFORE YOU GO

Books and Videos

If you like your history in novel form you'll enjoy James A. Michener's weighty *Hawaii* for its overall perspective; it's also available on audiocassette. Capt. James Cook's *A Voyage to the Pacific Ocean*, one of the first guidebooks to the Islands, contains many valid insights; *Shoal of Time*, by Gavan Daws, chronicles Hawaiian history from Cook's time to the 1960s. History also comes to life in the pages of *Travels in Hawaii*, by Robert Louis Stevenson. *History Makers of Hawaii*, by A. Grove Day, is a biographical dictionary of people who shaped the territory from past to present. To gain familiarity with the gods and goddesses who have also had a hand in this land's development, read *Hawaiian Mythology*, by Martha Beckwith. *Hawai'i's Story by Hawai'i's Queen*, the tale of the overthrow of the Hawaiian monarchy in Queen Lili'uokalani's own words, is poignant and thought-provoking. For a glimpse at military history, *Pearl Harbor: Fact and Reference Book*, by Terrance McCombs, is a collection of both well-known facts and lesser-known trivia. For a truly Hawaiian perspective, *Voices of Wisdom: Hawaiian Elders Speak*, by M. J. Harden shares interviews with some of Hawai'i's most respected elders, Hawai'i's traditional keepers of knowledge and wisdom.

A whole new genre of Hawaiian writing offers insights into island lifestyles through the use of pidgin prose and local settings. Paul Wood's essays, collected in *Four Wheels, Five Corners: Facts of Life in Upcountry Maui*, convey a real sense of place. Recent novels that capture the South Seas texture include *Shark's Dialogue*, by Kiana Davenport; this book weaves together multi-ethnic stories, legends, and ancient beliefs to create a mystical air. *Wild Meat and the Bully Burgers*, by Lois Ann Yamanaka, is a tale of growing up on the Big Island, told in an authentic native voice. Writers Paul Theroux, Barbara Kingsolver, and Maxine Hong Kingston are among those who share stories about the Islands in *Hawaii: True Stories of the Island Spirit*, a collection edited by Rick and Marcie Carroll.

Those interested in the outdoors will want to pick up *A Guide to Tropical and Semitropical Flora*, by Loraine Kuck and Richard Tongg. The *Handbook of Hawaiian Fishes*, by W. A. Gosline and Vernon Brock, is great for snorkelers. *Hawaii's Birds*, by the Hawai'i Audubon Society, is perfect for bird-watchers. *Hawaiian Hiking Trails*, by Craig Chisholm, is just the guide for day hikers and backpackers. Find your perfect place in the sand with *Hawaii's Best Beaches*, by John R. K. Clark, a guide to the 50th State's 50 best beaches. *Surfing: The Ultimate Pleasure*, by Leonard Lueras, covers everything about the sport, from its early history to the music and films of its later subculture.

Preparing your palate for an upcoming visit, or have you returned from the Islands in love with haute Hawaiian cuisine? *The New Cuisine of Hawaii*, by Janice Wald Henderson, is beautifully designed and features recipes from the 12 chefs credited with defining Hawai'i regional cuisine. One of these pioneers, celebrity chef Roy Yamaguchi, has opened a veritable empire of restaurants across the Islands. His cookbook *Roy's Feasts from Hawaii* provides an in-depth taste of the island in addition to some gorgeous photography and island background. Rachel Laudan's *The Foods of Paradise* describes local foods and their histories in addition to providing recipes. *Hawaiian Country Tables* by Kaui Philpotts spotlights vintage Island recipes and dishes and gives readers an unusual entrée into Hawai'i's history.

For swaying musicologists, there's *Hula Is Life, The Story of Maiki Aiu and Hālau Hulo o Maiki*, by Rita Aryioshi; it's the definitive book on hula's origins and development. Hawaiian music lovers might take note of the ideas presented in *Strains of Change: Impact of Tourism on Hawaiian Music*, by Elizabeth Tatar. *Hawaiian Traditions in Hawaii*, by Joan Clarke, is an illustrated book detailing ethnic celebrations in the Islands. Robert Shaw traces the history of the Islands through its tradition of quilting in this artful book *Hawaiian Quilt Masterpieces*. Instead of just taking home a lei, learn how to make one: *Hawaiian Lei Making*, by Laurie Shimizu Ide, offers a photographic guide and reference tool for making of floral leis. Albert J. Schütz's souvenir-worthy paperback *All About Hawaiian* is a good introduction to the authentic language of the Islands and recent efforts to preserve it. *Hawai'i Magazine* (✉ Box 55796, Boulder, CO 80222, ☎ 800/365-4421; subscription $17.97 for six issues) is an attractive bimonthly magazine devoted to the 50th state.

To view Hawaii on video before your arrival, take a look at *Forever Hawaii*, a video portrait of Hawai'i's six major islands.

For hikers, the video *Hawaii on Foot* with Robert Smith gives hikers a peek at some of the best trails on O'ahu, Maui, the Big Island, and Kaua'i. It is available from H.O.A. Publications (✉ 102-16 Kaui Pl., Kula 96796, ☎ 808/678-2664). For lovers of dance, hula comes alive in the *1999 Merrie Monarch Festival Highlights*. This hula festival, held each spring on the Big Island, is Hawai'i's most prestigious competition. The video is available from www.BooklinesHawaii.com, or by phone by calling ☎ 800/828-4852.

Movie buffs will enjoy *Made in Paradise: Hollywood's Films of Hawaii and the South Seas*, by Luis Reyes. It points out movie locations and pokes gentle fun at some of the misinformation popularized by Tinseltown's version of Island life. Guided tours of Kaua'i locations used in filming are provided by **Hawai'i Movie Tours** (☎ 800/628-8432). Its tours are highly recommended.

Most people automatically think of Elvis when the words "Hawai'i" and "movie" are mentioned in the same sentence. Elvis Presley's Hawaiian-filmed movies are *Girls! Girls! Girls!* (1962), *Paradise, Hawaiian Style* (1966), and *Blue Hawaii* (1962), which showcases O'ahu's picturesque Hanauma Bay and Kaua'i's Coco Palms Resort, the site of Elvis's celluloid wedding.

Films such as Shirley Temple's *Curly Top* (1935); *Waikiki Wedding* (1937), with Bing Crosby; and *Gidget Goes Hawaiian* (1962) feature Hawai'i's beaches, palm trees, and hula dancers. The Islands' winter waves have taken center stage in a legion of hang-ten films of which only *North Shore* (1987) is on video.

Military-theme movies filmed in Hawai'i include *Mister Roberts* (1955), starring Henry Fonda, Jack Lemmon, and James Cagney; and *Lt. Robin Crusoe, USN* (1966), with Dick Van Dyke. Some serious military films, often dealing with WWII, with Hawaiian locales frequently posing as the South Pacific, include *Between Heaven and Hell* (1956), starring Robert Wagner; *The Enemy Below* (1957), with Robert Mitchum; and John Wayne's *Donovan's Reef* (1963). *Tora! Tora! Tora!* (1971) re-created the December 7, 1941, bombing of Pearl Harbor. For *Flight of the Intruder* (1991), director John Milius turned taro farms at the base of Kaua'i's Mount Wai'ale'le into the rice paddies of Southeast Asia.

Hawai'i has repeatedly doubled for other places. Kaua'i's remote valleys and waterfalls and O'ahu's Kualoa Ranch portrayed a Costa Rican dinosaur preserve in Steven Spielberg's *Jurassic Park* (1993). The opening beach scene of that movie's sequel, *The Lost World* (1997), was also filmed on Kaua'i. Spielberg was no stranger to Kaua'i, though, having filmed Harrison Ford's escape via seaplane from Kaua'i's Menehune Fishpond in *Raiders of the Lost Ark*

(1981). The fluted cliffs and gorges of Kauaʻi's rugged Nā Pali coastline play the misunderstood beast's island home in *King Kong* (1976), and a jungle dweller of another sort, in *George of the Jungle* (1997), frolicked on Kauaʻi. Harrison Ford returned to the island for 10 weeks during the filming of *Six Days, Seven Nights* (1998), a romantic adventure set in French Polynesia.

Mitzi Gaynor washed that man right out of her hair on Kauaʻi's Lumahaʻi Beach in *South Pacific* (1958). And the tempestuous love scene between Burt Lancaster and Deborah Kerr in *From Here to Eternity* (1954) took place on Oʻahu's Halona Cove beach.

James Michener's story *Hawaii* (1967) chronicles the lives of the Islands' missionary families. *Picture Bride* (1995) tells the story of a young Japanese girl who arrives on the Islands to face harsh realities as the wife of a sugar plantation laborer she has only seen in a photograph.

Other movies with Hawaiʻi settings include *Black Widow* (1987), in which journalist Debra Winger travels to the Big Island's lava fields to prevent a murder; *Honeymoon in Vegas* (1992); *Under the Hula Moon* (1995); and *A Very Brady Sequel* (1997).

HAWAI'I AT A GLANCE

ca. AD 500 The first human beings to set foot on Hawaiian shores are Polynesians, who travel 2,000 mi in 60- to 80-ft canoes to the islands they name Havaiki after their legendary homeland. Researchers today believe they were originally from Southeast Asia, and that they discovered the South Pacific Islands of Tahiti and the Marquesas before ending up in Hawai'i.

ca. 1758 Kamehameha, the Hawaiian chief who unified the Islands, is born.

1778 In January, Capt. James Cook, commander of the H.M.S. *Resolution* and the consort vessel H.M.S. *Discovery*, lands on the island of Kaua'i and "discovers" it for the Western world. He names the archipelago the Sandwich Islands after his patron, the Earl of Sandwich. In November, he returns to the Islands for the winter, anchoring at Kealakekua Bay on the Big Island.

1779 In February, Cook is killed in a battle with Hawai'i's indigenous people at Kealakekua.

1785 The isolation of the Islands ends as British, American, French, and Russian fur traders and New England whalers come to Hawai'i. Tales spread of thousands of acres of sugarcane growing wild, and farmers come in droves from the United States and Europe.

1790 Kamehameha begins his rise to power with a series of bloody battles.

1791 Kamehameha builds Pu'ukoholā Heiau (temple) and dedicates it by sacrificing a rival chief he has killed.

1795 Using Western arms, Kamehameha wins a decisive confrontation on O'ahu. Except for Kaua'i (which he tries to invade in 1796 and 1804), this completes his military conquest of the Islands.

1810 The chief of Kaua'i acknowledges Kamehameha's rule, giving him suzerainty over Kaua'i and Ni'ihau. Kamehameha becomes known as King Kamehameha I, and he rules the unified Kingdom of Hawai'i with an iron hand.

1819 Kamehameha I dies, and his oldest son, Liholiho, rules briefly as Kamehameha II, with Ka'ahumanu, Kamehameha I's favorite wife, as co-executive. Ka'ahumanu persuades the new king to abandon old religious taboos, including those that forbade women to eat with men or to hold positions of power. The first whaling ships land at Lahaina on Maui.

1820 By the time the first missionaries arrive from Boston, Hawai'i's social order is beginning to break down. First, Ka'ahumanu and then Kamehameha II defy *kapu* (taboo) without attracting divine retribution. Hawaiians, disillusioned with their own gods, are receptive to the ideas of Christianity. The influx of Western visitors also introduces to Hawai'i Western diseases, liquor, and what some view as moral decay.

1824 King Kamehameha II and his favorite wife die of measles during a visit to England. Honolulu missionaries give both royals a Christian burial outside Kawaiaha'o Church, inspiring many Hawaiians to convert to the Protestant faith. The king's younger brother, Kau'ikea'ōuli, becomes King Kamehameha III, a wise and gentle sovereign who reigns for 30 years with Ka'ahumanu as regent.

1832 Ka'ahumanu is baptized and dies a few months later.

1840 The Wilkes Expedition, sponsored by the U.S. Coast and Geodetic Survey, pinpoints Pearl Harbor as a potential naval base.

1845 Kamehameha III and the legislature move Hawai'i's seat of government from Lahaina, on Maui, to Honolulu, on O'ahu.

1849 Kamehameha III turns Hawai'i into a constitutional monarchy, and the United States, France, and Great Britain recognize Hawai'i as an independent country.

1850 The Great Mahele, a land commission, reapportions the land to the crown, the government, chiefs, and commoners, introducing for the first time the Western principle of private ownership. Commoners are now able to buy and sell land, but this great division becomes the great dispossession. By the end of the 19th century, white men own four acres for every one owned by a native. Some of the commission's distributions continue to be disputed to this day.

1852 As Western diseases depopulate the Islands, a labor shortage occurs in the sugarcane fields. For the next nine decades, a steady stream of foreign labor pours into Hawai'i, beginning with the Chinese. The Japanese begin arriving in 1868, followed by Filipinos, Koreans, Portuguese, and Puerto Ricans.

1872 Kamehameha V, the last descendent of the king who unified the Islands, dies without heirs. A power struggle ensues between the adherents of David Kalākaua and William Lunalilo.

1873 Lunalilo is elected Hawai'i's sixth king in January. The bachelor rules only 13 months before dying of tuberculosis.

1874 Kalākaua vies for the throne with the Dowager Queen Emma, the half-Caucasian widow of Kamehameha IV. Kalākaua is elected by the Hawai'i Legislature, against protests by supporters of Queen Emma. American and British marines are called in to restore order, and Kalākaua begins his reign as the "Merrie Monarch."

1875 The United States and Hawai'i sign a treaty of reciprocity, assuring Hawai'i a duty-free market for sugar in the United States.

1882 King Kalākaua builds 'Iolani Palace, an Italian Renaissance–style structure, on the site of the previous royal palace.

1887 The reciprocity treaty of 1875 is renewed, giving the United States exclusive use of Pearl Harbor as a coaling station. Coincidentally, successful importation of Japanese laborers begins in earnest (after a false start in 1868).

1891 King Kalākaua dies and is succeeded by his sister, Queen Lili'uokalani, the last Hawaiian monarch.

1893 After a brief two-year reign, Lili'uokalani is removed from the throne by American business interests led by Lorrin A. Thurston (grandson of the missionary and newspaper founder Asa Thurston). Lili'uokalani is imprisoned in 'Iolani Palace for nearly eight months.

1894 The provisional government converts Hawai'i into a republic and proclaims Sanford Dole president.

1898 With the outbreak of the Spanish-American War, president William McKinley recognizes Hawai'i's strategic importance in the Pacific and moves to secure the Islands for the United States. On August 12, Hawai'i is officially annexed by a joint resolution of Congress.

1901 Sanford Dole is appointed first governor of the territory of Hawai'i. The first major tourist hotel, the Moana (now called the Sheraton Moana Surfrider), is built on Waikīkī Beach.

1903 James Dole (a cousin of Sanford Dole) produces nearly 2,000 cases of pineapple, marking the beginning of Hawai'i's pineapple industry. Pineapple eventually surpasses sugarcane as Hawai'i's number-one crop.

1907 Fort Shafter Base, headquarters for the U.S. Army, becomes the first permanent military post in the Islands.

1908 Dredging of the channel at Pearl Harbor begins.

1919 Pearl Harbor is formally dedicated by the U.S. Navy. Representing the Territory of Hawai'i in the U.S. House of Representatives, Prince Jonah Kūhiō Kalaniana'ole, the adopted son of Kapi'olani, the wife of Kalākaua, and with his brother one of the designated heirs to the throne of the childless Lili'uokalani, introduces the first bill proposing statehood for Hawai'i.

1927 Army lieutenants Lester Maitland and Albert Hegenberger make the first successful nonstop flight from the mainland to the Islands. Hawai'i begins to increase efforts to promote tourism, the industry that eventually dominates development of the Islands. The Matson Navigation Company builds the Royal Hawaiian Hotel as a destination for its cruise ships.

1929 Hawai'i's commercial interisland air service begins.

1936 Pan American World Airways introduces regular commercial passenger flights to Hawai'i from the mainland.

1941 At Pearl Harbor the U.S. Pacific Fleet is bombed by the Japanese, forcing U.S. entry into World War II. Nearly 4,000 men are killed in the surprise attack.

1942 James Jones, with thousands of others, trains at Schofield Barracks on Oʻahu. He later writes about his experience in *From Here to Eternity*.

1959 Congress passes legislation granting Hawaiʻi statehood. In special elections the new state sends to the U.S. House of Representatives its first American of Japanese ancestry, Daniel Inouye, and to the U.S. Senate its first American of Chinese ancestry, Hiram Fong. Later in the year, the first Boeing 707 jets make the flight from San Francisco in a record five hours. By year's end 243,216 tourists visit Hawaiʻi, and tourism becomes Hawaiʻi's major industry.

1986 Hawaiʻi elects its first native Hawaiian governor, John Waiheʻe.

1992 Hurricane ʻIniki, the most devastating hurricane to hit Hawaiʻi, tears through Kauaʻi on September 11. The island's people, infrastructure, gardens, and tourism industry have happily all since recovered.

1993 After native Hawaiians commemorate the 100th anniversary of the overthrow of Queen Liliʻuokalani with a call for sovereignty, Congress issues an apology to the Hawaiian people for the annexation of the Islands.

1997 After 34 years of planning, construction, and endless litigation, Oahu's H-3 "Trans-Koolau" freeway linking Pearl Harbor to the Windward side of Oʻahu finally opens. Opposition to the highway centered on the route through the Hālawa and Haiku valleys, areas of historical and religious significance to native Hawaiians. The price tag for this scenic roadway with a million-dollar view? $1.3 billion in state and federal tax dollars.

1998 The U.S.S. *Missouri* comes to her final resting place in Pearl Harbor. The battleship, on whose decks the Japanese signed their surrender agreement in World War II, is now a floating museum, permanently docked at Ford Island.

2000 Kilauea Volcano on the Big Island of Hawaiʻi greets the new year with a show of lava, making this the 18th year of its current eruptive phase and the longest phase of such activity in recorded volcanic history.

Hawaiian Islands

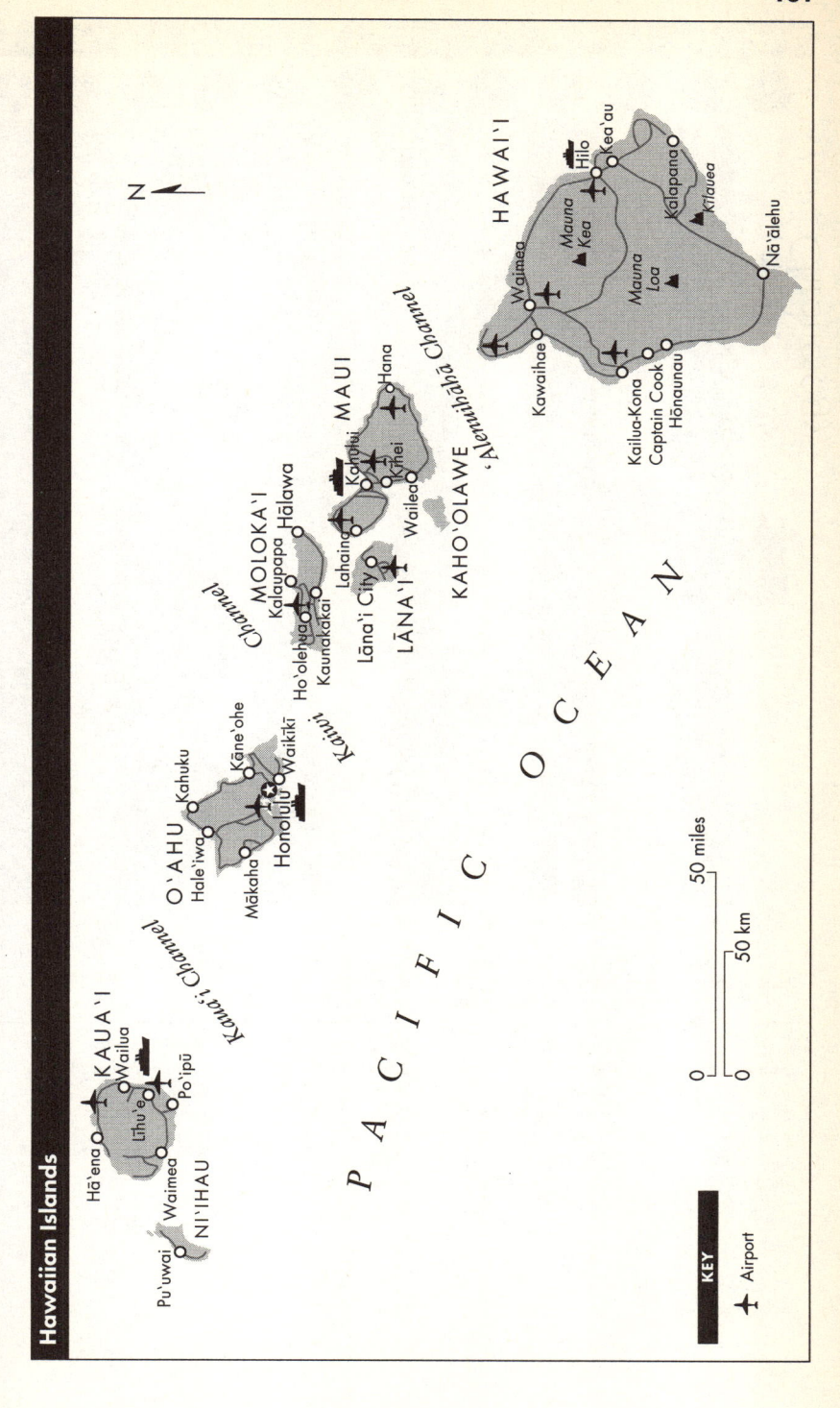

131

World Time Zones

Numbers below vertical bands relate each zone to Greenwich Mean Time (0 hrs.).
Local times frequently differ from these general indications,
as indicated by light-face numbers on map.

Algiers, **29**
Anchorage, **3**
Athens, **41**
Auckland, **1**
Baghdad, **46**
Bangkok, **50**
Beijing, **54**

Berlin, **34**
Bogotá, **19**
Budapest, **37**
Buenos Aires, **24**
Caracas, **22**
Chicago, **9**
Copenhagen, **33**
Dallas, **10**

Delhi, **48**
Denver, **8**
Dublin, **26**
Edmonton, **7**
Hong Kong, **56**
Honolulu, **2**
Istanbul, **40**
Jakarta, **53**

Jerusalem, **42**
Johannesburg, **44**
Lima, **20**
Lisbon, **28**
London (Greenwich), **27**
Los Angeles, **6**
Madrid, **38**
Manila, **57**

133

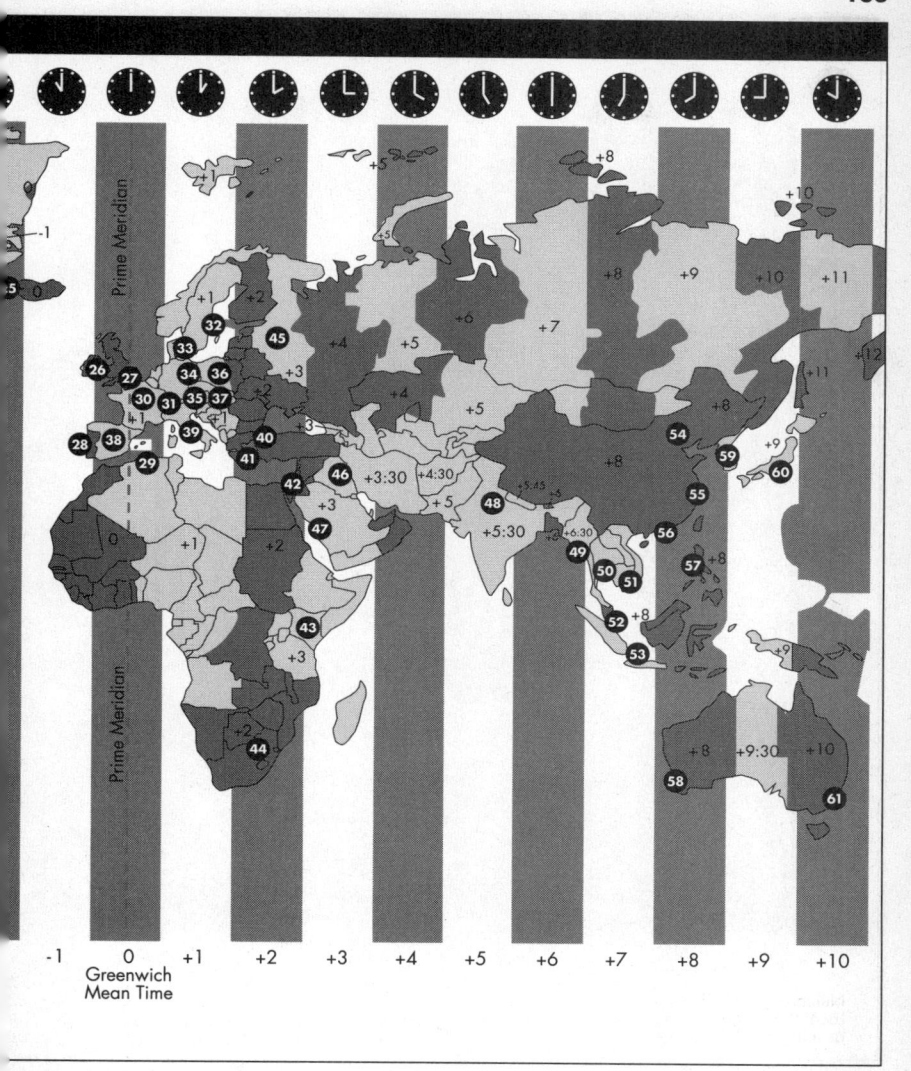

Mecca, **47**
Mexico City, **12**
Miami, **18**
Montréal, **15**
Moscow, **45**
Nairobi, **43**
New Orleans, **11**
New York City, **16**

Ottawa, **14**
Paris, **30**
Perth, **58**
Reykjavík, **25**
Rio de Janeiro, **23**
Rome, **39**
Saigon (Ho Chi Minh City), **51**

San Francisco, **5**
Santiago, **21**
Seoul, **59**
Shanghai, **55**
Singapore, **52**
Stockholm, **32**
Sydney, **61**
Tokyo, **60**

Toronto, **13**
Vancouver, **4**
Vienna, **35**
Warsaw, **36**
Washington, D.C., **17**
Yangon, **49**
Zürich, **31**

Maui

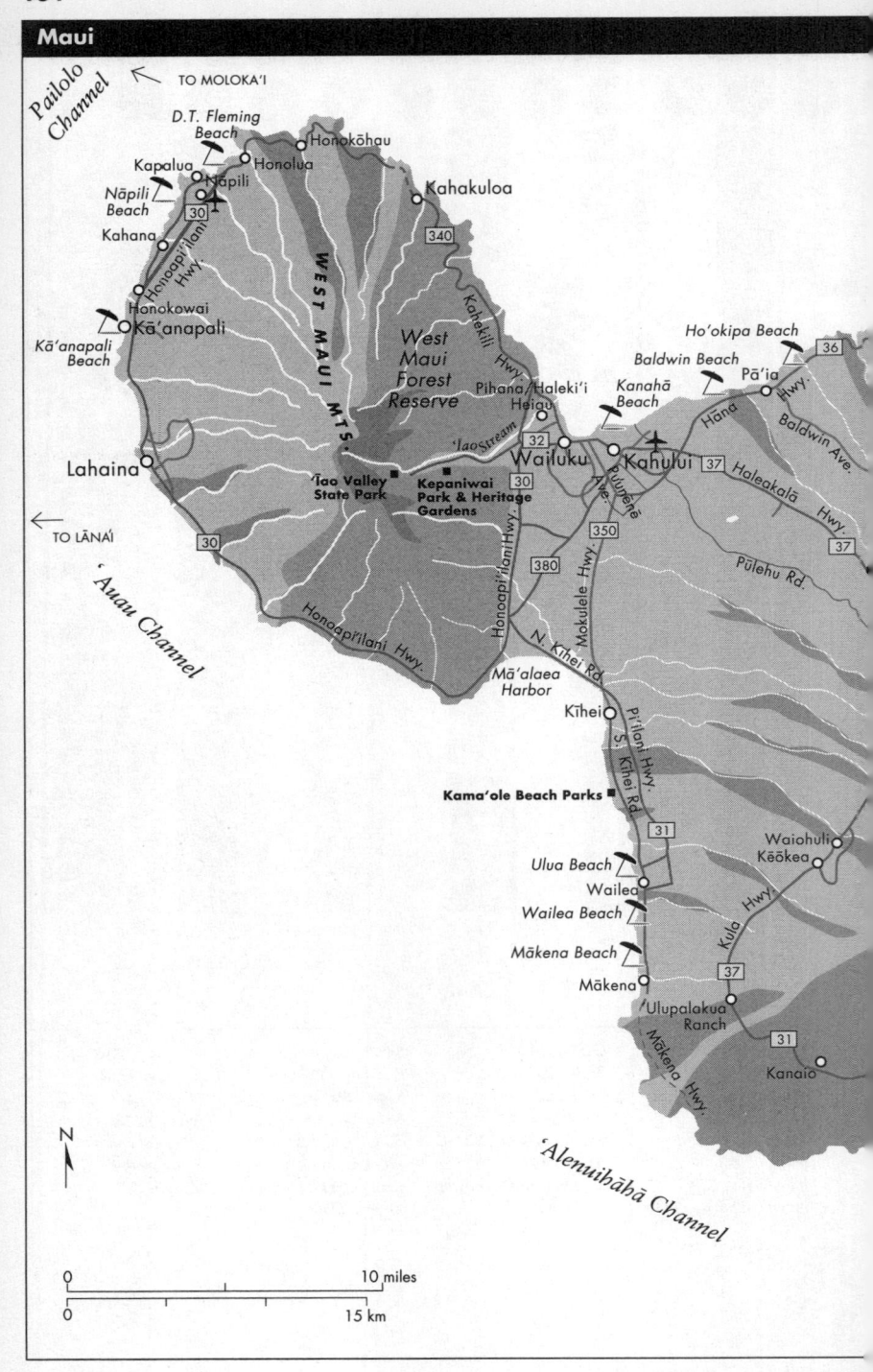

135

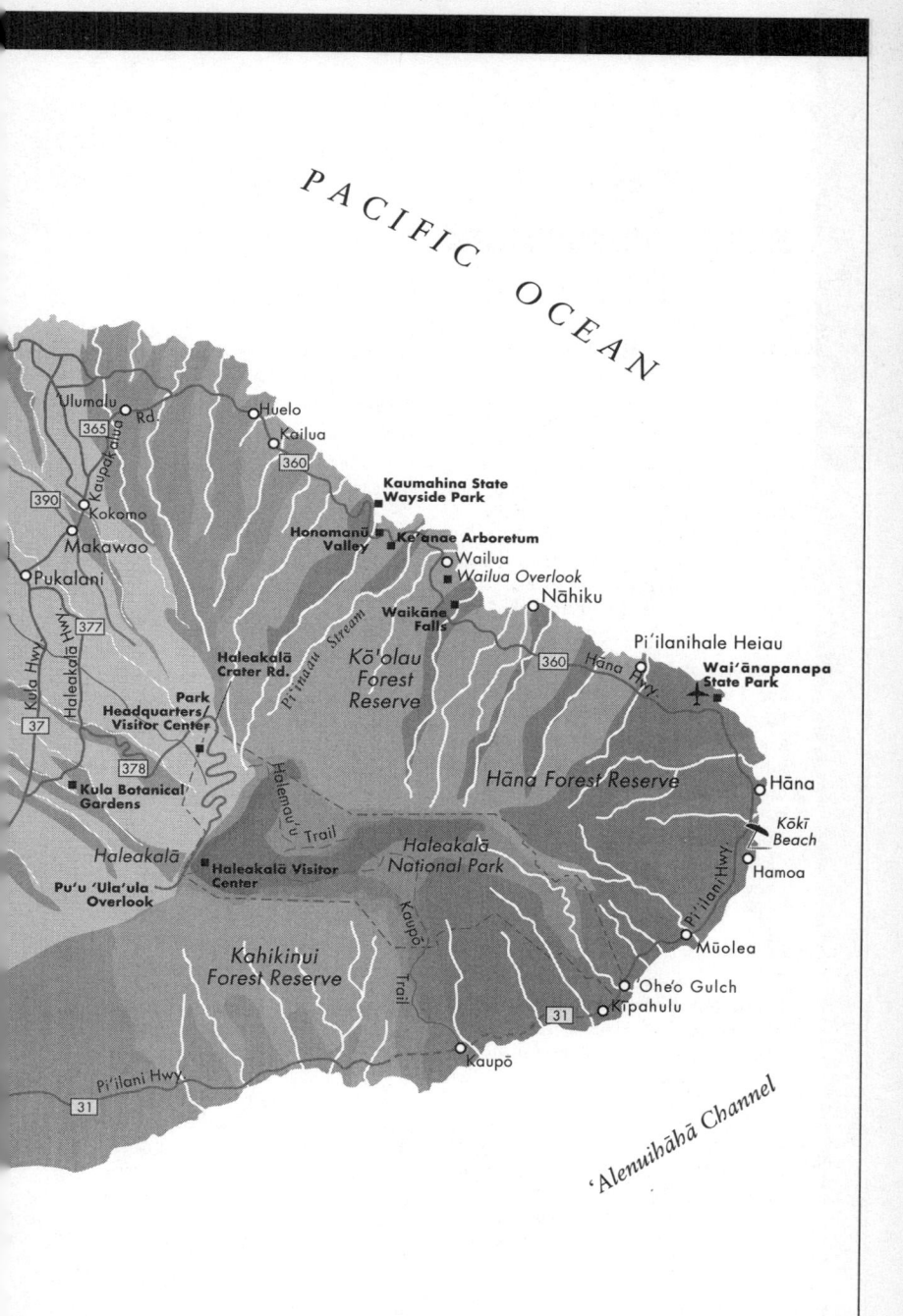

ESSENTIAL INFORMATION

AIR TRAVEL

Many of the major airline carriers serving Honolulu now fly direct to Maui, allowing you to bypass connecting flights out of Honolulu. From the mainland United States, American Airlines flies into Kahului, with one stop in Honolulu, from Dallas and Chicago and nonstop from Los Angeles; Delta has through service to Maui daily from Salt Lake City, Atlanta, and Los Angeles and one nonstop daily from Los Angeles; United flies nonstop to Kahului from Los Angeles and San Francisco; and Hawaiian Airlines has direct flights to Kahului from the U.S. West Coast.

Continental, Hawaiian, Northwest, and TWA all fly from the mainland to Honolulu, where Maui-bound passengers can connect with a 40-minute interisland flight. Honolulu–Kahului is one of the most heavily traveled air routes in the nation. Flights generally run about $50 one-way between Honolulu and Maui and are available from Hawaiian Airlines, Aloha Airlines, and Island Air.

BOOKING

When you book **look for nonstop flights** and **remember that "direct" flights stop at least once.** Try to avoid connecting flights, which require a change of plane.

CARRIERS

➤ MAJOR AIRLINES: **American** (☎ 800/433-7300). **Continental** (☎ 800/525-0280). **Delta** (☎ 800/221-1212). **Northwest** (☎ 800/225-2525). **TWA** (☎ 800/221-2000). **United** (☎ 800/241-6522).

➤ SMALLER AIRLINES: **Aloha Airlines** (☎ 808/244-9071; 800/367-5250 from the U.S. mainland). **Island Air** (☎ 800/652-6541). **Hawaiian Airlines** (☎ 808/871-6132, 800/367-5320, or 800/882-8811).

➤ DIRECT FLIGHTS FROM THE U.K.: **Air New Zealand** (☎ 0181/741-2299). **American** (☎ 0345/789-789). **Delta** (☎ 0800/414-767). **United** (☎ 0800/888-555). **Trailfinders** (✉ 42-50 Earls Court Rd., Kensington, London, W8 6FT, ☎ 020/7937-5400) can arrange bargain flights.

➤ WITHIN HAWAI'I: **Aloha Airlines** (☎ 800/367-5250), **Hawaiian Airlines** (☎ 800/367-5320), **Island Air** (☎ 800/323-3345), **Trans Air** (☎ 800/634-2094). **Pacific Wings** (☎ 888/575-4546).

CHECK-IN & BOARDING

Plan to **arrive at the airport 45 to 60 minutes before departure for interisland flights, 60 to 90 minutes for domestic flights, and at least 2 hours prior to departure for travel to international destinations.** Although the neighbor island airports are smaller and more casual than Honolulu International, during peak times they can also be quite busy. Prior to check-in, all luggage being taken out of Hawai'i must pass agricultural inspection. Fruit, plants, and processed foods that have been labeled and packed for export (including pineapples, papaya, coconuts, flowers, and macadamia nuts) are permitted. Fresh fruit and other agricultural items, including seed leis, are not, and will be confiscated.

Assuming that not everyone with a ticket will show up, airlines routinely overbook planes. When everyone does, airlines ask for volunteers to give up their seats. In return, these volunteers usually get a certificate for a free flight and are rebooked on the next flight out. If there are not enough volunteers, the airline must choose who will be denied boarding. The first to get bumped are passengers who checked in late and those flying on discounted tickets, so **get to the gate and check in as early as possible.**

Always **bring a government-issued photo I.D. to the airport.** You may be asked to show it before you are allowed to check in.

CUTTING COSTS

The least expensive airfares to Hawai'i must usually be purchased in advance and are nonrefundable. It's smart to **call a number of airlines, and when you are quoted a good price, book it on the spot.** The same fare may not be available the next day. Always **check different routings** and look into using different airports. Travel agents, especially low-fare specialists (☞ Discounts & Deals, *below*), are helpful.

Consolidators are another good source. They buy tickets for international flights at reduced rates from the airlines, then sell them at prices that beat the best fare available directly from the airlines. Sometimes you can even get your money back if you need to return the ticket. Carefully read the fine print detailing penalties for changes and cancellations, and **confirm your consolidator reservation with the airline.**

When you **fly as a courier,** you trade your checked-luggage space for a ticket deeply subsidized by a courier service. There are restrictions on when you can book and how long you can stay.

In Hawai'i, both Aloha Airlines and Hawaiian Airlines offer travelers multi-island air passes that allow unlimited interisland travel during a specific time period at a reduced rate.

➤ CONSOLIDATORS: **Cheap Tickets** (☎ 800/377–1000). **Discount Airline Ticket Service** (☎ 800/576–1600). **Unitravel** (☎ 800/325–2222). **Up & Away Travel** (☎ 212/889–2345). **World Travel Network** (☎ 800/409–6753).

➤ DISCOUNT PASSES: **Aloha Airlines** (☎ 800/367–5250). **Hawaiian Airlines** (☎ 800/367–5320).

FLYING TIMES

Flying time is about 10 hours from New York, 8 hours from Chicago, and 5 hours from Los Angeles.

HOW TO COMPLAIN

If your baggage goes astray or your flight goes awry, complain right away.

Most carriers require that you **file a claim immediately.**

➤ AIRLINE COMPLAINTS: U.S. Department of Transportation **Aviation Consumer Protection Division** (✉ C-75, Room 4107, Washington, DC 20590, ☎ 202/366–2220, airconsumer@ost.dot.gov, www.dot.gov/airconsumer). Federal Aviation Administration Consumer Hotline (☎ 800/322–7873).

AIRPORTS

Hawai'i's major airport is **Honolulu International,** on O'ahu, 20 minutes (9 mi) west of Waikīkī. To travel interisland from Honolulu, visitors depart from either the interisland terminal or the commuter-airline terminal. A free bus service, the Wiki Wiki Shuttle, operates between terminals.

Maui has two major airports: **Kahului Airport,** in the island's central town of Kahului, and **Kapalua–West Maui Airport.** The tiny town of **Hāna** in East Maui also has an airstrip, but it is only serviced by one commuter airline.

Kahului Airport is efficient and easy to navigate. Its main disadvantage is its distance from the major resort destinations in West Maui. It will take you about an hour, with traffic in your favor, to get to a hotel in Kapalua or Kā'anapali but only 20 to 30 minutes to go to Kīhei or Wailea. However, Kahului is the only airport on Maui that has direct service from the mainland.

If you're staying in West Maui, you probably want to fly into the **Kapalua–West Maui Airport.** The only way to get to the Kapalua–West Maui Airport is on an interisland flight from Honolulu, since the short runway accommodates only small planes. The little airport is set in the midst of a pineapple field with a terrific view of the ocean far below. Three rental-car companies have courtesy phones inside the terminal. Shuttles also run between the airport and the Kā'anapali and Kapalua resorts.

Hāna Airport isn't much more than a landing strip. Only commuter Aloha Island Air flies here, landing twice a day from Honolulu (via Moloka'i and Kahului) and departing 10 minutes later. The morning flight originates in Princeville, Kaua'i. If you are staying at the Hotel Hāna-Maui, your flight will be met, and if you reserved a rental car, the agent will usually know your arrival time and meet you.

Lāna'i Airport is small and centrally located. it handles a limited number of flights per day. Visitors to Lāna'i must first stop in O'ahu and change to an interisland flight.

➤ AIRPORT INFORMATION: O'ahu: **Honolulu International Airport** (☎ 808/836–6413 or 808/836–6411). Maui: **Kahului Airport** (☎ 808/872–3894 or 808/872–3830), **Kapalua–West Maui Airport** (☎ 808/669–0623), **Hāna Airport** (☎ 808/248–8205). Lāna'i: **Lāna'i Airport** (☎ 808/565–6757).

AIRPORT TRANSFERS

The best way to get from the airport to your destination—and to see the island itself—is in your own rental car. Most major car-rental companies have desks or courtesy phones at each airport (☞ Car Rental, *below*). They also can provide a map and directions to your hotel from the airport.

If you're staying at the Kā'anapali Beach Resort and fly into the Kapalua–West Maui Airport, you can take advantage of the resort's free shuttle and go back to the airport later to pick up your car. There is also the Trans Hawaiian Airporter Shuttle, which runs between Kahului Airport and the West Maui hotels daily 8–4. One-way fare for adults is $13. You should call 24 hours prior to departure.

Maui has more than two dozen taxi companies, and they make frequent passes through the airport. If you don't see a cab, you can call Yellow Cab of Maui or La Bella Taxi for islandwide service from the airport. Call Kīhei Taxi if you're staying in the Kīhei, Wailea, or Mākena areas. Charges from Kahului Airport to Kā'anapali run about $49; to Wailea, about $31; and to Lahaina, about $42.

➤ CONTACTS: **Trans Hawaiian Airporter Shuttle** (☎ 808/877–7308). **Yellow Cab of Maui** (☎ 808/877–7000). **La Bella Taxi** (☎ 808/242–8011). **Kīhei Taxi** (☎ 808/879–3000).

BIKE TRAVEL

Hawai'i's natural beauty, breathtaking coastal routes, and year-round fair weather make it attractive to explore by bike. However, on many roads, bicycle lanes are limited or nonexistent, and in the more populated areas, cyclists must contend with heavy traffic. On Maui, you can downhill cycle at Haleakalā crater, and on Lāna'i there's master off-road mountain biking. On these islands, you can rent bikes for solo cruising, join local cycling clubs for their weekly rides, or hit the road with outfitters for tours that go beyond the well-traveled paths.

➤ BIKE MAPS: **Mayor's Advisory Committee on Bicycling, Maui** (☎ 808/871–6886).

➤ BIKE RENTALS: **West Maui Cycles** (Maui, ☎ 808/661–9005).

BIKES IN FLIGHT

Most airlines accommodate bikes as luggage, provided they are dismantled and boxed. For bike boxes, often free at bike shops, you'll pay about $5 from airlines (at least $100 for bike bags). International travelers can sometimes substitute a bike for a piece of checked luggage at no charge; otherwise, the cost is about $100. Domestic and Canadian airlines charge $25–$50.

MOPEDS

You can rent mopeds on the West Side at Wheels R Us for $36 a day. On the South Shore, try Wheels USA at Rainbow Mall; rates are $25 for four hours or $31 until 4:30. Be especially careful navigating roads where there are no designated bicycle lanes. Note that helmets are optional on Maui, but eye protection is not.

➤ MOPED RENTALS: **Wheels R Us** (✉ 741 Waine'e St., Lahaina, ☎ 808/667–7751). **Wheels USA** (✉ 2439 S. Kīhei Rd., Kīhei, ☎ 808/875–1221).

BOAT TRAVEL

Approaching the Valley Isle on the deck of a ship is an unforgettable experience. You can book passage through American Hawai'i Cruises, which offers seven-day interisland cruises departing from Honolulu on the S.S. *Constitution* and the S.S. *Independence*. Or ask about the company's seven-day cruise-resort combination packages.

➤ BOAT INFORMATION: **American Hawai'i Cruises** (✉ 2 North Riverside Plaza, Chicago, IL 60606, ☎ 312/466–6000 or 800/765–7000).

FERRIES

There is daily ferry service between Lahaina, Maui, and Manele Bay, Lāna'i. The 9-mi crossing costs $50 round-trip and takes about 45 minutes or so, depending on ocean conditions (which can make this trip a rough one). Reservations are essential.

➤ FERRY INFORMATION: **Excursions/Lāna'i Passenger Ferry**, (☎ 808/661–3756).

BUS TRAVEL

Although Maui has no public transit system, a private company, Trans-Hawaiian Services, transports visitors around the West Maui and South Maui areas. One-way, round-trip, and all-day passes are available. Check with your hotel desk upon arrival for schedules.

➤ BUS INFORMATION: **Trans-Hawaiian Services** (☎ 808/877–0380 or 808/877–7308).

SHUTTLES

If you're staying in the right hotel or condo, there are a few shuttles that can get you around the area. The double-decker West Maui Shopping Express ferries passengers to and from Kā'anapali, Kapalua, Honokōwai, and Lahaina from 8 AM to 10 PM. The fare is $1 per person each way, and schedules are available at most hotels.

The Kā'anapali Trolley Shuttle runs within the resort between 9 AM and 11 PM and stops automatically at all hotels and at condos when requested. It's free. All Kā'anapali hotels have copies of schedules, or you can call the Kā'anapali Operation Association (☎ 808/661–7370).

The Wailea Shuttle and the Kapalua Shuttle run within their respective resorts and are free.

BUSINESS HOURS

Local business hours are generally 8 to 5 weekdays. Banks are generally open Monday through Thursday 8:30 to 3 and until 6 on Friday. Some banks have Saturday morning hours. ATM machines are plentiful and offer 24-hour money access.

Many self-serve gas stations now stay open around the clock, with full-service stations usually open from around 7 AM until 9 PM. U.S. post offices are open from 8:30 AM to 4:30 PM weekdays, 8:30 to noon on Saturdays.

MUSEUMS & SIGHTS

Most museums open their doors between 9 AM and 10 AM and stay open till 5 PM Tuesday through Saturday. Many museums operate with afternoon hours only on Sundays and close on Monday. Visitor attractions hours vary throughout the state, but most are open daily with the exception of major holidays like Christmas. **Check local newspapers upon arrival for attraction hours and schedules if visiting over holiday periods.** The local dailies carry a listing of "What's Open/What's Not" for those time periods.

SHOPS

Stores in resort areas can open as early as 8, with shopping-center opening hours varying from 9:30 to 10 on weekdays and Saturdays, a bit later on Sundays. Bigger malls stay open until 9 weekdays and Saturdays and close at 5 on Sundays. Boutiques in resort areas may stay open as late as 11.

CAMERAS & PHOTOGRAPHY

While you are traveling in Hawai'i, remember to **keep film out of direct sunlight and away from high-temperature areas** like the trunk of your car. Carry extra film and batteries for those jaunts to less populated island spots. **For underwater photography, "disposable" cameras can provide terrific photos** for those once-in-a-lifetime underwater experiences, at a fraction of the cost of purchasing or renting equipment.

Film developing is available on all islands. Many hotel-resort sundry stores offer the service, and larger department stores, like Long's Drugs, offer one-hour service for regular film developing and overnight service for panoramic film.

➤ PHOTO HELP: **Kodak Information Center** (☎ 800/242–2424). *Kodak Guide to Shooting Great Travel Pictures,* is available in bookstores or from Fodor's Travel Publications (☎ 800/533–6478; $16.50 plus $5.50 shipping).

EQUIPMENT PRECAUTIONS

Always **be prepared to turn on your camera or camcorder** to prove to security personnel that the device is real. Always **ask for hand inspection of film,** which becomes clouded after repeated exposure to airport X-ray machines, and **keep videotapes away from metal detectors.**

CAR RENTAL

You can rent anything from a $26-a-day econobox to a $1,100-a-day Ferrari. If you haven't booked a room-car package with your hotel, it's wise to **make reservations in advance,** especially if visiting the islands during peak seasons—summer and Christmas through Easter—or when coming for a major convention or sporting event.

Rates on Maui begin at $32 a day ($144 a week) for a compact car from one of the major companies. This does not include tax, insurance, and a $2-per-day road tax. You can get a better deal from one of the locally owned budget companies. You'll probably have to call for a shuttle from the airport, since few of these companies have rental desks there.

Budget, Dollar, and National have courtesy phones at the Kapalua–West Maui Airport; Hertz and Alamo are nearby. All of the above, plus Avis, have desks at or near Maui's major airport in Kahului. Roberts Tours offers car rentals through package tours. Quite a few locally owned companies rent cars on Maui, including Rent-A-Jeep, which will pick you up at Kahului Airport.

➤ MAJOR AGENCIES: **Alamo** (☎ 800/327–9633; 0181/759–6200 in the U.K.). **Avis** (☎ 800/331–1212; 800/879–2847 in Canada; 02/9353–9000 in Australia; 09/525–1982 in New Zealand). **Budget** (☎ 800/527–0700; 800/268–8900 in Canada; 0144/227–6266 in the U.K.). **Dollar** (☎ 800/800–4000; 0181/897–0811 in the U.K., where it is known as Eurodollar; 02/9223–1444 in Australia). **Hertz** (☎ 800/654–3131; 800/263–0600 in Canada; 0181/897–2072 in the U.K.; 02/9669–2444 in Australia; 03/358–6777 in New Zealand). **National InterRent** (☎ 800/227–7368; 0345/222525 in the U.K., where it is known as Europcar InterRent).

CUTTING COSTS

For a better rental deal, **check out local and national promotions as well as discounts offered through frequent-flyer programs, automobile clubs, or business or military affiliations.** Many rental companies in Hawai'i also offer customers coupons for discounts at various attractions that could save you money later on in your trip. To get the best deal, **book through a travel agent who will shop around.** Also **price local car-rental companies,** although the service and maintenance may not be as good as those of a major player. Remember to ask about required deposits, cancellation penalties, and drop-off charges if you're planning to pick up the car in one city and leave it in another. If you're traveling during a holiday period, also make sure that a confirmed reservation guarantees you a car.

Do **look into wholesalers,** companies that do not own fleets but rent in bulk from those that do and often offer better rates than traditional car-rental operations.

➤ LOCAL AGENCIES: **Roberts Tours** (☎ 808/523–9323). **Rent-A-Jeep** (☎ 808/877–6626). **Thrifty Car Rental** (☎ 808/831–2277).

➤ WHOLESALERS: **Auto Europe** (☎ 207/842–2000 or 800/223–5555, FAX 800–235–6321, www.autoeurope.com). **Kemwel Holiday Autos** (☎ 800/678–0678, FAX 914/825–3160, www.kemwel.com).

INSURANCE

When driving a rented car you are generally responsible for any damage to or loss of the vehicle as well as for any property damage or personal injury that you may cause. Before you rent see what coverage your personal auto-insurance policy and credit cards already provide.

For about $15 to $20 per day, rental companies sell protection, known as a collision- or loss-damage waiver (CDW or LDW), that eliminates your liability for damage to the car. In most states you don't need a CDW if you have personal auto insurance or other liability insurance. However, **make sure you have enough coverage to pay for the car.** If you do not have auto insurance or an umbrella policy that covers damage to third parties, purchasing liability insurance and a CDW or LDW is highly recommended.

REQUIREMENTS & RESTRICTIONS

In Hawai'i you must be 25 years of age to rent a car and have a valid driver's license and a major credit card. You'll pay extra for child seats (about $3 per day), which are compulsory for children under five, and for additional drivers (about $2 per day). Non-U.S. residents will need a reservation voucher, a passport, a driver's license, and a travel policy that covers each driver, when picking up a car.

In Hawai'i your unexpired mainland driver's license is valid for up to 90 days. If you plan to stay in the Islands for extended periods, apply for a Hawai'i driver's license ($18) at the State Department of Motor Vehicles office in Honolulu. You'll also have to take a $2 written exam. For drivers from foreign destinations, most car rental companies will accept a foreign driver's license printed in English. An international driver's license is readily accepted.

SURCHARGES

Before you pick up a car in one city and leave it in another, **ask about drop-off charges or one-way service fees,** which can be substantial. Note, too, that some rental agencies charge extra if you return the car before the time specified in your contract. To avoid a hefty refueling fee, **fill the tank just before you turn in the car,** but be aware that gas stations near the rental outlet may overcharge.

CAR TRAVEL

Most of the roads on Maui have two lanes. If you're going to attempt the partially paved, patched, and bumpy road between Hāna and 'Ulupalakua, you'll be better off with a four-wheel-drive vehicle, but be forewarned: rental-car companies prohibit travel on roads they've determined might damage the car, so if you break down, you're on your own for repairs. There are two other difficult roads on Maui: One is Highway 36, or the Hāna Highway, which runs 56 mi between Kahului and Hāna and includes more twists and turns than a person can count. The other is an 8-mi scenic stretch of one-lane highway between Kapalua and Wailuku on the north side of the West Maui mountains.

ROAD SERVICE

For emergency road service, AAA members may call ☎ 800/222–4357. A Honolulu-based dispatcher will send a tow truck, but you will need to tell the driver where to take your car. Don't forget to carry your membership card with you.

GASOLINE

Regardless of today's fluctuating gas prices, you can pretty much count on having to pay about 20% more at the pump for gasoline in the islands, self-serve or not, than on the U.S. mainland.

ROAD CONDITIONS

It's difficult to get lost in most of Hawai'i. Roads and streets, although they may challenge the visitor's tongue, are well marked. **Keep an eye open for the Hawai'i Visitors and Convention Bureau's red-caped warrior signs** that mark major visitor attractions and scenic spots. Ask for a map at the car-rental counter. Free visitor publications containing good-quality road maps can be found on all islands, too.

Maui has its share of impenetrable areas, although four-wheel-drive vehicles rarely run into problems on the island. Saddle roads run between the east and west landmasses composing Maui. Other highways follow the western coasts of East and West Maui. Although Lāna'i has fewer roadways, car rental is still worthwhile and will allow plenty of interesting sightseeing. **Opt for a four-wheel-drive vehicle** if dirt-road exploration holds any appeal.

RULES OF THE ROAD

Be sure to **buckle up.** Hawai'i has a strictly enforced seat-belt law for front-seat passengers. Children under 4 must be in a car seat (available from car-rental agencies). Children 18 and under, riding in the backseat, are also required by state law to use seat belts. The highway speed limit is usually 55 mph. In-town traffic moves from 25 to 40 mph. Jaywalking is very common, so be watchful for pedestrians, especially in congested areas. Unauthorized use of a parking space reserved for persons with disabilities can net you a $150 fine.

Asking for directions will almost always produce a helpful explanation from the locals, but you should be prepared for an island term or two. Instead of using compass directions, remember that Hawai'i residents refer to places as being either *mauka* (toward the mountains) or *makai* (toward the ocean) from one another. Other directions depend on your location; it all makes perfect sense once you get the lay of the land.

CHILDREN IN HAWAI'I

Its sunny beaches and many family-oriented cultural sites, activities, and attractions make the islands a very *keiki-* (child-) friendly place. Parents should **use caution on beaches and during water sports.** Even waters that appear calm can harbor powerful rip currents. And remember that the sun's rays are in operation full-force year-round here. Sunblock is essential. If you're renting a car, don't forget to **arrange for a car seat** when you reserve.

Most major resort chains in Hawai'i offer children's activity programs for kids ages 5–12. These kid clubs offer kids opportunities to learn about local culture, make friends with children from around the world, and to experience age-appropriate activities while giving moms and dads a "time-out." Upon arrival, **check out the daily local newspapers for children's events.**

FLYING

If your children are two or older, **ask about children's airfares.** As a general rule, infants under two not occupying a seat fly at greatly reduced fares or even for free. Experts agree that it's a good idea to use safety seats aloft for children weighing less than 40 pounds. Airlines set their own policies: U.S. carriers usually require that the child be ticketed, even if he or she is young enough to ride free, since the seats must be strapped into regular seats. Do **check your airline's policy about using safety seats during takeoff and landing.** And since safety seats are not allowed just everywhere in the plane, get your seat assignments early.

When reserving, **request children's meals or a freestanding bassinet** if you need them. But note that bulkhead seats, where you must sit to use the bassinet, may lack an overhead bin or storage space on the floor.

LODGING

Families cannot go wrong choosing resort locations that are part of larger hotel chains like Hilton, Sheraton, and Outrigger. Many of these resorts are located on the best beaches, have an array of activities created for kids, and are centrally located for visits to popular attractions. Many condominium resorts now also offer children's activities and amenities during holiday periods. Bed-and-breakfast lodgings give families some unique options, from Upcountry ranchland locations to private beachfront estates. Note that most hotels allow children under a certain age to stay in their parents' room at no extra charge, but others charge for them as extra adults. Be sure to **find out the cutoff age for children's discounts. Also check for special seasonal programs,** like "kids eat free" promotions.

➤ BEST CHOICES: **Aston Hotels** (☎ 800/922–5533, www.aston-hotels.com). **Four Seasons Resorts** (☎ 800/819–5053, www.fshr.com). **Hilton Hawaii** (☎ 800/445–8667, www.hilton.com/hawaii). **Hyatt Hawaii** (☎ 800/554–9288, www.hyatt.com). **Lanai Resorts** (☎ 800/321–4666, www.lanai-resorts.com). **Moloka'i Ranch** ☎ (800/254–8871, www.molokai-ranch.com). **Outrigger Hotels** (☎ 800/922–5533, www.outrigger.com). **Sheraton Resorts** (☎ 800/325–3535, www.sheratonhawaii.com).

SIGHTS & ATTRACTIONS

Top picks for children run the gamut from the natural attractions that kids can enjoy for free to some fairly expensive amusements. On Maui, kid favorites include the Sugar Cane Train in Kā'anapali, snorkeling at Molokini Island, watching the sunrise atop Haleakalā crater, driving the Road to Hāna for a dip in one of the Seven Sacred Pools, or whale-watching after a visit to the Maui Ocean Center. Lāna'i is a great island for adventurous kids. Four-wheel-drive off-road adventure tours take families to destinations like Shipwreck Beach and Manele Bay, where the dolphins sometimes come to play. Places that are especially appealing to children are indicated by a rubber-duckie icon in the margin.

COMPUTERS ON THE ROAD

Since Hawai'i is isolated in the middle of the Pacific Ocean, staying connected electronically to the world has always been a priority. New hotels and resorts, or those who have recently renovated in the islands, now offer in-room dataports. Many hotels that cater to the business traveler also have business centers with full computer setups that allow even the leisure traveler to check e-mail while away from home. **Check out the islands' new crop of Internet cafés.**

CONSUMER PROTECTION

Whenever shopping or buying travel services in Hawai'i, **pay with a major credit card** so you can cancel payment or get reimbursed if there's a problem. If you're doing business with a particular company for the first time, **contact your local Better Business Bureau and the attorney general's offices** in your own state and the company's home state as well. Have any complaints been filed? Finally, if you're buying a package or tour, always **consider travel insurance** that includes default coverage (☞ Insurance, *below*).

➤ BBBs: **Council of Better Business Bureaus** (✉ 4200 Wilson Blvd., Suite 800, Arlington, VA 22203, ☎ 703/276–0100, FAX 703/525–8277, www.bbb.org).

CRUISE TRAVEL

When Pan Am's amphibious *Hawai'i Clipper* touched down on Pearl Harbor's waters in 1936, it marked the beginning of the end of regular passenger-ship travel to the Islands. From that point on, the predominant means of transporting visitors would be by air, not by sea. Today, however, cruising to Hawai'i still holds a special appeal for those with the time and money to spare, and with a bit of research you can arrange passage aboard the luxury liners that call on Honolulu.

Cruises within the islands are available on the 1,021-passenger ship the S.S. *Independence,* under the direction of American Hawai'i Cruises. The liner's parent company, American Classic Voyages, has added a second vessel, under its new United States Lines brand, the 1,212-passenger M.S. *Patriot*. At press time, the ship was expected to begin its inaugural cruise December 9, 2000. Two additional cruise vessels are scheduled to be added to Island waters in 2002 and 2003. Seven-day cruises will now originate from both Honolulu and Maui, for visits to both these islands as well as ports of call on the Big Island and Kaua'i. To get the best deal on a cruise, **consult a cruise-only travel agency.**

➤ CRUISE LINES: For details on cruises that pass through Honolulu: **American Hawai'i Cruises** (☎ 800/765–7000). **Cunard** (☎ 800/221–4770). **Holland America** (☎ 800/426–0327). **Princess** (☎ 800/421–0522). **Royal Caribbean Cruise Line** (☎ 800/327–6700). **Royal Cruise Line** (☎ 415/956–7200).

CUSTOMS & DUTIES

When shopping, **keep receipts** for all purchases. Upon reentering the country, **be ready to show customs officials what you've bought.** If you feel a duty is incorrect or object to the way your clearance was handled, note the inspector's badge number and ask to see a supervisor. If the problem isn't resolved, write to the appropriate authorities, beginning with the port director at your point of entry.

IN AUSTRALIA

Australian residents who are 18 or older may bring home $A400 worth of souvenirs and gifts (including jewelry), 250 cigarettes or 250 grams of tobacco, and 1,125 ml of alcohol (including wine, beer, and spirits). Residents under 18 may bring back $A200 worth of goods. Prohibited items include meat products. Seeds, plants, and fruits need to be declared upon arrival.

➤ INFORMATION: **Australian Customs Service** (Regional Director, ✉ Box 8, Sydney, NSW 2001, ☎ 02/9213–2000, FAX 02/9213–4000).

IN CANADA

Canadian residents who have been out of Canada for at least 7 days may bring home C$500 worth of goods duty-free. If you've been away less than 7 days but more than 48 hours, the duty-free allowance drops to C$200; if your trip lasts 24–48 hours, the allowance is C$50. You may not pool allowances with family members. Goods claimed under the C$500 exemption may follow you by mail; those claimed under the lesser exemptions must accompany you. Alcohol and tobacco products may be included in the 7-day and 48-hour exemptions but not in the 24-hour exemption. If you meet the age requirements of the province or territory through which you reenter Canada, you may bring in, duty-free, 1.14 liters (40 imperial ounces) of wine or liquor *or* 24 12-ounce cans or bottles of beer or ale. If you are 16 or older you may bring in, duty-free, 200 cigarettes and 50 cigars. Check ahead of time with Revenue Canada or the Department of Agriculture for policies regarding meat products, seeds, plants, and fruits.

You may send an unlimited number of gifts worth up to C$60 each duty-free to Canada. Label the package UNSOLICITED GIFT—VALUE UNDER $60. Alcohol and tobacco are excluded.

➤ INFORMATION: **Revenue Canada** (✉ 2265 St. Laurent Blvd. S, Ottawa, Ontario K1G 4K3, ☎ 613/993–0534; 800/461–9999 in Canada, FAX 613/957–8911, www.ccra-adrc.gc.ca).

IN HAWAI'I

Plants and plant products are subject to regulation by the Department of Agriculture, both on entering and leaving Hawai'i. Pineapples and coconuts with the packer's agricultural inspection stamp pass freely; papayas must be treated, inspected, and stamped. All other fruits are banned for export to the U.S. mainland. Flowers pass except for gardenia, rose leaves, jade vine, and mauna loa. Also banned are insects, snails, soil, cotton, cacti, sugarcane, and all berry plants.

You should **leave dogs and other pets at home.** A strict 30-day quarantine is imposed to keep out rabies, which is nonexistent in Hawai'i.

IN NEW ZEALAND

Homeward-bound residents 17 or older may bring back $700 worth of souvenirs and gifts. Your duty-free allowance also includes 4.5 liters of wine or beer; one 1,125-ml bottle of spirits; and either 200 cigarettes, 250 grams of tobacco, 50 cigars, or a combination of the three up to 250 grams. Prohibited items include meat products, seeds, plants, and fruits.

➤ INFORMATION: **New Zealand Customs** (Custom House, ✉ 50 Anzac Ave., Box 29, Auckland, New Zealand, ☎ 09/359–6655, FAX 09/359–6732).

IN THE U.K.

From countries outside the EU, including the United States, you may bring home, duty-free, 200 cigarettes or 50 cigars; 1 liter of spirits or 2 liters of fortified or sparkling wine or liqueurs; 2 liters of still table wine; 60 ml of perfume; 250 ml of toilet water; plus £136 worth of other goods, including gifts and souvenirs. If returning from outside the EU, prohibited items include meat products, seeds, plants, and fruits.

➤ INFORMATION: **HM Customs and Excise** (✉ Dorset House, Stamford St., Bromley, Kent BR1 1XX, ☎ 0171/202–4227).

IN THE U.S.

➤ INFORMATION: **U.S. Customs Service** (✉ 1300 Pennsylvania Ave. NW, Washington, DC 20229, www.customs.gov; inquiries, ☎ 202/354–

1000; complaints c/o ✉ Office of Regulations and Rulings; registration of equipment c/o ✉ Resource Management, ☎ 202/927–0540).

DISABILITIES & ACCESSIBILITY

The Society for the Advancement of Travel for the Handicapped has named Hawai'i the most accessible vacation spot for people with disabilities. Ramped visitor areas and specially equipped lodgings are relatively common in the Islands. The Hawa'i Center for Independent Living publishes the "Aloha Guide to Accessibility," listing addresses and telephone numbers for support-service organizations and rates the Islands' hotels, beaches, shopping and entertainment centers, and major visitor attractions. The guide costs $15 but is available in sections for $3–$5 per section. Part I (general information) is free. Vision-impaired travelers who use a guide dog no longer have to worry about quarantine restrictions. All you need to do is present documentation that the animal is a trained guide dog and has a current inoculation record for rabies.

➤ LOCAL RESOURCES: **Hawai'i Center for Independent Living** (✉ 414 Kauwili St., Suite 102, Honolulu 96817, ☎ 808/522–5400). For accessibility information on Neighbor Islands: **Disability and Communications Access Board** offices on Kaua'i (✉ 3060 'Eiwa St., Room 207, Līhu'e 96766, ☎ 808/274–3308), and Maui (✉ 54 High St., Wailuku 96793, ☎ 808/984–8219).

LODGING

Travelers with disabilities and people using wheelchairs will find it easy to get around Hawai'i's resorts and hotels. If choosing a smaller hotel or a condo or apartment rental, inquire about ground-floor accommodations and **always check to see if rooms will accommodate wheelchairs and if bathrooms are accessible.** Many hotels now offer special-needs rooms featuring larger living spaces and bathrooms equipped for guests who require additional assistance.

RESERVATIONS

When discussing accessibility with an operator or reservations agent, **ask hard questions.** Are there any stairs, inside *or* out? Are there grab bars next to the toilet *and* in the shower/tub? How wide is the doorway to the room? To the bathroom? For the most extensive facilities meeting the latest legal specifications, **opt for newer accommodations.**

SIGHTS & ATTRACTIONS

Many of Hawai'i's sights and attractions are accessible to travelers with disabilities. On Maui, **Accessibility Vans of Hawaii** can help travelers plan activities from snorkeling to whale-watching.

TRANSPORTATION

Paratransit Services (HandiVan) will take you to a specific destination—not on sightseeing outings—in vans with lifts and lock-downs. With a Handi-Van Pass, one-way trips cost $1.50. Passes are free and can be obtained from the Department of Transportation Services (⊙ weekdays 7:45–4:30); you'll need a doctor's written confirmation of your disability or a paratransit ID card. Handi-Cabs of the Pacific also operates ramp-equipped vans with lock-downs in Honolulu. Fares are $9 plus $2.25 per mile for curbside service. Reservations at least one day in advance are required by all companies, so do advance planning.

Those who prefer to do their own driving may rent hand-controlled cars from Avis (reserve 24 hrs ahead) and Hertz (24- to 72-hr notice required). Mainlanders can use the windshield card from their own state to park in spaces reserved for people with disabilities.

➤ CONTACTS: **Paratransit Services (HandiVan)** (☎ 808/456–5555). **Department of Transportation Services** (✉ 711 Kapi'olani Blvd., Honolulu 96819, ☎ 808/523–4083). **Handi-Cabs of the Pacific** (☎ 808/524–3866). **Avis** (☎ 800/331–1212.) **Hertz** (☎ 800/654–3131).

➤ COMPLAINTS: **Disability Rights Section** (✉ U.S. Department of Justice, Civil Rights Division, Box 66738, Washington, DC 20035-6738, ☎ 202/514–0301 or 800/514–0301; TTY 202/514–0301 or 800/514–0301, FAX 202/307–1198) for general complaints. **Aviation Consumer Protection Division** (☞ Air Travel, *above*) for airline-related problems. **Civil Rights Office**

(✉ U.S. Department of Transportation, Departmental Office of Civil Rights, S-30, 400 7th St. SW, Room 10215, Washington, DC 20590, ☎ 202/366–4648, FAX 202/366–9371) for problems with surface transportation.

TRAVEL AGENCIES

In the United States, the Americans with Disabilities Act requires that travel firms serve the needs of all travelers. Some agencies specialize in working with people with disabilities.

▶ TRAVELERS WITH MOBILITY PROBLEMS: **Access Adventures** (✉ 206 Chestnut Ridge Rd., Rochester, NY 14624, ☎ 716/889–9096, dltravel@prodigy.net), run by a former physical-rehabilitation counselor. **Accessible Vans of the Rockies** (✉ 2040 W. Hamilton Pl., Sheridan, CO 80110, ☎ 303/806–5047 or 888/837–0065, FAX 303/781–2329, www.access-able.com/avr/avrockies.htm). **Accessible Vans of Hawaii, Activity and Travel Agency** (✉ 296 Alamaha St., Suite C, Kahului, HI 96732, ☎ 808/871–7785 or 800/303–3750, FAX 808/871–7536, avavans@maui.net, www.accessible-vanshawaii.com). **CareVacations** (✉ 5-5110 50th Ave., Leduc, Alberta T9E 6V4, ☎ 780/986–6404 or 877/478–7827, FAX 780/986–8332, www.carevacations.com), for group tours and cruise vacations. **Flying Wheels Travel** (✉ 143 W. Bridge St., Box 382, Owatonna, MN 55060, ☎ 507/451–5005 or 800/535–6790, FAX 507/451–1685, thq@ll.net, www.flyingwheels.com).

▶ TRAVELERS WITH DEVELOPMENTAL DISABILITIES: **New Directions** (✉ 5276 Hollister Ave., Suite 207, Santa Barbara, CA 93111, ☎ 805/967–2841 or 888/967–2841, FAX 805/964–7344, newdirec@silcom.com, www.silcom.com/newdirec/). **Sprout** (✉ 893 Amsterdam Ave., New York, NY 10025, ☎ 212/222–9575 or 888/222–9575, FAX 212/222–9768, sprout@interport.net, www.gosprout.org).

DISCOUNTS & DEALS

Be a smart shopper and **compare all your options** before making decisions. A plane ticket bought with a promotional coupon from travel clubs, coupon books, and direct-mail offers may not be cheaper than the least expensive fare from a discount ticket agency.

DISCOUNT RESERVATIONS

To save money, **look into discount reservations services** with toll-free numbers, which use their buying power to get a better price on hotels, airline tickets, even car rentals. When booking a room, always **call the hotel's local toll-free number** (if one is available) rather than the central reservations number—you'll often get a better price. Always ask about special packages or corporate rates.

▶ AIRLINE TICKETS: ☎ 800/FLY-4-LESS. ☎ 800/FLY-ASAP.

▶ HOTEL ROOMS: **Players Express Vacations** (☎ 800/458–6161, www.playersexpress.com). **RMC Travel** (☎ 800/245–5738, www.rmcwebtravel.com). **Steigenberger Reservation Service** (☎ 800/223–5652, www.srs-worldhotels.com). **Turbotrip.com** (☎ 800/473–7829, www.turbotrip.com).

PACKAGE DEALS

Don't confuse packages and guided tours. When you buy a package, you travel on your own, just as though you had planned the trip yourself. Fly/drive packages, which combine airfare and car rental, are often a good deal.

ECOTOURISM

Hawai'i's connection to its environment is spiritual, cultural, and essential to its survival. You'll find a rainbow of natural attractions to explore, from the ribbon of beaches that surround its shorelines to the summits of its volcanoes, where lava shows after dark are spectacular. Maui offers travelers the sophistication of shoreline resorts at Kaanapali and Wailea, the exhilaration of a rain-forest hike in Hāna, and the cool Upcountry climes of Kula at the base of Haleakalā crater. Lāna'i, one of the least developed islands, offer adventures best experienced on foot and by four-wheel-drive vehicle, or even by mule. Eco-touring in Hawai'i gives visitors the opportunity to learn from local guides who are familiar with the *aina* (land) and Hawai'i's unique cultural heritage. Many of these tours take clients to locations less traveled, so it helps to be in good physical shape.

➤ LOCAL RESOURCES: **Hawai'i Ecotourism Association** (☎ 877/300–7058). **Alternative-Hawai'i** (www.Alternative-Hawaii.com) offers an ecotravel cyberguide.

EMERGENCIES

➤ EMERGENCY NUMBERS: **Police, fire, or ambulance**, ☎ 911. **Coast Guard Rescue Center**, ☎ 800/552–6458.

ETIQUETTE AND BEHAVIOR

In 2001, Hawai'i celebrates 42 years of statehood, so residents can be pretty sensitive to visitors who refer to their own hometowns "back in the States." In a destination as exotic as Hawai'i, this slip of the tongue is easy to make. But remember, when in Hawai'i, **refer to the contiguous 48 as "the mainland" and not as the United States.**

FOOD & DRINK

Dining out in Hawai'i can be a vacation all its own. The islands are home to a world of cuisines, and restaurants range from casual to gorgeously gourmet. A new emphasis on Hawai'i regional cuisine is a boon, giving you a chance to seek out the chefs and restaurants who put an emphasis on the islands unique and abundant harvest.

Price categories are as follows:

CATEGORY	COST*
$$$$	over $60
$$$	$40–$60
$$	$20–$40
$	under $20

*per person for a three-course meal, excluding drinks, service, and 4.17% sales tax

RESERVATIONS & DRESS

Go tropical when dressing up to dine out in Hawai'i. Aloha shirts and long pants for men and island-style dresses or casual resort wear are standard attire for evenings in most hotel restaurants and local eateries at dinner. For breakfast and lunch, T-shirts, shorts, and footwear are acceptable.

Reservations are always a good idea: we mention them only when they're essential or not accepted. Book as far ahead as you can, and reconfirm as soon as you arrive. We mention dress only when men are required to wear a jacket or a jacket and tie.

SPECIALTIES

Fish, fruit, and fresh island-grown products are at the heart of a cuisine that was born here, known as both Pacific Rim and Hawai'i regional cuisine. Expect to find an array of traditional world cuisines enhanced by island chefs to add the flavor of the tropics to the mix. Here, *pupu* are appetizers, and a "plate lunch" is standard midday fare which, be it fish or beef, is accompanied by two scoops of rice and a side of macaroni salad.

WINE, BEER & SPIRITS

Hawai'i has a new generation of microbreweries that can be found throughout Maui. Many restaurants also have on-site microbreweries. On Maui, check out the Tedeschi Vineyards; there you can tour a beautiful island estate and get a taste of that sweet pineapple wine. The drinking age in Hawai'i is 21 years of age, and a photo ID must be presented to purchase alcoholic beverages. Bars are open until 2 AM, and venues with a cabaret license can stay open until 4 AM. No matter what you might see in the local parks, drinking alcohol in public parks or on the beaches is illegal. It is also illegal to have open containers of alcohol in motor vehicles.

GAY & LESBIAN TRAVEL

➤ LOCAL RESOURCES: **Pacific Ocean Holidays** (✉ Box 88245, Honolulu 96830, ☎ 808/923–2400 or 800/735–6600, www.gayHawaii.com) not only arranges independent travel in the Islands, but publishes the *Pocket Guide to Hawai'i*, distributed free in the state at gay-operated venues and available for $5 by mail for one issue, $12 for a yearly subscription of three issues.

A few small hotels and some bed-and-breakfasts in Hawai'i are favored by gay and lesbian visitors. A computerized Gay Community listing compiled by **GLEA** (Gay & Lesbian Education Advocacy Foundation, ✉ Box 37083, Honolulu 96837, ☎ 808/532–9000)

is available by contacting them by phone or at the address listed above.

➤ GAY- & LESBIAN-FRIENDLY TRAVEL AGENCIES: **Different Roads Travel** (✉ 8383 Wilshire Blvd., Suite 902, Beverly Hills, CA 90211, ☎ 323/651–5557 or 800/429–8747, FAX 323/651–3678, leigh@west.tzell.com). **Kennedy Travel** (✉ 314 Jericho Turnpike, Floral Park, NY 11001, ☎ 516/352–4888 or 800/237–7433, FAX 516/354–8849, main@kennedytravel.com, www.kennedytravel.com). **Now Voyager** (✉ 4406 18th St., San Francisco, CA 94114, ☎ 415/626–1169 or 800/255–6951, FAX 415/626–8626, www.nowvoyager.com). **Skylink Travel and Tour** (✉ 1006 Mendocino Ave., Santa Rosa, CA 95401, ☎ 707/546–9888 or 800/225–5759, FAX 707/546–9891, skylinktvl@aol.com, www.skylinktravel.com), serving lesbian travelers.

HEALTH

Hawai'i is known as the Health State. The life expectancy here is 79 years, the longest in the nation. Balmy weather makes it easy to remain active year-round, and the low-stress aloha attitude certainly contributes to general well-being. When visiting the Islands, however, here are a few health issues to keep in mind.

The Hawaii State Department of Health recommends that, when hiking or spending time in the sun, **drink 4 ounces of water every 15 minutes to avoid dehydration.** Use sunblock, wear sunglasses, and protect your head with a visor or hat for shade. Visitors not acclimated to warm, humid weather should allow plenty of time for rest stops and liquid refueling. When visiting freshwater streams, be aware of the tropical disease leptospirosis. Symptoms include fever, headache, nausea, and red eyes. If left untreated it can cause liver and kidney damage, respiratory failure, internal bleeding, and even death. To avoid this, don't swim or wade in freshwater streams or ponds if you have open sores and don't drink from any freshwater steams and ponds you encounter.

In the islands, fog is a rare occurrence, but there can often be "vog." This is the haze that is airborne by gases released from the volcanos. These volcanic pollutants can play havoc with respiratory and other health conditions. If susceptible, plan indoor activities, drink plenty of warm fluids, and get emergency assistance if needed.

Doctors on Call serves West Maui. A walk-in clinic at Whalers Village, West Maui Health Care Center was created by two doctors in 1980 to treat visitors to West Maui. Kīhei Clinic Medical Services is in the central part of the Valley Isle and geared toward working with visitors in Kīhei and Wailea.

➤ INFORMATION: **Doctors on Call** (✉ Hyatt Regency Maui, Nāpili Tower, Suite 100, Kā'anapali, ☎ 808/667–7676).**West Maui Health Care Center** (✉ 2435 Kā'anapali Pkwy., Suite H-7, Kā'anapali, ☎ 808/667–9721; ☉ Daily 8 AM–10 PM). **Kīhei Clinic Medical Services** (✉ 2349 S. Kīhei Rd., Suite D, Kīhei, ☎ 808/879–1440).

➤ HOSPITALS: **Hāna Medical Center** (✉ Hāna Hwy., Hāna, ☎ 808/248–8294). **Kula Hospital** (✉ 204 Kula Hwy., Kula, ☎ 808/878–1221). **Maui Memorial Hospital** (✉ 221 Mahalani, Wailuku, ☎ 808/244–9056).

DIVERS' ALERT

Do not fly for 24 hours after scuba diving.

PESTS AND OTHER HAZARDS

The islands have their share of bugs who enjoy the tropical climate as much as people do. When spending time outdoors in hiking areas, **use a strong mosquito repellant and wear long-sleeve tops and long pants.** In very damp, wet places you may encounter centipedes. In the islands they usually come in two colors—brown and blue. Their sting can be powerful. If hiking or traveling in remote areas, always carry a first-aid kit and appropriate medications for sting reactions.

HOLIDAYS

Major national holidays include New Year's Day (Jan. 1); Martin Luther King, Jr., Day (3rd Mon. in Jan.); Presidents' Day (3rd Mon. in Feb.); Memorial Day (last Mon. in May); Independence Day (July 4); Labor Day

(1st Mon. in Sept.); Thanksgiving Day (4th Thurs. in Nov.); Christmas Eve and Christmas Day (Dec. 24 and 25); and New Year's Eve (Dec. 31). In addition, Hawai'i celebrates Prince Kuhio Day (March 26); King Kamehameha Day (June 11); and Admission Day (3rd Fri. in August). State, city, and county offices as well as many local companies are closed for business.

INSURANCE

The most useful travel-insurance plan is a comprehensive policy that includes coverage for trip cancellation and interruption, default, trip delay, and medical expenses (with a waiver for preexisting conditions).

Without insurance you will lose all or most of your money if you cancel your trip, regardless of the reason. Default insurance covers you if your tour operator, airline, or cruise line goes out of business. Trip-delay covers expenses that arise because of bad weather or mechanical delays. Study the fine print when comparing policies.

British and Australian citizens need extra medical coverage when traveling overseas. Always **buy travel policies directly from the insurance company**; if you buy them from a cruise line, airline, or tour operator that goes out of business you probably will not be covered for the agency or operator's default, a major risk. Before making any purchase, **review your existing health and home-owner's policies** to find what they cover away from home.

➤ TRAVEL INSURERS: In the U.S.: **Access America** (✉ 6600 W. Broad St., Richmond, VA 23230, ☏ 804/285–3300 or 800/284–8300, FAX 804/673–1583, www.previewtravel.com), Travel Guard International (✉ 1145 Clark St., Stevens Point, WI 54481, ☏ 715/345–0505 or 800/826–1300, FAX 800/955–8785, www.noelgroup.com). In Canada: **Voyager Insurance** (✉ 44 Peel Center Dr., Brampton, Ontario L6T 4M8, ☏ 905/791–8700; 800/668–4342 in Canada).

➤ INSURANCE INFORMATION: In the U.K.: **Association of British Insurers** (✉ 51–55 Gresham St., London EC2V 7HQ, ☏ 0171/600–3333, FAX 0171/ 696–8999, info@abi.org.uk, www.abi.org.uk). In Australia: **Insurance Council of Australia** (☏ 03/9614–1077, FAX 03/9614–7924).

LANGUAGE

Studying the Hawaiian language is not needed for a vacation in the islands since English is spoken here. For more about it, see Hawaiian Vocabulary at the end of the book. The history of Hawai'i includes waves of immigrants who have settled here over centuries, each bringing their English. If you listen closely, you'll know what is being said by the inflections and body language. For an informative and hilarious view of things Hawaiian, check out Jerry Hopkins's series of books titled, *Pidgin to the Max* and *Fax to the Max,* available at most local bookstores.

LEI GREETINGS

When you walk off a long flight nothing quite compares with a Hawaiian lei greeting. Though the tradition has created an expectation that everyone receives this floral garland when they step off the plane, the state of Hawai'i cannot greet each of its nearly 7 million annual visitors. Still, it's easy to **arrange for a lei ceremony for yourself or your companions before you arrive.** Contact one of the companies below if you are not part of a package that provides it.

➤ LEI GREETERS: **Greeters of Hawai'i** (✉ Box 29638, Honolulu 96820, ☏ 808/836–0161; 808/834–7667 for airport desk, FAX 800/736–5665); 48-hours' notice needed, $19.95 to $29.95 per person, add $10 for late notification. **Aloha Lei Greeters** (☏ 808/951–9990 or 800/367–5255 FAX 808/951–9992); $12 to $29 per person, one week's notice needed. **Kama'aina Ali'i, Flowers & Greeters** (✉ 3159-B Koapaka St., Honolulu, ☏ 808/836–3246 or 800/367–5183 FAX 808/836–1804); $13.50 for a greeting on Maui or Lāna'i.

LODGING

No matter what your budget, there is a place for you in Hawai'i. Large city-size resorts grace the islands' most scenic shores. Family-style condominiums offer spaciousness and many of the amenities of fine hotels, and it's possible to find many at reasonable prices. The islands offer visitors an opportunity to experience some of the world's most beautiful hotel locations, along with more intimate accommodations like bed-and-breakfasts. A number of hostel-style accommodations, ranches, and tent camps are good for those seeking an off-the-beaten path vacation.

The lodgings we list are the cream of the crop in each price category. We always list the facilities that are available, but we don't specify whether they cost extra. When pricing accommodations, always ask what's included.

CATEGORY	COST*
$$$$	over $200
$$$	$125–$200
$$	$75–$125
$	under $75

*All prices are for a standard double room, excluding 11.41% tax and service charges.

APARTMENT & VILLA RENTALS

If you want a home base that's roomy enough for a family and comes with cooking facilities, **consider a furnished rental.** These can save you money, especially if you're traveling with a group. Home-exchange directories sometimes list rentals as well as exchanges.

▶ INTERNATIONAL AGENTS: **Hideaways International** (✉ 767 Islington St., Portsmouth, NH 03801, ☎ 603/430–4433 or 800/843–4433, ᶠᴬˣ 603/430–4444 info@hideaways.com www.hideaways.com; membership $99). **Hometours International** (✉ Box 11503, Knoxville, TN 37939, ☎ 865/690–8484 or 800/367–4668, hometours@aol.com, www.thor.he.net/hometour/). **Vacation Home Rentals Worldwide** (✉ 235 Kensington Ave., Norwood, NJ 07648, ☎ 201/767–9393 or 800/633–3284, ᶠᴬˣ 201/767–5510, vhrww@juno.com, www.vhrww.com). **Villas and Apartments Abroad** (✉ 1270 Avenue of the Americas, 15th floor, New York, NY 10020, ☎ 212/897–5045 or 800/433–3020, ᶠᴬˣ 212/897–5039, vaa@altour.com, www.vaanyc.com).

B & B S

B&Bs have made heavy inroads into the Hawaiian market in the past several years, and offer visitors an accommodations alternative that is unique, charming, intimate, and spotlights Hawai'i's diverse cultural melting pot.

Before you choose this alternative, however, **decide exactly how much privacy you desire and what amenities you require** to be comfortable. Most of these accommodations book well in advance, require a 50% deposit prior to arrival, and do not accept credit cards.

Consulting a reservations service in the islands can help you to find the B&B that will meet your personal expectations. There is a small fee for these services, but they provide you a professional point of contact should something go wrong. These services can also assist with interisland travel and car-rental arrangements.

The Maui Visitors Bureau refers callers to Bed & Breakfast Hawai'i. Bed and Breakfast Honolulu has statewide listings, with about 50 B&Bs on Maui. Bed & Breakfast Maui-Style has listings for about 50 B&Bs on Maui. Island Bed & Breakfast, headquartered on Kaua'i, has listings throughout the state and handles about 35 B&Bs on Maui. A directory is available for $12.95.

▶ RESERVATION SERVICES: **Bed and Breakfast Hawai'i** (✉ Box 449, Kapa'a, Kaua'i 96746 ☎ 800/733–1632, ☎ 808/822–7771, ᶠᴬˣ 808/822–2723). **Bed and Breakfast Honolulu** (statewide) (✉ 3242 Kā'ohinani Dr., Honolulu 96817, ☎ 808/595–7533 or 800/288–4666, ᶠᴬˣ 808/595–2030). **Bed & Breakfast Maui-Style** (☎ 808/879–7865, ᶠᴬˣ 808/874–0831).

Go Native Hawai'i (2009 W. Holmes Rd., Suite #9, Lansing, MI 48910, ☎ 800/662–8483). **Hawai'i's Best B&Bs** (✉ Box 563, Kamuela 96743, ☎ 808/885–0550 or 800/262–9912, ᶠᴬˣ 808/885–0559), specializing in upscale properties. **Island Bed & Breakfast** (☎ 808/822–7771 or 800/733–1632). **Pacific Hawai'i**

Bed and Breakfast (✉ 99-1661 Aiea Heights Dr., Aiea, Oʻahu 96701, ☎ 808/261–0532 or 800/999–6026).

CAMPING

A variety of national, state, and county parks are available, some with bathroom and cooking facilities, others a bit more primitive. The National Park Service and Division of State Parks of the Hawaiʻi Department of Land and Natural Resources (☞ National and State Parks, *below*) can provide more information; details on local camping are available from the individual counties. You can pack up your own sleeping bag and bring it along, or you can rent camping equipment at any number of local companies

➤ CAMPING AND RV FACILITIES: State Parks Division, Hawaiʻi State Department of Land and Natural Resources (☎ 808/587–0300).

CONDOMINIUMS

Hawaiʻi is known for developing the resort condominium concept in the early 1970s and continues to maintain its status as a leader in the field. Besides large living areas and full kitchens, many condos now offer front-desk and daily maid services. Nearly 100 companies in Hawaiʻi and around the U.S. rent out condominium space in the islands. Your travel agent will be the most helpful in finding the condo you desire.

Maui also has condos you can rent through central booking agents. Most agents represent more than one condo complex (some handle single-family homes as well), so be specific about what kind of price, space, facilities, and amenities you want. Listed below are multiproperty agents.

➤ RENTAL AGENTS: **Ameri Resort Management, Inc.** (✉ 5500 Honoapiʻilani Rd., Kapalua 96761, ☎ 808/669–5635 or 800/786–7387). **Aston Hotels & Resorts** (✉ 2255 Kūhiō Ave., 18th fl., Honolulu 96815, ☎ 800/342–1551). **Castle Resorts and Hotels** (✉ 1150 S. King St., Honolulu, 96814, ☎ 800/367–5004, ℻ 800/477–2329). **Destination Resorts** (✉ 3750 Wailea Alanui Dr., Wailea 96753, ☎ 800/367–5246). **Hawaiian Apartment Leasing Enterprises** (✉ 479 Ocean Ave., Laguna Beach, CA 92651, ☎ 714/497–4253 or 800/854–8843). **Hawaiian Resorts, Inc.** (✉ 1270 Ala Moana Blvd., Honolulu 96814, ☎ 800/367–7040; 800/877–7331 in Canada). **Hawaiʻi Condo Exchange** (✉ 1817 El Cerrito Pl., Los Angeles 90068, ☎ 323/436–0300 or 800/442–0404). **Kīhei Maui Vacations** (✉ Box 1055, Kīhei 96753, ☎ 800/542–6284). **Marc Resorts Hawaiʻi** (✉ 2155 Kalakaua Ave., Suite 706, Honolulu 96815, ☎ 800/535–0085). **Maui Windsurfari** (✉ 425 Koloa St., Kahului 96732, ☎ 808/871–7766 or 800/736–6284). **Vacation Locations Hawaiʻi** (✉ Box 1689, Kīhei, Maui 96753, ☎ 808/874–0077 or 800/522–2757).

HOME EXCHANGES

If you would like to exchange your home for someone else's, **join a home-exchange organization,** which will send you its updated listings of available exchanges for a year and will include your own listing in at least one of them. It's up to you to make specific arrangements.

➤ EXCHANGE CLUBS: **HomeLink International** (✉ Box 650, Key West, FL 33041, ☎ 305/294–7766 or 800/638–3841, ℻ 305/294–1448, usa@homelink.org, www.homelink.org; $98 per year). **Intervac U.S.** (✉ Box 590504, San Francisco, CA 94159, ☎ 800/756–4663, ℻ 415/435–7440, www.intervac.com; $89 per year includes two catalogues).

HOSTELS

No matter what your age, you can **save on lodging costs by staying at hostels.** In some 5,000 locations in more than 70 countries around the world, Hostelling International (HI), the umbrella group for a number of national youth-hostel associations, offers single-sex, dorm-style beds and, at many hostels, rooms for couples and family accommodations.

Membership in any HI national hostel association, open to travelers of all ages, allows you to stay in HI-affiliated hostels at member rates; one-year membership is about $25 for adults (C$26.75 in Canada, £9.30 in the U.K., $30 in Australia, and $30 in New Zealand). Hostels run about $10–$25 per night. Members have priority if the hostel is full. They're also eligible for discounts around the world, even on rail and bus travel in some countries.

▶ ORGANIZATIONS: **Hostelling International—American Youth Hostels** (✉ 733 15th St. NW, Suite 840, Washington, DC 20005, ☎ 202/783-6161, FAX 202/783-6171, www.hiayh.org). **Hostelling International—Canada** (✉ 400-205 Catherine St., Ottawa, Ontario K2P 1C3, ☎ 613/237-7884, FAX 613/237-7868, www.hostellingintl.ca). **Youth Hostel Association of England and Wales** (✉ Trevelyan House, 8 St. Stephen's Hill, St. Albans, Hertfordshire AL1 2DY, ☎ 01727/855215 or 01727/845047, FAX 01727/844126, www.yha.uk). **Australian Youth Hostel Association** (✉ 10 Mallett St., Camperdown, NSW 2050, ☎ 02/9565-1699, FAX 02/9565-1325, www.yha.com.au). **Youth Hostels Association of New Zealand** (✉ Box 436, Christchurch, New Zealand, ☎ 03/379-9970, FAX 03/365-4476, www.yha.org.nz).

HOTELS

You can find most major hotel brands in Hawai'i, plus large, locally based operators, such as Aston Hotels and Resorts and Outrigger Hotels Hawai'i, as well as a number of independents. The result is an extensive range of rooms, from rock-bottom economy units to luxurious suites. All hotels listed have private bath unless otherwise noted.

▶ TOLL-FREE NUMBERS: **Best Western** (☎ 800/528-1234, www.bestwestern.com). **Choice** (☎ 800/221-2222, www.hotelchoice.com). **Colony** (☎ 800/777-1700. www.colony.com), **Days Inn** (☎ 800/325-2525. www.daysinn.com). **Doubletree and Red Lion Hotels** (☎ 800/222-8733, www.doubletreehotels.com). **Embassy Suites** (☎ 800/362-2779, www.embassysuites.com). **Fairfield Inn** (☎ 800/228-2800, www.marriott.com). **Four Seasons** (☎ 800/332-3442, www.fourseasons.com). **Hilton** (☎ 800/445-8667, www.hiltons.com). **Holiday Inn** (☎ 800/465-4329, www.holiday-inn.com). **Howard Johnson** (☎ 800/654-4656, www.hojo.com). **Hyatt Hotels & Resorts** (☎ 800/233-1234, www.hyatt.com). **La Quinta** (☎ 800/531-5900, www.laquinta.com). **Marriott** (☎ 800/228-9290, www.marriott.com). **Nikko Hotels International** (☎ 800/645-5687, www.nikko.com). **Radisson** (☎ 800/333-3333, www.radisson.com). **Ramada** (☎ 800/228-2828. www.ramada.com), **Renaissance Hotels & Resorts** (☎ 800/468-3571, www.hotels.com). **Sheraton** (☎ 800/325-3535, www.sheraton.com).

MEDIA

Although Hawai'i sits in the middle of the Pacific Ocean, it remains connected globally with a variety of media, including network television, cable television, Web-based media, newspapers, magazines, and radio. Many of the resorts and hotels throughout the islands include an additional visitor-information channel on your in-room television. Consult your in-room directory for channel and scheduling information and to find out the special activities or events that might be happening during your visit.

NEWSPAPERS & MAGAZINES

Each of the islands has its own daily newspapers. They can be picked up through many hotel bell desks, in sundry stores, restaurants, cafés and at newspaper stands located throughout the islands. Many hotels will deliver one to your room upon request. On Maui, the main paper is *The Maui News*. There are a variety of free visitor publications and guides available throughout the islands. Check out local bookstores for other magazines.

RADIO & TELEVISION

Radio airwaves on the islands are affected by natural terrain, so don't expect to hear one radio station islandwide. Sometimes, just driving from the leeward to the windward coasts is enough to lose the signal. For Hawaiian music on Maui, tune your FM radio dial to 93.5 KPOA. News junkies can get their fill by tuning to the AM stations 1110 KAOI or 1570 KUAU, and National Public Radio enthusiasts can tune to the FM station 90.7 KKUA.

Television channels in the islands are plentiful between network and cable channels. Channel allocation varies by island and location, so check daily island newspapers or your in-room hotel television guide for station selection.

MONEY MATTERS

Expect to pay 50¢ for a daily newspaper, $1 to ride the bus anywhere on Oʻahu, and from $45 on up to attend a lūʻau. Museums throughout the islands vary in size and admission fees, the large ones cost between $8 and $15 per entry. Smaller ones can cost from $3 to $6. Prices throughout this guide are given for adults. Substantially reduced fees are almost always available for children, students, and senior citizens.

ATMS

Automatic teller machines for easy access to cash are everywhere on the islands. For a directory of locations, call 800/424-7787 for the Cirrus network or 800/843-7587 for the Plus network.

CREDIT CARDS

Most major credit cards are accepted throughout the islands and are required to rent a car. When making reservations, double-check to ensure that the lodging, restaurant, or attraction you are planning to visit accepts them. In smaller concessions, bed-and-breakfasts, and fast-food outlets, expect to pay cash. Throughout this guide, the following abbreviations are used: **AE**, American Express; **D**, Discover; **DC**, Diner's Club; **MC**, Master Card; and **V**, Visa.

➤ REPORTING LOST CARDS: **American Express** (☎ 800/528-4800). **Discover** (☎ 800/347-2683). **Diner's Club** (☎ 800/234-6377). **Master Card** (☎ 800/307-7309). **Visa** (☎ 800/847-2911).

NATIONAL AND STATE PARKS

Hawaiʻi is home to seven national parks. On Maui, Haleakalā National Park houses Haleakalā volcanic crater and some of the world's most beautiful sunrises.

Hawaiʻi's 52 state parks encompass over 25,000 acres on five islands, and include many of its most beautiful beaches and coastal areas.

Look into discount passes to save money on park entrance fees. The Golden Eagle Pass ($50) gets you and your companions free admission to all national parks for one year. (Camping and parking are extra). Both the Golden Age Passport ($10), for those 62 and older, and the Golden Access Passport (free), for travelers with disabilities, entitle holders to free entry to all national parks, plus 50% off fees for the use of many park facilities and services. You must show proof of age and of U.S. citizenship or permanent residency (such as a U.S. passport, driver's license, or birth certificate) and, if requesting Golden Access, proof of disability. All three passes are available at all national parks wherever entrance fees are charged. Golden Eagle and Golden Access passes are also available by mail.

➤ PASSES BY MAIL: **National Park Service** (✉ National Park Service National Office, 1849 C St. NW, Washington, DC 20240-0001, ☎ 202/208-4747).

➤ STATE PARKS: Details of state parks and historic areas come from the **State Parks Division, Hawaiʻi State Department of Land and Natural Resources** (✉ 1151 Punchbowl St., Room 310, Honolulu, 96813; ✉ Box 621, Honolulu, 96809; ☎ 808/587-0300).

PACKING

Hawaiʻi is casual: sandals, bathing suits, and comfortable, informal clothing are the norm. In summer, synthetic slacks and shirts can be uncomfortably warm. You'll easily find a bathing suit in Hawaiʻi, but **bring a bathing cap with you if you wear one.** You can waste hours searching for one.

There's a saying in the Hawaiian Islands that when a man wears a suit during the day, he's either going for a loan or he's a lawyer trying a case. Only a few upscale restaurants require a jacket for dinner, and none requires a tie. The aloha shirt is accepted dress in Hawaiʻi for business and most social occasions. Shorts are acceptable daytime attire, along with a T-shirt or polo shirt. Golfers should remember that many courses have

Smart Travel Tips A to Z

dress codes requiring a collared shirt; call courses you're interested in for details. If you're visiting in winter or planning to visit a volcano area, **bring a sweater or jacket.** Trade winds cool things off when the sun goes down, and things get chilly above 10,000 ft.

Probably the most important thing to tuck in your suitcase is sunscreen. The ultraviolet rays here are powerful: doctors advise putting on sunscreen when you get up in the morning. Don't forget to **reapply sunscreen periodically during the day,** since perspiration can wash it away. There are many tanning oils on the market in Hawai'i, including coconut and *kukui* (the nut from a local tree) oils, but doctors warn that they merely sauté your skin. Hats and sunglasses offer important sun protection, too. Both are easy to find in island shops. All major hotels in Hawai'i provide beach towels.

In your carry-on luggage, **pack an extra pair of eyeglasses or contact lenses and enough of any medication you take** to last the entire trip. You may also ask your doctor to write a spare prescription using the drug's generic name, since brand names may vary from country to country. In luggage to be checked, **never pack prescription drugs or valuables.** To avoid customs delays, carry medications in their original packaging. And don't forget to carry with you the addresses of offices that handle refunds of lost traveler's checks.

CHECKING LUGGAGE

How many carry-on bags you can bring with you is up to the airline. Most allow two, but not always, so make sure that everything you carry aboard will fit under your seat or in the overhead bin, and get to the gate early.

If you are flying internationally, note that baggage allowances may be determined not by piece but by weight—generally 88 pounds (40 kilograms) in first class, 66 pounds (30 kilograms) in business class, and 44 pounds (20 kilograms) in economy.

Airline liability for baggage is limited to $1,250 per person on flights within the United States. On international flights it amounts to $9.07 per pound or $20 per kilogram for checked baggage (roughly $640 per 70-pound bag) and $400 per passenger for unchecked baggage. You can buy additional coverage at check-in for about $10 per $1,000 of coverage, but it excludes a rather extensive list of items, shown on your airline ticket.

Before departure, **itemize your bags' contents** and their worth, and label the bags with your name, address, and phone number. Inside each bag, **pack a copy of your itinerary.** At check-in, **make sure that each bag is correctly tagged** with the destination airport's three-letter code. If your bags arrive damaged or fail to arrive at all, file a written report with the airline before leaving the airport.

PASSPORTS & VISAS

➤ CONTACTS: **U.S. Embassy Visa Information Line** (☎ 01891/200–290; calls cost 49p per minute, 39p per minute cheap rate) for U.S. visa information. **U.S. Embassy Visa Branch** (✉ 5 Upper Grosvenor Sq., London W1A 1AE) for U.S. visa information; send a self-addressed, stamped envelope. **U.S. Consulate General** (✉ Queen's House, Queen St., Belfast BTI 6EO) if you live in Northern Ireland. **Office of Australia Affairs** (✉ 59th floor, MLC Centre, 19–29 Martin Pl., Sydney, NSW 2000) if you live in Australia. **Office of New Zealand Affairs** (✉ 29 Fitzherbert Terr., Thorndon, Wellington) if you live in New Zealand.

PASSPORT OFFICES

The best time to apply for a passport or to renew is in fall and winter. Before any trip, check your passport's expiration date, and, if necessary, renew it as soon as possible.

➤ AUSTRALIAN CITIZENS: **Australian Passport Office** (☎ 131–232, www.dfat.gov.au/passports).

➤ CANADIAN CITIZENS: **Passport Office** (☎ 819/994–3500 or 800/567–6868, www.dfait-maeci.gc.ca/passport).

➤ NEW ZEALAND CITIZENS: **New Zealand Passport Office** (☎ 04/494–0700, www.passports.govt.nz).

➤ U.K. CITIZENS: **London Passport Office** (☎ 0990/210–410) for fees and documentation requirements and to request an emergency passport.

SAFETY

Hawai'i is one of the world's safer tourist destinations, but remember that crimes do occur. It's wise to **follow the same commonsense safety precautions you would normally follow** in your own hometown. There are some spots on every island that you might wish to avoid. Hotel and visitor center staff can provide information should you decide to head out on your own to more of the remote areas. Rental cars are magnets for break-ins, so don't leave any valuables in the car, not even in a locked trunk. When hiking, **stay on marked trails,** no matter how alluring the temptation might be to stray. Since weather conditions can cause landscapes to become muddy, slippery, and tenuous, staying on marked trails will lessen the possibility of a fall or getting lost. Ocean safety is of utmost importance when visiting an island destination. Don't swim alone, and **follow the international signage posted at beaches that alert swimmers** to strong currents, man-of-war jellyfish, sharp coral, high surf, and dangerous shorebreaks. At coastal lookouts along cliff tops, heed the signs indicating that waves can climb over the ledges. Check with lifeguards at each beach for current conditions, and if the red flags are up, indicating swimming and surfing is not allowed, **don't attempt to swim.** Waters that look calm on the surface can harbor strong currents and undertows.

LOCAL SCAMS

Be wary of those hawking "too good to be true" prices on everything from car rentals to visitor attractions. Many of these offers are just a lure to get you in the door for time-share presentations. When handed a flyer, read the fine print before you make your decision to participate.

SENIOR-CITIZEN TRAVEL

Hawai'i is steeped in a tradition that gives great respect to elders, or *kapuna*, and considers them "keepers of the wisdom." For seniors, traveling in Hawai'i offers discounts, special senior-oriented activities, and easy access. Many lodging facilities offer discounts for members of the American Association of Retired Persons (AARP). No matter where you visit, be it visitor attractions, museums, restaurants, or movie theaters, inquire about their senior-citizen discounts. They can save you a bundle. To qualify for age-related discounts, **mention your senior-citizen status up-front** when booking hotel reservations (not when checking out) and before you're seated in restaurants (not when paying the bill). When renting a car, ask about promotional car-rental discounts, which can be cheaper than senior-citizen rates.

➤ EDUCATIONAL PROGRAMS: **Elderhostel** (✉ 75 Federal St., 3rd floor, Boston, MA 02110, ☎ 877/426–8056, FAX 877/426–2166, www.elderhostel.org).

SHOPPING

SMART SOUVENIRS

Aloha shirts and resort wear, Hawaiian music recordings, shell leis, coral jewelry, traditional quilts, island foods, Kona coffee, and koa-wood products are just a few of the gifts that visitors to Hawai'i treasure. For the more elegant gift items, check out the Hawaiian boutiques located in major island shopping centers as well as those tucked away in smaller shopping areas in residential districts. Island craft fairs and swap meets offer a bargain bazaar of standard items like T-shirts and tiki statues as well as the original works of local artisans.

STUDENTS IN HAWAI'I

Hawai'i is a popular destination for exchange students from around the world. Contact your hometown university about study and internship possibilities. To check out the student scene in the islands, stop by any of the University of Hawai'i campuses, the community college campuses, and read the *Honolulu Weekly* upon arrival for club and event information. Be sure to ask about discounts for students at all museums and major attractions and be prepared to show ID to qualify.

➤ I.D.s & SERVICES: **Council Travel** (CIEE; ✉ 205 E. 42nd St., 14th floor, New York, NY 10017, ☎ 212/822–2700 or 888/268–6245, FAX 212/822–

2699, info@councilexchanges.org, www.councilexchanges.org) for mail orders only, in the U.S. **Travel Cuts** (⊠ 187 College St., Toronto, Ontario M5T 1P7, ☎ 416/979–2406 or 800/667–2887, www.travelcuts.com) in Canada.

TAXES

There is a 4.17% state sales tax on all purchases, including food. A hotel room tax of 7.25%, combined with the sales tax of 4.17%, equals an 11.42% rate added onto your hotel bill. A $2-per-day road tax is also assessed on each rental vehicle.

TIME

Hawai'i is on Hawaiian Standard Time, 5 hours behind New York, 2 hours behind Los Angeles, and 10 hours behind London.

When the U.S. mainland is on daylight saving time, Hawai'i is not, so add an extra hour of time difference between the islands and mainland destinations.

TIPPING

Tip cab drivers 15% of the fare. Standard tips for restaurants and bar tabs runs from 15% to 20% of the bill, depending on the standard of service. Bellman at hotels usually receive $1 per bag, more if you have bulky items like bicycles and surfboards. Tip the hotel room maid $1 per night, paid daily. Tip the doorman $1 for assistance with taxis and tips for concierge vary depending on the service.

TOURS & PACKAGES

Because everything is prearranged on a prepackaged tour or independent vacation, you'll spend less time planning—and often get it all at a good price. Packages that include any combination of lodging, airfare, meals, sightseeing, car rental, and even sports activities and entertainment are popular in Hawai'i and are often considerably cheaper than piecing the vacation together à la carte. Honeymoon packages that include everything from the actual wedding ceremony to extras like special suites, champagne, flowers, and romantic dinners are offered by some resorts and hotels. Do some homework, ask questions, and make sure that the package suits your tastes and budget.

BOOKING WITH AN AGENT

Travel agents are excellent resources. But it's a good idea to collect brochures from several agencies as some agents' suggestions may be influenced by relationships with tour and package firms that reward them for volume sales. If you have a special interest, **find an agent with expertise in that area.** American Society of Travel Agents (☞ Travel Agencies, *below*) has a database of specialists worldwide.

Make sure your travel agent knows the accommodations and other services of the place they're recommending. Do some homework on your own, too: local tourism boards can provide information about lesser-known and small-niche operators, some of which may sell only direct.

BUYER BEWARE

Each year consumers are stranded or lose their money when tour operators—even large ones with excellent reputations—go out of business. So **check out the operator.** Ask several travel agents about its reputation, and try to **book with a company that has a consumer-protection program.** (Look for information in the company's brochure.) In the United States, members of the National Tour Association and the United States Tour Operators Association are required to set aside funds to cover your payments and travel arrangements in the event that the company defaults. It's also a good idea to choose a company that participates in the American Society of Travel Agents' Tour Operator Program (TOP); ASTA will act as mediator in any disputes between you and your tour operator.

Remember that the more your package or tour includes the better you can predict the ultimate cost of your vacation. Make sure you know exactly what is covered, and **beware of hidden costs.** Are taxes, tips, and transfers included? Entertainment and excursions? These can add up.

➤ TOUR-OPERATOR RECOMMENDATIONS: **American Society of Travel Agents** (☞ Travel Agencies, *below*). **National Tour Association** (NTA; ⊠ 546 E. Main St., Lexington, KY 40508, ☎ 606/226–4444 or 800/682–

8886, www.ntaonline.com). **United States Tour Operators Association** (USTOA; ✉ 342 Madison Ave., Suite 1522, New York, NY 10173, ☎ 212/599–6599 or 800/468–7862, FAX 212/599–6744, ustoa@aol.com, www.ustoa.com).

TOURS IN MAUI

AERIAL TOURS

Helicopter flight-seeing excursions can take you over the West Maui mountains, Hāna, and Haleakalā. This is a beautiful, exciting way to see the island, and the *only* way to see some of its most dramatic areas. Tour prices usually include a videotape of your trip so you can relive the experience at home. Prices run from about $100 for a half-hour rain-forest tour to $250 for a two-hour mega-experience that includes a champagne toast on landing.

It takes about 90 minutes to travel inside the volcano, then down to the village of Hāna. Some companies stop in secluded areas for refreshments. Helicopter-tour operators throughout the state come under sharp scrutiny for passenger safety and equipment maintenance. Noise levels are a concern as well; residents have become pretty vocal about regulating this kind of pollution. Don't be afraid to ask about a company's safety record, flight paths, age of equipment, and level of operator experience.

Blue Hawaiian Helicopters has provided aerial adventures in Hawai'i since 1985, and it has the best service and safety record. Its ASTAR helicopters are air-conditioned and have noise-canceling headsets for all passengers. Hawai'i Helicopters flies fast, twin-engine jet helicopters. Sunshine Helicopters offers a Moloka'i flight in its "Black Beauty" aircraft.

➤ AERIAL TOUR OPERATORS: **Blue Hawaiian Helicopters** (✉ Kahului Heliport, Hangar 105, Kahului 96732, ☎ 808/871–8844). **Hawai'i Helicopters** (✉ Kahului Heliport, Hangar 106, Kahului 96732, ☎ 808/877–3900, 800/994–9099, or 800/367–7095). **Sunshine Helicopters** (✉ Kahului Heliport, Hangar 107, Kahului 96732, ☎ 808/871–0722 or 800/544–2520).

ART TOURS

A free guided tour of the Hyatt Regency Maui's art collection and gardens starts at 11 on Monday, Wednesday, and Friday. It takes you through the Hyatt's public spaces, adorned with a constantly changing multimillion-dollar collection of Asian and Pacific art. Among the treasures to be found are Chinese cloisonné; Japanese dragon pots; Thai elephant bells; Hawaiian quilts; and battle shields and masks from Papua, New Guinea. If you're not fond of group tours, just pick up a copy of the hotel's "Art Guide" for a do-it-yourself experience.

Exploring the spectacular $30 million art collection housed on the grounds of the Grand Wailea is like entering an international art museum. Sculptures, artifacts, stained-glass windows, a 200,000-piece ceramic tile mosaic, paintings, and assorted works by Fernand Léger, Fernando Botero, and noted Hawaiian artists make this excursion a must for art lovers. The tour leaves from the resort's Napua Art Gallery at 10 every Tuesday and Friday and is free for guests of the resort. Nonguests pay $6.

➤ ART TOURS: **Hyatt Regency Maui** (✉ 200 Nokea Kai Dr., Kā'anapali, ☎ 808/661–1234). **Grand Wailea** (✉ 3850 Wailea Alanui Dr., Wailea, ☎ 808/875–1234).

CRATER TOURS

Groups assemble at a Haleakalā ranger station at 7:30, then walk 4–10 mi to where Craig Moore and his crew have unpacked the horses, set up the campsite, and organized a social hour. A second day is spent exploring the crater. The third day is a hike back out of the crater. Gourmet breakfasts and dinners are served. A basic three-day, two-night package is $500 per person, or talk to Moore about special arrangements and interests, including shorter treks, hikes, van tours, and his Haleakalā crater mule rides.

➤ CRATER TOUR OPERATOR: **Craig Moore** (☎ 808/878–1743).

DOWNHILL BIKING TOURS

After instruction in safety fundamentals, don a helmet, get on a bicycle atop Haleakalā volcano, and coast down. Lunch or breakfast is included, depending on what time you start.

▶ DOWNHILL BIKING TOUR OPERATORS: **Maui Downhill** (✉ 199 Dairy Rd., Kahului 96732, ☎ 808/871–2155 or 800/535–2453; 📠 $95–$115). **Maui Mountain Cruisers.** (☎ 808/871–6014; 📠 $86–$99, van riders $55).

GROUND TOURS

This is a big island to see in one day, so tour companies combine various sections—either Haleakalā, ʻIao Needle, and Central Maui, or West Maui and its environs—in various tour packages. Contact companies for a brochure of their current offerings. Very often your hotel has a tour desk to facilitate arrangements.

A tour of Haleakalā and Upcountry is usually a half-day excursion, and is offered in several versions by different companies for about $50 and up. The trip often includes stops at a protea farm and at Tedeschi Vineyards and Winery, the only place in Hawaiʻi where wine is made. A Haleakalā sunrise tour starts before dawn so that visitors get to the top of the dormant volcano before the sun peeks over the horizon. Some companies throw in champagne to greet the sunrise.

A tour of Hāna is almost always done in a van, since the winding road to Hāna just doesn't provide a comfortable ride in bigger buses. Of late, Hāna has so many of these one-day tours that it seems as if there are more vans than cars on the road. Tour costs run $70–$120.

Most of the tour guides have been in the business for years. Some were born in the Islands and have taken special classes to learn more about their culture and lore. They expect a tip ($1 per person at least), but they're just as cordial without one. Be sure to ask how many stops you'll get on your tour, or you may be disappointed to find that all your sightseeing is done through a window.

Polynesian Adventure Tours uses large buses with floor-to-ceiling windows. The drivers are fun characters who really know the island. Roberts Hawaiʻi Tours is one of the state's largest tour companies, and its staff can arrange tours with bilingual guides if asked ahead of time. Trans Hawaiian Services manages to keep its tours personal despite its size.

▶ GROUND TOUR OPERATORS: **Polynesian Adventure Tours** (✉ 400 Hāna Hwy., Kahului 96732, ☎ 808/877–4242 or 800/622–3011). **Roberts Hawaiʻi Tours** (✉ Box 247, Kahului 96732, ☎ 808/871–6226 or 800/767–7551). **Trans Hawaiian Services** (✉ 720 Iwilei Rd., Suite 101, Honolulu 96817, ☎ 800/533–8765).

HIKING TOURS

Hike Maui is the oldest hiking company in the Islands, and its rain-forest, mountain-ridge, crater, coastline, and archaeological-snorkel hikes are led by such knowledgeable folk as ethnobotanists and marine biologists. Prices range from $75 to $125 for hikes of five to 10 hours, including lunch. Hike Maui supplies waterproof day packs, rain ponchos, first-aid gear, and water bottles.

▶ HIKING TOUR OPERATOR: **Hike Maui** (✉ Box 330969, Kahului 96733, ☎ 808/879–5270, FAX 808/893–2515,www.hikemaui.com).

HORSEBACK TOURS

Several companies on Maui offer horseback riding that's far more appealing than the typical hour-long trudge over a boring trail with 50 other horses.

Frank Levinson started Adventures on Horseback in the 1980s with five-hour outings into secluded parts of Maui. The tours traverse ocean cliffs on Maui's north shore, follow the slopes of Haleakalā, and pass along streams, through rain forests, and near waterfalls, where riders can stop for a dip in a freshwater pool.

Charley's Trail Rides & Pack Trips require that riders must weigh under 200 pounds. Charley's overnighters go from Kaupō—a *tiny* village nearly 20 mi past Hāna—up the slopes of Haleakalā to the crater.

Pony Express Tours will take you on horseback into Haleakalā Crater. The half-day ride goes down to the crater floor for a picnic lunch. The full-day excursion covers 12 mi of terrain and visits some of the crater's weird formations. You don't need to be an experienced rider, but the longer ride can be tough if you're unathletic. The company also offers one- and two-hour rides on Haleakalā Ranch.

➤ HORSEBACK TOUR OPERATORS: **Adventures on Horseback** (✉ Box 1771, Makawao 96768, ☎ 808/242–7445; 💰 $175 including breakfast, lunch, and refreshments). **Charley's Trail Rides & Pack Trips** (✉ c/o Kaupō Ranch, Kaupō 96713, ☎ 808/248–8209; 💰 $40–$160). **Pony Express Tours** (✉ Box 535, Kulā 96790, ☎ 808/667–2200 or 808/878–6698; 💰 $40–$160).

PERSONAL GUIDES

Rent-a-Local is *the* best way to see Maui—through the eyes of the locals. Started by Laurie Robello, who is part Hawaiian, the company now has excellent guides who will drive your car on a tour tailored to your interests. Temptation Tours president Dave Campbell has targeted members of the affluent older crowd (though almost anyone would enjoy these tours) who don't want to be herded onto a crowded bus. He provides exclusive tours in his plush six-passenger limovan and specializes in full-day tours to Haleakalā and Hāna. Dave's "Ultimate" Hāna tour includes lunch at Hotel Hāna-Maui.

➤ GUIDE CONTACTS: **Rent-a-Local** (✉ 333 Dairy Rd., #102, Kahului 96732, ☎ 808/877–4042 or 800/228–6284; 💰 $199 for 2 people, $25 for each additional person). **Temptation Tours** (✉ 211 'Āhinahina Pl., Kula 96790, ☎ 808/877–8888. 💰 $110–$249).

PINEAPPLE PLANTATION TOURS

A Pineapple Plantation Tour takes you right into the fields in a company van. The 2½-hour trip gives you firsthand experience of the operation and its history, some incredible views of the island, and the chance to pick a fresh pineapple for yourself. Tours go out morning and afternoon, weekdays, from the Kapalua Logo Shop.

➤ PLANTATION TOUR OPERATOR: **Pineapple Plantation Tour** (✉ Kapalua Resort Activity Desk, ☎ 808/669–8088. 💰 $26).

WALKING TOURS

The Lahaina Restoration Foundation has published a walking-tour map for interested visitors. The map will guide you to the most historic sites of Lahaina, some renovated and some not. Highlights of the walk include the Jodo Mission, the Brig *Carthaginian II*, the Baldwin Home, and the Old Court House. These are all sights you could find yourself, but the map is free and full of historical tidbits, and it makes the walk easier.

➤ WALKING TOURS INFORMATION: **Lahaina Restoration Foundation** (✉ Baldwin Home, 696 Front St., Lahaina, ☎ 808/661–3262).

TRANSPORTATION AROUND HAWAI'I

Renting a car is definitely recommended for those who plan to move beyond their hotel beach chair. **Reserve your vehicle in advance.** Most major companies have airport counters and complimentary transportation for pickup/drop-off back at the airport upon departure.

TAXIS

Taxis can be found at island airports, through your hotel doorman, in the more popular resort areas, or by contacting local taxi companies by telephone. Flag-down fees are $2 and each additional mile is $1.70. Most companies will also provide a car and driver for half-day or day-long island tours if you don't want to rent a car, and a number of companies also offer personal guides. Remember, however, that rates are quite steep for these services, ranging from $100 to $200 dollars and up.

For short hops between hotels and restaurants, taxis can be convenient, but you'll have to call ahead. Even busy West Maui doesn't have curbside taxi service. West Maui Taxi and Yellow Cab of Maui service the entire island, but you'd be smart to consider using them just for the areas where they're located. Ali'i Cab specializes in West Maui, and Kīhei Taxi serves Central Maui.

➤ TAXI COMPANIES: **West Maui Taxi** (✉ 761 Kumukahi St., Lahaina, ☎ 808/667–2605). **Yellow Cab of Maui** (✉ Kahului Airport, ☎ 808/877–7000). **Aliʻi Cab** (✉ 75 Kūʻai Pl., Lahaina, ☎ 808/661–3688). **Kīhei Taxi** (✉ Kīhei, ☎ 808/879–3000).

LIMOUSINES

Arthur's Limousine Service offers a chauffeured superstretch Lincoln complete with bar and two TVs for $88 per hour. Arthur's fleet also includes less grandiose Lincoln Town Cars for $65 per hour with a two-hour minimum. If you want to stretch out with a company on the South Shore, call Wailea Limousine Service. Despite the name, this company also provides limousines to the Lahaina area.

➤ LIMOUSINE COMPANIES: **Arthur's Limousine Service** (✉ 283H Lalo St., Kahului 96732, ☎ 808/871–5555 or 800/345–4667). **Wailea Limousine Service** (☎ 808/875–4114; 808/661–4114 for Lahaina).

TRAVEL AGENCIES

A good travel agent puts your needs first. Look for an agency that has been in business at least five years, emphasizes customer service, and has someone on staff who specializes in your destination. In addition, **make sure the agency belongs to a professional trade organization.** The American Society of Travel Agents (ASTA), with 27,000 agents in some 170 countries, is the largest and most influential in the field. Operating under the motto "Integrity in Travel," it maintains and enforces a strict code of ethics. ASTA also maintains a Web site that includes a directory of agents. (If a travel agency is also acting as your tour operator, *see* Buyer Beware *in* Tours & Packages, *above.*)

➤ LOCAL AGENT REFERRALS: **American Society of Travel Agents** (ASTA; ☎ 800/965–2782 24-hr hot line, FAX 703/684–8319, www.astanet.com). **Association of British Travel Agents** (✉ 68–71 Newman St., London W1P 4AH, ☎ 0171/637–2444, FAX 0171/637–0713, abta.co.uk, www.abtanet.com). **Association of Canadian Travel Agents** (✉ 1729 Bank St., Suite 201, Ottawa, Ontario K1V 7Z5, ☎ 613/521–0474, FAX 613/521–0805, acta.ntl@sympatico.ca). **Australian Federation of Travel Agents** (✉ Level 3, 309 Pitt St., Sydney 2000, ☎ 02/9264–3299, FAX 02/9264–1085, www.afta.com.au). **Travel Agents' Association of New Zealand** (✉ Box 1888, Wellington 10033, ☎ 04/499–0104, FAX 04/499–0827, taanz@tiasnet.co.nz).

VISITOR INFORMATION

Before you go, contact the Hawaiʻi Visitors & Convention Bureau for general information, free brochures that include an accommodations and car-rental guide, and an entertainment and dining listing containing one-line descriptions of bureau members. Take a virtual visit to Hawaiʻi on the Web, which can be most helpful in planning your vacation. The HVCB site has a calendar section that allows you to see what local events are in place during the time of your stay.

Aunty Aloha's Breakfast Lūʻau is a fun and tasty way to learn about exciting and often unpublicized things to do on Maui. The orientation includes live Hawaiian music, a hula show, a comical slide show, and an all-you-can-eat island-style breakfast and runs weekdays at 8:15 AM. The cost is $13.95, and you can get two tickets for the price of one if you attend on their first morning in Maui. Visitor Channel Seven televises visitor information 24 hours a day, including video tours, restaurant previews, and activities information.

➤ TOURIST INFORMATION: **Aunty Aloha's Breakfast Lūʻau** (✉ Kāʻanapali Beach Hotel, Kāʻanapali, ☎ 808/242–8437 or 800/993–8338). **Hawaiʻi Visitors & Convention Bureau** (✉ 2270 Kalakaua Ave., Suite 801, Honolulu, 96817, ☎ 808/923–1811). For brochures, ☎ 800/464–2924. In the U.K. contact the **Hawaiʻi Visitors & Convention Bureau** (✉ Box 208, Sunbury, Middlesex, TW16 5RJ, ☎ 020/8941–4009). Send a £2 check or postal order for an information pack. **Maui Visitors Bureau** (✉ 1727 Wili Pā Loop, Wailuku 96793, ☎ 808/244–3530, FAX 808/244–1337, www.visitmaui.com).

WEB SITES

Do check out the World Wide Web when you're planning. You'll find everything from current weather forecasts to virtual tours of famous cities. Fodor's Web site, www.fodors.com, is a great place to start your on-line travels. When you see a 🐾 in this book, go to www.fodors.com/urls for an up-to-date link to that destination's site. For more information on Hawai'i, visit www.goHawaii.com, the official Web site of the Hawai'i Convention and Visitors Bureau.

Other sites to check out include www.visitmaui.com (Maui County Visitors Bureau) and www.cruise-Hawaii.com (for information on cruise vessels sailing interisland). www.Hawaii.net has links to more than 100 Hawaiian sites (click on Visitor Center). www.search-Hawaii.com has an engine that can search all linked Hawaiian Web pages by topic or word.

Visit www.hsHawaii.com for the Hawai'i State vacation planner; www.Hawaii.gov, the state's official Web site, for all information on the destination, including camping; and www.nps.gov for national parks information.

WHEN TO GO

Maui's long days of sunshine and fairly mild year-round temperatures make it an all-seasons destination. In resort areas near sea level, the average afternoon temperature during the coldest winter months of December and January is 75°F; during the hottest months of August and September the temperature often reaches 92°F. Winter is the season when most travelers prefer to head for the islands. This high season also means that fewer travel bargains are available; room rates average 10%–15% higher during this season than the rest of the year.

The only weather change most areas experience during the December–February span is rainfall, though the sun is rarely hidden behind the clouds for a solid 24-hour period. Haleakalā Weather Forecast gives up-to-date reports on sea conditions and weather forecasts for the road to Hāna and for 'Īao Valley State Park. National Weather Service/Maui Forecast covers the islands of Maui, Moloka'i, and Lāna'i.

➤ WEATHER: **Haleakalā Weather Forecast** (☏ 808/871–5054). **National Weather Service/Maui Forecast** (☏ 808/877–5111).

CLIMATE

The following are average maximum and minimum temperatures for Honolulu; the temperatures throughout the Hawaiian Islands are similar.

➤ FORECASTS: **Weather Channel Connection** (☏ 900/932–8437), 95¢ per minute from a Touch-Tone phone.

HONOLULU, O'AHU

Jan.	80F	27C	May	85F	29C	Sept.	88F	31C
	65	18		70	21		73	23
Feb.	80F	27C	June	86F	30C	Oct.	87F	31C
	65	18		72	22		72	22
Mar.	81F	27C	July	87F	31C	Nov.	84F	29C
	69	21		73	23		69	21
Apr.	83F	28C	Aug.	88F	31C	Dec.	81F	27C
	69	21		74	23		67	19

FESTIVALS AND SEASONAL EVENTS

➤ DEC.: **Nā Mele O Maui** (Maui; ☏ 808/661–3271): The first week of December, this Hawaiiana festival at Kā'anapali features arts and crafts, and schoolchildren competing in Hawaiian song and hula performances. **Bodhi Day** (all islands; ☏ 808/522–9200): The traditional Buddhist Day of Enlightenment is celebrated at temples statewide; visitors are welcome. **Festival of Lights** (all islands; ☏ 808/667–9175). Islands deck out the lights to celebrate the season, with electric light parades, decorated city buildings, and events that last throughout December. **Christmas** (all islands): Hotels outdo each other in such extravagant exhibits and events as Santa arriving by outrigger canoe. **First Night Maui** (Maui; ☎ 808/244–9166): An alcohol-free New Year's Eve street festival of arts and entertainment at dozens of downtown locations.

➤ JAN.: **Rivals.com Hula Bowl Game** (Maui; ☎ 808/947–4141): This annual college all-star football classic is followed by a Hawaiian-style concert.

➤ JAN.–FEB.: **Chinese New Year Celebrations** (all islands; ☎ 808/667–9175): The Chinese New Year is welcomed with a Narcissus Festival pageant, coronation ball, cooking demonstrations, fireworks, and lion dances.

➤ MAR.: **East Maui Taro Festival** (Maui; ☎ 808/248–8972): Held in Hana, this festival focuses on all things taro, including poi. **Prince Kuhio Day** (all islands; ☎ 808/822–5521): March 26, a local holiday, honors Prince Kuhio, a member of Congress who might have become king if Hawai'i had not become a U.S. territory and later a state.

➤ APR.: **Celebration of the Arts** (Maui; ☎ 808/669–6200): For three days the Ritz-Carlton Kapalua pays tribute to Hawai'i's culture with hula and chanting demonstrations, art workshops, a lū'au, and Hawaiian music and dance concerts. Most activities are free.

The 'Ulupalakua Thing! (Maui; ☎ 808/875–0457): Maui County holds its annual agriculture trade show and sampling, hosted by Tedeschi Winery, on the lovely grounds of 'Ulupalakua Ranch. **Buddha Day** (all islands; ☎ 808/536–7044): Flower pageants are staged at Island Buddhist temples to celebrate Buddha's birth.

➤ MAY: **Lei Day** (all islands; ☎ 808/547–7393): This annual flower-filled celebration on May 1 includes music, hula, food, and lei-making competitions, with lots of exquisite leis on exhibit and for sale.

➤ JUNE: **King Kamehameha Day** (all islands; ☎ 808/586–0333): Kamehameha united all the Islands and became Hawai'i's first king. Parades and fairs abound, and twin statues of the king—in Honolulu on O'ahu and in Hāwī on the Big Island—are draped in giant leis.

➤ JULY: **Kapalua Wine and Food Symposium** (Maui; ☎ 800/669–0244): Wine and food experts and enthusiasts gather for tastings, discussions, and gourmet dinners at the Kapalua Resort. **Makawao Statewide Rodeo** (Maui; ☎ 808/572–1895): This old-time Upcountry rodeo, held at the Oskie Rice Arena in Makawao on the July 4th weekend, includes a parade and three days of festivities. **Independence Day** (all islands): The national holiday on July 4 is celebrated with fairs, parades, and, of course, fireworks. Special events include an outrigger canoe regatta featuring 30 events held on and off Waikīkī Beach.

➤ JULY–AUG.: **Bon Odori Season** (all islands; ☎ 808/661–4304): Buddhist temples invite everyone to festivals that honor ancestors and feature Japanese o-bon dancing.

➤ AUG.: The **Maui Onion Festival** (Maui; ☎ 808/875–0457): This lighthearted and food-filled celebration of Maui's most famous crop takes place at Whalers Village, Kā'napali. **Admission Day** (all islands): The state holiday, the third Friday in August, recognizes Hawai'i's attainment of statehood in 1959.

➤ SEPT.: **Maui Music Festival** (Maui; ☎ 800/245–9229): On Labor Day weekend, well-known contemporary jazz, Hawaiian, and other musicians converge on the Kā'anapali Beach Resort for two days of nonstop music on several outdoor stages. **Maui Writers Conference** (Maui; ☎ 808/879–0061): Best-selling authors and powerhouse agents and publishers offer advice—and a few contracts—to aspiring authors and screenwriters at this Labor Day Weekend gathering. **Taste of Lahaina** (Maui; ☎ 808/667–9175): Maui's best chefs compete for top cooking honors, and samples of their entries are sold at a lively open-air party featuring live entertainment.

➤ SEPT.–OCT.: **Aloha Festivals** (all islands; ☎ 808/545–1771): This traditional celebration, started in 1946, preserves Hawaiian native culture. Crafts, music, dance, pageantry, street parties, and canoe races are all part of the festival.

➤ OCT.: **Aloha Classic World Wave-sailing Championships** (Maui; ☎ 808/575–9151): Top windsurfers from around the globe gather at Hoʻokipa Beach for this professional tour's final event of the season. **Maui Country Fair** (Maui; ☎ 808/875–0457): This decades-old annual event is very popular. Rides, games, entertainment, and exhibits are at the War Memorial Complex, Kahului.

WORDS AND PHRASES

Vocabulary

Although an understanding of Hawaiian is by no means required on a trip to the Aloha State, a *malihini*, or newcomer, will find plenty of opportunities to pick up a few of the local words and phrases. Traditional names and expressions are widely used in the Islands, thanks in part to legislation enacted in the early '90s to encourage the use of the authentically spelled Hawaiian language. Visitors are likely to read or hear at least a few words each day of their stay. Such exposure enriches a trip to Hawai'i.

With a basic understanding and some uninhibited practice, anyone can have enough command of the local tongue to ask for directions and to order from a restaurant menu. One visitor announced she would not leave until she could pronounce the name of the state fish, the *humuhumunukunukuāpua'a*. Luckily, she had scheduled a nine-day stay.

Simplifying the learning process is the fact that the Hawaiian language contains only eight consonants—H, K, L, M, N, P, W, and the silent *'okina*, or glottal, stop, written '—plus the five vowels. All syllables, and therefore all words, end in a vowel. Each vowel, with the exception of a few diphthongized double vowels such as *au* (pronounced "ow") or *ai* (pronounced "eye"), is pronounced separately. Thus *'Iolani* is four syllables (ee-oh-la-nee), not three (yo-la-nee). Although some Hawaiian words have only vowels, most also contain some consonants, but consonants are never doubled.

Pronunciation is simple. Pronounce *A* "ah" as father; *E* "ay" as in weigh; *I* "ee" as in marine; *O* "oh" as in no; *U* "oo" as in true.

Consonants mirror their English equivalents, with the exception of W. When the letter begins any syllable other than the first one in a word, it is usually pronounced as a V. *'Awa*, the Polynesian drink, is pronounced "ava"; *'ewa* is pronounced "eva."

Nearly all long Hawaiian words are combinations of shorter words; they are not difficult to pronounce if you segment them into shorter words. *Kalaniana'ole*, the highway running east from Honolulu, is easily understood as *Kalani ana 'ole*. Apply the standard pronunciation rules—the stress falls on the next-to-last syllable of most two- or three-syllable Hawaiian words—and Kalaniana'ole Highway is as easy to say as Main Street.

Now about that fish. Try *humu-humu nuku-nuku āpu a'a*.

The other unusual element in Hawaiian language is the *kahakō*, or macron, written as a short line (¯) placed over a vowel. Like the accent (´) in Spanish, the kahakō puts emphasis on a syllable that would normally not be stressed. The most familiar example is probably *Waikīkī*. With no macrons, the stress would fall on the middle syllable; with only one macron, on the last syllable, the stress would fall on the first and last syllables. Some words become plural with the addition of a macron, often on a syllable that would have been stressed anyway. No Hawaiian word becomes plural with the addition of an *S*, since that letter does not exist in *'ōlelo Hawai'i* (which is Hawaiian for "Hawaiian language").

What follows is a glossary of some of the most commonly used Hawaiian words. Don't be afraid to give them a try. Hawaiian residents appreciate visitors who at least try to pick up the local language.

'a'ā: rough, crumbling lava, contrasting with *pāhoehoe*, which is smooth.
'ae: yes.
aikane: friend.
akamai: smart, clever, possessing savoir faire.
akua: god.
ala: a road, path, or trail.
ali'i: a Hawaiian chief, a member of the chiefly class.
aloha: love, affection, kindness. Also a salutation meaning both greetings and farewell.
'ānuenue: rainbow.
'a'ole: no.
'auwai: a ditch.
auwē: alas, woe is me!
'ehu: a red-haired Hawaiian.
'ewa: in the direction of 'Ewa plantation, west of Honolulu.
hala: the pandanus tree, whose leaves (*lau hala*) are used to make baskets and plaited mats.
halau: school.
hale: a house.
hale pule: church, house of worship.
hana: to work.
haole: originally a stranger or foreigner. Since the first foreigners were Caucasian, *haole* now means a Caucasian person.
hapa: a part, sometimes a half; often used as a short form of *hapa haole*, to mean a person who is part-Caucasian; thus, the name of a popular local band, whose members represent a variety of ethnicities.
hau'oli: to rejoice. *Hau'oli Makahiki Hou* means Happy New Year. *Hau'oli lā hānau* means Happy Birthday.
heiau: an outdoor stone platform; an ancient Hawaiian place of worship.
holo: to run.
holoholo: to go for a walk, ride, or sail.
holokū: a long Hawaiian dress, somewhat fitted, with a yoke and a train. Influenced by European fashion, it was worn at court, and at least one local translates the word as "expensive mu'umu'u."
holomū: a post–World War II cross between a *holokū* and a *mu'umu'u*, less fitted than the former but less voluminous than the latter, and having no train.
honi: to kiss, a kiss. A phrase that some tourists may find useful, quoted from a popular *hula*, is *Honi Ka'ua Wikiwiki:* Kiss me quick!
honu: turtle.
ho'omalimali: flattery, a deceptive "line," bunk, baloney, hooey.
huhū: angry.
hui: a group, club, or assembly. A church may refer to its congregation as a *hui* and a social club may be called a *hui*.
hukilau: a seine; a communal fishing party in which everyone helps to drive the fish into a huge net, pull it in, and divide the catch.
hula: the dance of Hawai'i.
iki: little.
ipo: sweetheart.
ka: the. This is the definite article for most singular words; for plural nouns, the definite article is usually *nā*. Since there is no *S* in Hawaiian, the article may be your only clue that a noun is plural.
kahuna: a priest, doctor, or other trained person of old Hawai'i, endowed with special professional skills that often included the gift of prophecy or other supernatural powers; plural: kāhuna.
kai: the sea, saltwater.
kalo: the taro plant from whose root poi is made.
kama'āina: literally, a child of the soil, it refers to people who were born in the Islands or have lived there for a long time.

kanaka: originally a man or humanity in general, it is now used to denote a male Hawaiian or part-Hawaiian, but is occasionally taken as a slur when used by non-Hawaiians. *Kanaka maoli*, originally a full-blooded Hawaiian person, is used by some native Hawaiian rights activists to embrace part-Hawaiians as well.

kāne: a man, a husband. If you see this word on a door, it's the men's room. If you see *kane* on a door, it's probably a misspelling; that is the Hawaiian name for the skin fungus, Tinea.

kapa: also called by its Tahitian name, *tapa*, a cloth made of beaten bark and usually dyed and stamped with a repeat design.

kapakahi: crooked, cockeyed, uneven. You've got your hat on *kapakahi*.

kapu: keep out, prohibited. This is the Hawaiian version of the more widely known Tongan word *tabu* (taboo).

kapuna: grandparent.

keiki: a child; *keikikāne* is a boy, *keikiwahine* a girl.

kona: the leeward side of the Islands, the direction (south) from which the *kona* wind and *kona* rain come.

kula: upland.

kuleana: a homestead or small plot of ground on which a family has been installed for some generations without necessarily owning it. By extension, *kuleana* is used to denote any area or department in which one has a special interest or prerogative. You'll hear it used this way: If you want to hire a surfboard, see Moki; that's his *kuleana*. And conversely: I can't help you with that; that's not my *kuleana*.

lā: sun.

lamalama: to fish with a torch.

lānai: a porch, a balcony, an outdoor living room. Almost every house in Hawai'i has one. Don't confuse this two-syllable word with the three-syllable name of the island, Lāna'i.

lani: heaven, the sky.

lau hala: the leaf of the *hala* or pandanus tree, widely used in Hawaiian handicrafts.

lei: a garland of flowers.

limu: sun.

lolo: stupid.

luna: a plantation overseer or foreman.

mahalo: thank you.

makai: toward the ocean.

malihini: a newcomer to the Islands.

mana: the spiritual power that the Hawaiian believed inhabited all things and creatures.

manō: shark.

manuwahi: free, gratis.

mauka: toward the mountains.

mauna: mountain.

mele: a Hawaiian song or chant, often of epic proportions.

Mele Kalikimaka: Merry Christmas (a transliteration from the English phrase).

Menehune: a Hawaiian pixie. The *Menehune* were a legendary race of little people who accomplished prodigious work, such as building fishponds and temples in the course of a single night.

moana: the ocean.

mu'umu'u: the voluminous dress in which the missionaries enveloped Hawaiian women. Now made in bright printed cottons and silks, it is an indispensable garment in a Hawaiian woman's wardrobe. Culturally sensitive locals have embraced the Hawaiian spelling but often shorten the spoken word to "mu'u." Most English dictionaries include the spelling "muumuu," and that version is a part of many apparel companies' names.

nani: beautiful.

nui: big.

ohana: family.
'ono: delicious.
pāhoehoe: smooth, unbroken, satiny lava.
Pākē: Chinese. This *Pākē* carver makes beautiful things.
palapala: document, printed matter.
pali: a cliff, precipice.
pānini: prickly pear cactus.
paniolo: a Hawaiian cowboy, a rough transliteration of *español,* the language of the Islands' earliest cowboys.
pau: finished, done.
pilikia: trouble. The Hawaiian word is much more widely used here than its English equivalent.
puka: a hole.
pupule: crazy, like the celebrated Princess Pupule. This word has replaced its English equivalent in local usage.
pu'u: volcanic cinder cone.
waha: mouth.
wahine: a female, a woman, a wife, and a sign on the ladies' room door; plural: *wāhine.*
wai: freshwater, as opposed to saltwater, which is *kai.*
wailele: waterfall.
wikiwiki: to hurry, hurry up. (Since this is a reduplication of *wiki,* quick, neither W is pronounced as a V.).

Note: Pidgin is the unofficial language of Hawai'i. It is a Creole language, with its own grammar, evolved from the mixture of English, Hawaiian, Japanese, Portuguese, and other languages spoken in 19th-century Hawai'i, and it is heard everywhere: on ranches, in warehouses, on beaches, and in the hallowed halls (and occasionally in the classrooms) of the University of Hawai'i.

KEY WORDS ON THE MENU

Vocabulary

Much of the Hawaiian language encountered during a stay in the Islands will appear on restaurant menus and lists of lūʻau fare. Here's a quick primer.

ʻahi: locally caught yellowfin tuna.
aku: skipjack, bonito tuna.
ʻamaʻama: mullet; it's hard to get but tasty.
bento: a box lunch.
chicken lūʻau: a stew made from chicken, taro leaves, and coconut milk.
haupia: a light, gelatinlike dessert made from coconut.
imu: the underground ovens in which pigs are roasted for lūʻau.
kālua: to bake underground.
kaukau: food. The word comes from Chinese but is used in the Islands.
kim chee: pickled Chinese cabbage made with garlic and hot peppers.
Kona coffee: coffee grown in the Kona district of the Big Island.
laulau: literally, a bundle. *Laulau* are morsels of pork, butterfish, or other ingredients wrapped with young taro shoots in ti leaves for steaming.
lilikoʻi: passion fruit; a tart, seedy yellow fruit that makes delicious desserts, jellies, and sherbet.
lomilomi: to rub or massage; also a massage. Lomilomi salmon is fish that has been rubbed with onions and herbs, commonly served with minced onions and tomatoes.
lūʻau: a Hawaiian feast, also the leaf of the taro plant used in preparing such a feast.
lūʻau leaves: cooked taro tops with a taste similar to spinach.
mahimahi: mild-flavored dolphinfish, not the marine mammal.
mai tai: fruit punch with rum, from the Tahitian word for "good."
malasada: a Portuguese deep-fried doughnut without a hole, dipped in sugar.
manapua: dough wrapped around diced pork.
manō: shark.
niu: coconut.
ʻōkolehao: a liqueur distilled from the ti root.
onaga: pink or red snapper.
ono: a long, slender mackerel-like fish; also called wahoo.
ʻono: delicious; also hungry.
ʻopihi: a tiny shellfish, or mollusk, found on rocks; also called limpets.
pāpio: a young ulua or jack fish.
pohā: Cape gooseberry. Tasting a bit like honey, the pohā berry is often used in jams and desserts.
poi: a paste made from pounded taro root, a staple of the Hawaiian diet.
poke: chopped, pickled raw fish and seafood, tossed with herbs and seasonings.
pūpū: Hawaiian hors d'oeuvre.
saimin: long thin noodles and vegetables in broth, often garnished with small pieces of fish cake, scrambled egg, luncheon meat, and green onion.
sashimi: raw fish thinly sliced and usually eaten with soy sauce.
ti leaves: a member of the agave family, used to wrap food in cooking and removed before eating.
uku: deep-sea snapper.
ulua: a member of the jack family that also includes pompano and amberjack. Also called crevalle, jack fish, and jack crevalle.

INDEX

Icons and Symbols

★   Our special recommendations
✕   Restaurant
🏠   Lodging establishment
✕🏠   Lodging establishment whose restaurant warrants a special trip
🦆   Good for kids (rubber duck)
☞   Sends you to another section of the guide for more information
✉   Address
☎   Telephone number
⊙   Opening and closing times
💰   Admission prices
🌐   Sends you to www.fodors.com/urls for up-to-date links to the property's Web site

Numbers in white and black circles ③ ❸ that appear on the maps, in the margins, and within the tours correspond to one another.

A

A Pacific Cafe ✕, 50
A Saigon Café ✕, 49
Aerial tours, 157
'Ainahau 🏠, 61
Air travel, 104–105, 136–138, 142
Airport Flower & Fruit Co., 88
Airports, 104–105, 137–138
Akamai Trading, 103–104
Alexander & Baldwin Sugar Museum, 26, 28–29
Aloha Classic World Wave Sailing Championships, 82
Aloha Lani Inn 🏠, 63–64
America II Sunset Sail, 67
Ancient Graveyard, 102
Ann Fielding's Snorkel Maui, 79
Anthony's Coffee Company ✕, 41
'Ānuenue Room ✕, 46
Apartment and villa rentals, 150
Art galleries, 86–87, 89
Art in the Park, 86
Art Night, 86
Art tours, 157
Arts, 67–70, 101
ATMs, 153
Azeka Place Shopping Center, 85

B

Bailey House, 28–29
Baldwin Beach, 73
Baldwin Home, 22–23
Baldwin Theatre Guild, 70
Bambula Inn 🏠, 62
Banyan Tree, 22–23
Bars and clubs, 66–67
Bay Club ✕, 43–44
Beaches, 72–73, 79
  Hāna, 39
  Lāna'i, 93, 97–99
  North Shore, 73
  South Shore, 19, 32, 72–73
  West Maui, 72
Bed-and-breakfasts, 61–64, 150–151
Bella Luna Restaurant ✕, 50
Bicycling, 73–74, 102, 138, 157–158
BJ's Chicago Pizza ✕, 47
Black Rock (lava cone), 79
Bloom Cottage 🏠, 61
Blue Ginger Cafe ✕, 99
Blue Ginger Vacation Rental 🏠, 101
Blue Water Rafting, 78
Boat travel, 138–139
Bodysurfing, 72–73
Brick Palace (Lahaina), 22–23
Brig *Carthaginian II*, 22, 24
Bus travel, 139
Business hours, 139
By the Sea B&B 🏠, 62

C

Cafe O'Lei ✕, 30
Cameras and photography, 139–140
Camping, 74, 102, 151
Captain's Retreat 🏠, 100
Car rentals, 140–141
  Lāna'i, 105
Car travel, 141–142
  Lāna'i, 104–105
Casanova Italian Restaurant and Deli ✕, 51, 66
Cathedrals dive site, 103
Cavendish Golf Course, 101
Caves, 79
Celebration of the Whales (art show), 86
Central Maui
  restaurants, 48–49
  sightseeing in, 26–31
Challenge at Mānele, 102
Charley's Saloon ✕, 41
Cheeseburger in Paradise ✕, 67
Chez Paul ✕, 46
Children, traveling with, 142
Churches, 22, 26, 29–30
Cinderella *(yacht)*, 78

Climate, 161
Clothing, shopping for, 87–88
Computers, 143
Condominiums, 53, 151
Consumer protection, 142
Court House (Lahaina), 22, 24
Crafts, shopping for, 88–89, 103–104
Crater Observatory, 33
Crater tours, 157
Credit cards, 153
  key to abbreviations, 153
Cruises, 78, 138–139, 143
Customs and duties, 143–145

D

Da Kine Hawaiian Pro Am (windsurfing), 82
David Paul's Lahaina Grill ✕, 46
Deep-sea fishing, 77, 102
Destination Lāna'i, 98, 105–106
Dining. ☞ Restaurants
Dinner cruises, 67
Disabilities and accessibility, 145–146
Discounts and deals, 137, 140, 146
Dive sites, 79, 103
Dreams Come True 🏠, 101
D.T. Fleming Beach, 72
Duties, 143–145

E

East Maui
  hotels, 60–61
  restaurants, 50–51
Ecotourism, 146–147
Ed Robinson's Diving Adventures, 78
Ekena 🏠, 61
Elleair Golf Course, 75
EMC Maui Kā'anapali Classic SENIOR PGA Golf Tournament, 82
Emergencies, 147
  Lāna'i, 105
Enchanting Floral Gardens, 33–34
Erik's Seafood Grotto ✕, 47
Etiquette and behavior, 147
Eucalyptus Ladder, 102
Experience at Kō'ele, 102

F

Feast at Lele, 68
Ferries, 104, 139
Festivals and seasonal events, 69, 86, 161–163
  Lāna'i, 93

Index

Film festival, 68
Finest Kind Inc. (fishing charter), 77
Fishing, 77, 102
Fitness centers, 75
Five Caves, 79
505 Front Street, 22, 24
Flea markets, 88
Formal Dining Room ✕, 99
Fort (Lahaina), 22, 24
Four Seasons Resort 🏨, 58
Four-wheel-drive vehicles, rentals
Lāna'i, 105

G

Garden of the Gods, 93, 95, 97
Gardens, 33–34, 36–38, 41
Lāna'i, 93, 95, 97
Gay and lesbian travel, tips for, 147–148
Gerard's ✕, 46
Gifts with Aloha, 104
Golden Bamboo Ranch 🏨, 62
Golf, 75, 80, 82
Lāna'i, 92, 101–102
Grand Wailea 🏨, 58
Ground tours, 158
GTE Hawaiian Tel Hall of Fame, 80
Guesthouses, 61–64
Guided tours, 105

H

Ha'ikū, 19, 37, 38
Haimoff & Haimoff Creations in Gold, 89
Hale Ho'okipa Inn, 63
Hale Pa'ahao (Old Prison), 22, 24
Hale Pa'i, 22, 24
Haleakalā Crater, 74
Haleakalā Highway, 18–19, 33–34
Haleakalā National Park, 18, 33–35
Haleakalā Visitor Center, 33
Haleki'i-Pihana Helau State Monument, 26, 29
Halfway to Hāna House 🏨, 64
Hāli'imaile General Store ✕, 50–51
Halulu Heiau, 94
Hāmoa Bay House & Bungalow 🏨, 61
Hāna, 19, 37–41, 39, 73
Hāna Airport, 39, 137–138
Hāna Cultural Center, 89
Hang gliding, 76
Hang Gliding Maui, 76
Hapa's Brewhaus & Restaurant ✕, 49, 67
Happy Divers, 78
Hard Rock Cafe, 67
Hawai'i Nature Center, 74

Hawaiian Pro Am Windsurfing, 82
Health issues, 148
Heavenly Hāna Inn 🏨, 61
Henry Clay's Rotisserie ✕, 99
High Goal Benefit polo match, 82
Hiking, 74, 102, 158
Lāna'i, 92
Hilo Hattie, 87
Hinatea Sportfishing, 77
Holidays, 148–149
Home exchanges, 151
Honolua Bay, 79, 80
Honolua Surf Company, 87
Honolulu International Airport, 137
Honomanū Bay, 37, 39
Ho'okipa Beach, 19, 37, 39, 73, 80
Ho'omana'o Challenge Outrigger Sailing Canoe World Championship, 82
Horseback Riding, 102, 158–159
Hosmer Grove, 74
Hospitals, 105
Hostels, 151–152
Hot Island Glassblowing Studio & Gallery, 86–87
Hotel Hāna-Maui 🏨, 38, 39, 60
Hotel Lāna'i 🏨, 101
Hotels, 38–39, 52–64, 142–143, 145, 149–152
East Maui, 60–61
guest houses and bed-and-breakfasts, 61–64
Lāna'i, 100
price categories, 150
South Shore, 58–60
West Maui, 53–58
Huelo, 37, 39
Hui No'eau Visual Arts Center, 33, 36, 87
Hula dancing, 69
Hula Grill ✕, 46–47
Hula Moons ✕, 49
Hulopo'e Beach, 98, 103
Hyatt Regency Maui 🏨, 53, 76

I

'Īao Theater, 26, 29
'Īao Valley State Park, 19, 28, 29
Icons and symbols, 168.
☞ Also Web sites
I'o ✕, 47
'Ihilani ✕, 99
Insurance, 140–141, 149
International Food and Clothing Center, 103
Island Marine, 81
Island View 🏨, 63

J

Jasmine Garden 🏨, 100
Jazz, 66

Jessica's Gems, 89
Jewelry, shopping for, 89
Joe's Bar & Grill ✕, 48

K

Ka Hula Piko festival, 69
Ka Lima O Maui, 82
Ka'ahumanu Center, 85
Ka'ahumanu Church, 26, 29–30
Kā'anapali, 19, 22, 24
Kā'anapali Ali'i 🏨, 53
Kā'anapali Beach, 72
Kā'anapali Beach Hotel 🏨, 57
Kā'anapali Golf Course, 75
Kahakuloa, 19, 22, 25
Kahale's Beach Club, 66
Kahanu Garden, 41
Kahe'a Heiau, 97
Kahului, 26, 30
Kahului Airport, 137
Kahului Harbor, 26, 30
Kalahaku Overlook, 33
Kama'ole I, II, and III beach parks, 72–73
Kama'ole Sands 🏨, 58–59
Kānepu'u Preserve, 93, 95, 97
Kanahā Beach, 73
Kapalua, 19, 22, 25
Kapalua Bay Hotel 🏨, 53, 55
Kapalua Bay Villas 🏨, 56
Kapalua Beach, 72
Kapalua Betsy Nagelsen Tennis Invitational, 83
Kapalua Clambake Pro-Am, 80
Kapalua Golf Club, 75
Kapalua Jr. Vet/Sr. Tennis Championships, 83
Kapalua Tennis Club, 83
Kapalua Tennis Garden, 76
Kapalua-West Maui Airport, 137
Kaulana Cocktail Cruise, 67
Kaumahina State Wayside Park, 37, 39–40
Kaumālapa'u Harbor, 93–95
Kaunolū, 93–95
Kaupō Road, 38
Kayaking, 77
Kea Lani Hotel Suites & Villas 🏨, 59
Ke'anae Arboretum, 19, 37, 40
Ke'anae Overlook, 37, 40
Keōmuku, 97–98
Keōpūolani Park, 26, 30
Kepaniwai Park & Heritage Gardens, 28, 30
Kiele V charter, 78
Kīhei, 32
Kīhei Kalama Village Marketplace, 89
Kīlauea Point National Wildlife Refuge, 35
Kimo's ✕, 48

Index

Kōkī Beach, 73
Komoda Store & Bakery ×, 36
Kūʻau Cove Plantation 🏨, 63
Kula Botanical Gardens, 33, 36
Kula Hawaii 🏨, 60–61
Kula Lodge ×, 36
Kula View 🏨, 63

L

La Pérouse Bay, 19, 32
Lahaina, 19, 25
Lahaina and Kāʻanapali & Pacific Railroad, 25
Lahaina Cannery Mall, 85
Lahaina Center, 85
Lahaina Civic Center, 76
Lahaina Coolers ×, 43
Lahaina Divers, 78
Lahaina Galleries, 87
Lahaina Inn 🏨, 58
Lahaina Para-Sail, 76
Lahaina Printsellers Ltd., 88
Lahaina Scrimshaw, 89
Lānaʻi, 90–106
 emergencies, 105
 guided tours, 105
 hotels, 92, 100–101
 nightlife and the arts, 101
 North and East region, 95, 97–100
 restaurants, 92, 99–100
 shopping, 103–104
 sightseeing, 92–99
 South and West region, 93–95, 99
 sports, 92, 101–103
 timing the visit, 93
 transportation, 104–105
 visitor information, 105–106
Lānaʻi Airport, 138
Lānaʻi Art Studio, 104
Lānaʻi City, 93, 97–98
Lānaʻi City Service, 103–105
Lānaʻi Ecoadventure Center, 102
Lānaʻi Pine Sporting Clays Range, 102
Lānaʻi Theater and Playhouse, 101
Language, 149
Lei greetings, 149
Leleiwi Overlook, 33
Liberty House, 87
Lightning Bolt Maui, 80
Limousines, 160
Lindbergh, Charles, grave of, 38
Local Motion Surfing, 83
Lodge at Kōʻele 🏨, 100–101, 101, 102, 104
Lodging. ☞ Hotels
Longhi's ×, 43
Luʻahiwa Petroglyphs, 93–95
Luana Kai 🏨, 60
Lūʻaus, 68, 70

Lucky Strike Charters, 77
Luggage, tips for checking, 154

M

Māʻalaea Small Boat Harbor, 32
Māʻalaea Waterfront Restaurant ×, 50
Mahana Naʻia, 78
Makai Bar, 66
Makani ʻOluʻolu Cottage 🏨, 64
Makawao, 19, 33, 36
Makawao Steak House ×, 51
Mākena Beach State Park, 19, 32
Mākena Golf Course, 75
Mākena Tennis Club, 76–77
Mama's Fish House ×, 51
Mana Foods ×, 41
Mānele Bay, 94–95
Mānele Bay Hotel 🏨, 100, 101, 104
Marco's Grill & Deli ×, 48
Market Street, 30
Martin Lawrence Galleries, 87
Master Touch Gallery, 89
Master's Reading Room, 22, 25
Maui
 itinerary recommendations, 18–19
 timing the visit, 19
Maui Academy of Performing Arts, 70
Maui Arts and Culture Center, 26, 30, 66
Maui Bake Shop & Deli Ltd., 29
Maui Beach & Tennis Club, 77
Maui Brews, 67
Maui Coast Hotel 🏨, 59
Maui Community Theatre, 80
Maui Crafts Guild, 87
Maui Dive Shop, 78
Maui Divers, 89
Maui Family YMCA, 75
Maui Film Festival, 68
Maui Hands, 87
Maui Lu Resort 🏨, 60
Maui Mall, 85–86
Maui Marketplace, 86
Maui Marriott 🏨, 56
Maui Myth and Magic Theatre, 68
Maui Ocean Activities, 80
Maui Ocean Center, 19, 32
Maui Philharmonic Society, 70
Maui Prince 🏨, 59
Maui Race Series, 82–83
Maui Rusty Pro, 83
Maui Sea Kayaking, 77
Maui Swap Mart, 88
Maui Swiss Cafe ×, 25

Maui Symphony Orchestra, 70
Maui Tropical Plantation and Country Store, 28, 29
Maui Visitors Bureau, 106
Maui Windsurf Company, 80
Maui Windsurfari, 80
Mauian Hotel 🏨, 57
Maui-Molokaʻi Sea Cruises, 78
Maui's Best, 88
Media, 152–153
Mercedes Golf Championship, 80
Merrie Monarch Hula Festival, 69
Mōkapu Beach, 73, 79
Molokini Center, 79
Molokini Lounge, 66
Money, 153
Moose McGillycuddy's, 67
Mopeds, 138
Mountain biking, 102
Munro Trail, 95, 97–98, 102
Museums, 139
Music, 66–67, 70, 96
Myths and legends of Hawaii, 27

N

Naha, 97–98
Nāhiku, 37, 40
Nāpili Bay, 79
Nāpili Beach, 72
Nāpili Kai Beach Club Keiki Hula Show, 68
Nāpili Kai Beach Club 🏨, 56
National parks, 153
Newspapers and magazines, 152
Nightlife, 66–70, 101
North Shore
 beaches, 72–73

O

Ocean Activities Center, 77, 79, 80, 81
Ocean Riders, 78
ʻOheʻo Gulch, 19, 38, 40, 74
Ola's Makawao, 88
Old Cowboy Trail, 102
Old Laihaina Lūʻau, 68
Old Wailuku Inn 🏨, 62
Ole Surfboards, 80
Olinda Country Cottage & Inn 🏨, 62
Orient Express ×, 48
Oskie Rice Memorial Tournament, 82
Outrigger Wailea Resort 🏨, 59
Outrigger-canoe races, 82

P

Pacific Dive Shop, 78
Pacific Whale Foundation, 81
PacificʻO ×, 48, 66

Packing, tips for, *153–154*
Pā'ia, *19, 37, 40*
Pā'ia Fishmarket ✕, *41*
Papaka Sporting Clays, *76*
Papakea Beach Resort ⌺, *57–58*
Parasailing, *76*
Passports, *154–155*
Peace of Maui ⌺, *63*
Pele's Other Garden ✕, *100*
Personal tour guides, *159*
Pests and other hazards, *148*
Picnics ✕, *40–41*
Pi'ilanihale Heiau, *38, 41*
Pine Isle Market, *103*
Pineapple plantation tours, *159*
Pioneer Inn ⌺, *58*
Plane travel, *104–105, 136–138, 142*
Plantation House Restaurant ✕, *47*
Plantation Inn ⌺, *57*
Polihua Beach, *98–99*
Polipoli Forest, *74*
Polli's ✕, *51*
Polo, *82*
Polo Beach, *73, 79*
Price categories
for dining, *147*
for lodging, *150*
Pride Charters, *67, 81*
Puahokamoa Stream, *37, 41*
Pu'u Ōla'i, *79*
Pu'u'Ula'ula Overlook, *34, 36*

Q
Quilters Corner, *89*

R
Radio and television, *152–153*
Rafting, *77–78*
Red Lantern ✕, *43*
Renaissance Wailea Beach Resort ⌺, *59–60*
Restaurant Matsu ✕, *48*
Restaurants, *25, 36, 41, 43–51, 147*
American, *4, 43*
Central Maui, *48–49*
Chinese, *43*
Continental, *43, 46, 49*
dinner and sunset cruises, *67*
East Maui, *50–51*
eclectic, *49*
French, *46*
Hawai'i Regional/Pacific Rim, *46–47, 50–51*
Italian, *47–48, 50–51*
Japanese, *48*
Lāna'i, *99–100*
Lū'au, *68, 70*
Mexican, *51*
price categories, *147*
seafood, *50–51*
South Shore, *49–50*

steak, *48, 51*
Thai, *49*
West Maui, *43, 46–48*
Reyn's (clothing store), *87*
Richard's Shopping Center, *103*
Ritz-Carlton, Kapalua ⌺, *56*
Rock music, *66–67*
Rodeos, *82*
Royal Lahaina Resort ⌺, *56*
Royal Lahaina Tennis Ranch, *77*
Roy's Kahana Bar & Grill ✕, *47*
Ruth's Chris Steak House ✕, *48*

S
Saeng's Thai Cuisine ✕, *49*
Safety issues, *155*
Sail Hawai'i, *78*
Sailing, *78*
Sandalwood Golf Course, *75*
Scotch Mist Charters, *67, 78*
Scuba diving, *78–79, 102–103, 148*
Lāna'i, *92*
Seabury Hall Performance Studio, *70*
Seamen's Hospital, *22, 25*
Seasons ✕, *49*
Second Wind (surfboard rental), *80*
Senior Skins golf game, *82*
Senior-citizen travel, *156*
Sergeant Major Reef, *103*
SGT Leisure, *88*
Sheraton Maui ⌺, *56–57*
Shipwreck Beach, *93, 97–99, 102*
Shopping, *85–89, 156*
business hours, *139*
clothing, *87–88*
food shopping, *88*
gifts, *88*
grocery stores, *86*
Hawaiian crafts, *88–89*
jewelry, *89*
Lāna'i, *103–104*
shopping centers, *85–86*
specialty stores, *86–87*
Shops at Wailea, *86*
Shuttles, *139*
Siam Thai ✕, *49*
Silver Cloud Guest Ranch ⌺, *62*
"Slaughterhouse" Beach, *72*
Snorkel Bob's, *79*
Snorkeling, *79, 103*
Lāna'i, *92*
South Shore, *31–33*
beaches, *72–73*
hotels, *58–60*
restaurants, *49–50*
Spinning Dolphin Fishing Charters, *102–103*
Sporting clays, *76, 102*
Sports, *72–83, 101–103*

Spring House, *22, 25*
Stables at Kō'ele, *102*
State parks, *153*
Students, travel tips for, *156–157*
Sunset cruises, *67*
Surfing, *80, 82–83*
Swan Court ✕, *43*
Symbols and icons, *168*. ☞ *Also* Web sites

T
Take Home Maui, *88*
Taxes, *157*
Taxis, *104–105, 159–160*
Tedeschi Vineyards and Winery, *19, 33, 36–37*
Tennis, *76–77, 83*
Theater, *70*
Time zones, *157*
Tipping, *157*
Tour of the Stars, *66*
Tours and packages, *157–159*
Trattoria Ha'ikū ✕, *51*
Travel agencies, *146, 160*
Trilogy Excursions, *78, 102–103*
Tropical Tantrum Outlet Store, *88*
Tsunami, *67*
24 Hour Fitness, *75*

U
Ulua Beach, *73, 79*

V
Videos and camcorders, *140*
Viewpoints, *87*
Village Gallery, *87*
Visas, *154–155*
Visiting Artist Program, *101*
Visitor information, *160*
Lāna'i, *105–106*

W
Wai'ānapanapa State Park, *38, 41*
Waiehu Municipal Golf Course, *75*
Waikāne Falls, *37, 41*
Wailea, *19, 32*
Wailea Beach, *73, 79*
Wailea Golf Club, *75*
Wailea Tennis Club, *77, 83*
Wailea Villas ⌺, *60*
Wailua Overlook, *19, 37, 41*
Wailuku, *19, 26, 31*
Waimoku Falls, *74*
Waiola Church and Cemetery, *22, 26*
Walking tours, *159*
Warren & Annabelle's ⌺, *68–69*
Water sports, *77–80, 102–103*
Waterfalls, *37, 74*

Web sites, *160–161*
Lāna'i, 94
West Maui
beaches, 72
hotels, 53–58
restaurants, 43, 46–48
sightseeing in, 19, 22–26

West Maui Para-Sail, *76*
Westin Maui 🏨, *57*
Whalers Village, *86*
Whale-watching, *81*
Wildlife, *35*
Wilson Kapalua Open Tennis Tournament, *83*

Windjammer Cruises, *67*
Windmill Beach, *79*
Windsurfing, *80, 82–83*
Wine Corner ✕, *41*
Wo Hing Museum, *22, 26*
World Class (cutter), *78*
World Gym, *75*

NOTES

FODOR'S MAUI AND LĀNA'I 2001

EDITOR: Alice K. Thompson

Editorial Contributors: DeSoto Brown, Gary Diedrichs, Amy Karafin, Helayne Schiff, Sophia Schweitzer, Marty Wentzel, Pablo Madera, Margaret M. Wunsch

Editorial Production: Frank Walgren

Maps: David Lindroth, *cartographer*; Rebecca Baer and Bob Blake, *map editors*

Design: Fabrizio La Rocca, *creative director*; Guido Caroti, *art director*; Jolie Novak, *photo editor*; Melanie Marin, *photo researcher*

Cover Design: Pentagram

Production/Manufacturing: Angela L. McLean

COPYRIGHT

Copyright © 2001 by Fodor's Travel Publications.

Fodor's is a registered trademark of Random House, Inc. All rights reserved under International and Pan-American Copyright Conventions. Published in the United States by Fodor's Travel Publications, a division of Random House, Inc., New York, and simultaneously in Canada by Random House of Canada Limited, Toronto. Distributed by Random House, Inc., New York.

No maps, illustrations, or other portions of this book may be reproduced in any form without written permission from the publisher.

ISBN 0–679–00625–7

ISSN 1525–5042

Grateful acknowledgment is made to the following for permission to reprint previously published material: "The Aloha Shirt: A Colorful Swatch of Island History," by DeSoto Brown, reprinted from *Aloha* magazine, copyright © October 1987 Davick Publications.

SPECIAL SALES

Fodor's Travel Publications are available at special discounts for bulk purchases for sales promotions or premiums. Special editions, including personalized covers, excerpts of existing guides, and corporate imprints, can be created in large quantities for special needs. For more information, contact your local bookseller or write to Special Markets, Fodor's Travel Publications, 280 Park Avenue, New York, NY 10017. Inquiries from Canada should be directed to your local Canadian bookseller or sent to Random House of Canada, Ltd., Marketing Department, 2775 Matheson Boulevard East, Mississauga, Ontario L4W 4P7. Inquiries from the United Kingdom should be sent to Fodor's Travel Publications, 20 Vauxhall Bridge Road, London SW1V 2SA, England.

PRINTED IN THE UNITED STATES OF AMERICA

10 9 8 7 6 5 4 3 2 1

IMPORTANT TIP

Although all prices, opening times, and other details in this book are based on information supplied to us at press time, changes do occur all the time in the travel world, and Fodor's cannot accept responsibility for facts that become outdated or for inadvertent errors or omissions. So **always confirm information when it matters,** especially if you're making a detour to visit a specific place.

PHOTOGRAPHY

Stone: *Terry Donnelly, cover (The Cove, Ahihi Bay, Maui).*

Steve Brinkman, *10C, 14G.*

Corbis: *Douglas Peebles, 13D. Neil Rabinowitz, 4–5.*

Kapalua Land Company, Ltd., *2 top left, 10A.*

Four Seasons Resort, *3 top left, 3 top right, 14E.*

Robert Holmes, *10B.*

The Image Bank: *John Lewis Stage, 7E. Alvis Upitis, 13E.*

Bob Krist, *11E.*

Lahaina Inn: *Maria Demarest, 14C.*

Wayne Levin, *11F.*

Maui Ocean Center, *Dean Lee, 6A.*

Maui Visitors Bureau: *2 bottom left, 6B, 8 bottom left. Ron Dahlquist, 2 top right, 2 bottom center, 9D, 14D, 14I. Ray Mains, 2 bottom right, 3 bottom left, 3 bottom right, 14A, 14B, 14F. Patrick McFeeley, 14H.*

T. Novak-Clifford, *14J.*

Photo Resource Hawaii: *Rick Carroll, 12A. Jim Cazel, 7C. Franco Salmoiraghi, 12B, 12C.*

David Sanger Photography: *1, 8B, 9C.*

Stone: *Rob Boudreau, 16. Greg Huglin, 9 top. Joe McBride, 9E. David Robbins, 11D. Traveler's Resource, 8A.*

Nik Wheeler, *7D.*

ABOUT OUR WRITERS

Every trip is a significant trip. Acutely aware of that fact, we've pulled out all stops in preparing *Fodor's Maui and Lāna'i 2001*. To help you zero in on what to see in Maui and Lāna'i, we've gathered some great color photos. To show you how to put it all together, we've created great itineraries and neighborhood walks. And to direct you to the places that are truly worth your time and money, we've rallied the team of endearingly picky know-it-alls we're pleased to call our writers. Having seen all corners of Maui and Lāna'i, they're real experts. If you knew them, you'd poll them for tips yourself.

Pablo Madera, our Maui updater, is a freelance journalist, jazz drummer, and ethnobotanist who has made Maui his home base for 25 years. When he's not pursuing projects on various Pacific islands, he tries to keep up with banana production on his small farm, which is off the road to Hāna.

Big Island resident **Sophia Schweitzer** is our updater for Lāna'i. Sophia is a freelance food, wine, health and fitness, and travel writer whose work has appeared in magazines across the country. She is educational writer for *Wine X*, a lifestyle magazine for the new generation, and has just finished coauthoring a book about the Big Island.

Maggie Wunsch, our Smart Travel Tips updater, is a 27-year resident of Hawai'i whose writings about the Islands have appeared on radio, local and national television, and in both consumer and travel-trade publications. Maggie grew up in Asia and Europe and fell in love with Hawai'i in 1961 when, at the age of 6, she first met the Pacific Ocean on the beach fronting the Halekūlani Hotel. Her fascination with Hawai'i and the Pacific continues to this day.

Don't Forget to Write

We love feedback—positive and negative—and follow up on all suggestions. So contact the Maui and Lāna'i editor at editors@fodors.com or c/o Fodor's, 280 Park Avenue, New York, NY 10017. Have a wonderful trip!

Karen Cure
Editorial Director